THE ENGLISH

J. B. PRIESTLEY

HEINEMANN · LONDON

WILLIAM HEINEMANN LTD
15 QUEEN ST, MAYFAIR, LONDON W1X 8BE
LONDON MELBOURNE TORONTO
JOHANNESBURG AUCKLAND

DESIGNED AND PRODUCED BY
GEORGE RAINBIRD LIMITED
MARBLE ARCH HOUSE
44 EDGWARE ROAD
LONDON W2

PICTURE RESEARCH: MARY ANNE NORBURY
DESIGN: JUDITH ALLAN

FIRST PUBLISHED SEPTEMBER 1973
SECOND PRINTING OCTOBER 1973
THIRD PRINTING AUGUST 1974

THE TEXT WAS SET BY
JARROLD AND SONS LIMITED, NORWICH
THE BOOK PRINTED BY
BUTLER AND TANNER LIMITED, FROME
AND BOUND BY
DORSTEL PRESS LIMITED, HARLOW

THE COLOUR PLATES AND JACKET WERE
ORIGINATED AND PRINTED BY
WESTERHAM PRESS LIMITED
WESTERHAM, KENT, ENGLAND

SBN 434 60359 7

Colour Plates:
(reverse of frontispiece) The English Cabbage Rose (*Rosa centifolia*)
referred to by Chaucer and Shakespeare. Watercolour drawing by
Alfred Parsons, R.A., from *The Genus Rosa* by Ellen Willmott, F.L.S. (1914)

(frontispiece) Landscape study, watercolour drawing by John Constable

CONTENTS

❁

LIST OF COLOUR PLATES

❀

ACKNOWLEDGMENTS

❀

Acknowledgments are made to the owners and photographers of pictures and prints whose names are given on pages 249 to 252. Quotations in the text have been taken from the following copyright works, and acknowledgment is made to: William Collins Sons & Company Limited and Sir Neville Cardus for the quotation from his *Autobiography*; Constable & Company Limited and Charles Scribner's Sons for the quotation from *Soliloquies in England*, and *Later Soliloquies* by George Santayana; and Eyre & Spottiswoode (Publishers) Limited for the quotation from *Life Worth Living: Some Phases of an Englishman* by C. B. Fry.

PREFACE

This is quite a different kind of book from my three informal social histories – *The Prince of Pleasure*, *The Edwardians* and *Victoria's Heyday*. However, it has been my good fortune to have been so ably assisted once again by Mary Anne Norbury (Mrs Sanders), collecting the illustrations, and by Mr John Hadfield, who has not only supervised the illustrating and general format but has also been even more valuable than ever as an editor. So I take this opportunity to offer my grateful thanks to these two colleagues and friends.

J.B.P.

504.92

THE ENGLISH SECRET

❧

THIS is not a history of the English but an informal attempt to explain the English. The text will not even try to be impersonal. But that does not mean it will be one-sided, with 'Land of Hope and Glory' boasting away in the background. I may have – as indeed I do have – a strong and deep affection for my own country and its people; but I have never been a professional patriot and I don't propose to turn myself into one at this late hour. Counsel for the prosecution will have his turn here. What I want to do is to be as detached as it is reasonably possible to be, not waving a flag in the reader's face. If I generalize, sometimes ignoring exceptions, it will be because I want to save space and time and keep everything bouncing along. No doubt both prejudices and inconsistencies will invade the text. But after all I am an Englishman writing about the English, who have contrived for centuries to be prickly with prejudices and yet at the same time hazily inconsistent. And this of course, among other things, will have to be explained.

After much pondering, it seemed to me I had to decide between two ways of beginning this book and tackling the subject. Either I had, so to speak, to wade in at the shallow end, or I had to take a chance and dive in at the deep end. If I adopted the first method, then I would obviously begin by quoting a lot of opinions about and judgments of the English, both from home and abroad and covering some centuries. I would then try to make sense out of them, poking around to discover, if possible, a common denominator. And this is the shallow end indeed. The alternative, diving at once into the deep end, was less obvious, harder and bolder, perhaps a rash gamble; but more attractive to me and, I can only hope, to most readers. It meant ignoring for the time being all those opinions and snap judgments, cutting clean through them to arrive as close as possible to the essential Englishness of the English, to find the all-important clue, to reveal the secret. So here we go.

'Unknown Gentleman with Two Children' (detail), 1799, by Henry Edridge

{11}

Because we have to go deep, a brief reference to depth psychology might be helpful; but it will be Jung's and not Freud's. So I suggest that in the English psyche the barrier between consciousness and the unconscious is not fixed, high and strong, and indeed is not really complete, so that the conscious and the unconscious often merge as if they were two English counties sharing irregular misty boundaries. We can put it another way, keeping clear of depth psychology, and declare that the English depend more upon instinct and intuition than other West Europeans do. They are not unreasonable, but they are hardly ever strictly rational, and almost always they suspect the closed-in creations of pure rationality: they prefer the open-ended. It is essentially English not to allow the intellect to go its own way and decide everything: it must submit to some shaping and colouring by the instinctive and the intuitive. All this does not make them better or worse than other Europeans, but, as so many foreign observers have testified, it does make them *different*.

I am convinced that here we have the essence of Englishness, the great clue, the guiding thread in the maze. Clearly it is not enough merely to announce a belief; I hope to offer adequate proof as we go along. Some points should be made at once. For example, to be suspicious of the purely rational, of the force of logic, of the despotic intellect, and always to take into account what is instinctive or intuitive, suggests a cast and habit of mind that are feminine, not belonging to the robustly masculine image that Englishmen have projected down the centuries. However, this leaves me unshaken. It is possible to be aggressively over-masculine outside, if only to hide or simply to protect the feminine element inside. But we shall see. We shall also see – coming to the next point – that from time to time the general style and behaviour of certain distinct classes, or of some small but important groups, will obviously break the pattern, perhaps deliberately turning everything topsy-turvy. And this explains why so many conclusions about the English, hastily arrived at and never based on a wide and perceptive study of the whole nation, have gone so badly wrong. On the other hand, I believe that once we accept this central idea of the English character, temperament, habit of mind, national psyche, not rejecting the feminine element to be found here, we shall make progress where there has been so much confusion. So I hope to show that various contradictions and inconsistencies that have left so many foreign observers bewildered, and have at times even baffled the English themselves, will lose their hard edges and begin to fade away, like so much of the English landscape.

Something else must be understood. Because I have offered this clue to our Englishness, on about as deep a level as a work like this could explore, I am not pretending that the English have never changed. There

'The Bench', 1758, by William Hogarth

have always been changes – at least three of them, quite important, during my own lifetime. But these differences, obvious enough above ground, don't go down and strike at the roots. For better or worse, this Englishness I have defined, this deep-level common denominator, this enduring secret, still profoundly influences the national character and its general style of life.

The English still have no written constitution: their legal system is not based on any definite code but on the complicated inheritance of Common Law. There are some advantages here, notably a certain flexibility and some safeguards for the liberty of the individual not found among many other nations. But for all the boasting – and this is an area in which English politicians and lawyers have been very boastful – the ordinary citizen suffers from some serious disadvantages. He rarely understands what rights he enjoys, having no written constitution or definite code to which he can appeal. Litigation can be slow and appallingly expensive. English judges may at times successfully defy the government, in defence of Common Law, but at too many other times they unduly inflate themselves into becoming judges of everything and everybody, a role they were never appointed to play. We could rewrite Robert Burton's famous remark about women and horses, and say that England is a harvest field for lawyers and a barren, dark labyrinth for laymen. And if I have overweighted the disadvantages, perhaps it is

because for so many years I have heard public men, especially lawyers, declare that the English legal system 'is the envy of the world'. I am not competent to judge between rival systems, but I must say that during many years of travel abroad I was never around when this envy was being expressed.

Indeed, it is possible to regard these large complacent statements, so dear to politicians and their audiences after dinner, as examples of an English weakness – or perhaps vice. It belongs to the shadow side of Englishness and for the most part to the middle ranks of society. The best name for it is self-deception. This must not be confused with plain deception. There is an important difference between a man who, knowing exactly what he is doing, is bent on deceiving you, and a man who, not aware of what he is up to, is busy deceiving himself. (This second man is almost always more dangerous, especially in public affairs.) Now obviously a man whose consciousness, so to speak, is like a clear lighted space, untroubled by mysterious promptings and warning shadows from the unconscious, will feel that he knows himself and his motives, and will be free from the grosser forms of self-deception. Not

{14}

understanding the peculiar Englishness I have described, more open to the unconscious, compelled to take into account the instinctive or the intuitive, this foreign observer will probably conclude that the English are hypocrites. Now it would be absurd to pretend that some measure of hypocrisy doesn't exist among the English – after all, we cannot help remembering Mr Pecksniff – but it is quite wrong to confuse hypocrisy on the grand Tartuffean scale, and its clear-sighted, self-regarding motives, with the vague muddle that encourages so much English self-deception.

It is this confusion that largely explains the charge of perfidy brought against English politicians and officials, especially those responsible for the Foreign Office. Such men, it has been commonly imagined abroad, must be immensely clever, subtle schemers, hypocritical and wicked. And at least nine times out of ten this is quite wrong. More than once, ultra-cautious and aware of all manner of checks and balances not understood abroad, bewildered into timidity, the Foreign Office has refused to make clear direct statements that might have prevented a war. But more often than not it has been revealing the peculiar English cast of mind and not any Machiavellian depths of duplicity. Outside public affairs, I have noticed that Europeans settling in England – especially Central Europeans – start by thinking the English stupid and then begin to wonder if these islanders aren't cunning and rather treacherous; or they may reverse this, bringing the sly-clever judgment with them but afterwards deciding that the English are stupid. Such visitors are mistaken at both ends: by and large the English are neither stupider nor cleverer – only *different*.

Before I come to the defence of Englishness, there are two examples of English self-deception that are worth a mention. The first is the illusion, shared occasionally by some foreigners, that the English are astonishingly *practical*, far more so than their neighbours across the water. I have never discovered any evidence that supports this conclusion. Certainly the English in general are more practical, better able to cope realistically with this life, than many other peoples I have known, from Egypt to Tahiti. But far more practical than, let us say, the French, the Dutch, the Germans, the Swedes, the Swiss? Not at all! Anybody who knows these and several other nations, the English included, will also know that you can find among them some notable examples of sharp common sense, convenient arrangements to be welcomed and admired, and at the same time can discover lingering displays of daftness bewildering the visitor. I could provide plenty of examples of the deft and the daft, home and abroad, but readers who have travelled at all can amuse themselves providing their own examples. However, there is one question we ought to ask ourselves. When and how did the English achieve this spurious reputation of being so supremely practical? (But we mustn't confuse this with political pragmatism, to which I shall come later.) I think the legend grew in the later years of the eighteenth century and the earlier decades of the nineteenth, swelling with the triumphs (so-called) of the Industrial Revolution. People commanding such markets must be supremely practical. But this does not apply to a whole nation. Napoleon made the same mistake when he contemptuously dismissed the English as a 'nation of shopkeepers'. They are in fact nothing of the kind; they would be far better off at this moment if they had been more enthusiastic shopkeepers and salesmen; and the French themselves, I would say, have in general more of the keen shopkeeper's outlook and mentality. The English have been at their best at the inventing and originating end, and at their worst at the exploiting and selling end.

The second illusion is of more recent date and belongs to the middle classes, the upper and lower classes rarely cherishing it. This piece of self-deception assumes that the English are kinder, altogether more tender-hearted, than members of other nations, and that if they have a fault it is that they are inclined to be too soft with their enemies, even when at war. Many of the English – a high proportion of women among them – who eagerly swallow this legend are thinking about horses, dogs and cats and not about people, children and all. There has long been, and probably still is, a brutal strain in the English. For example, while there may be worse prisons abroad than there are in England, undoubtedly there are many that are much better. Again, right up to our own time conditions in the English fighting services and their punishments were harsher than they were in other West European forces. Here I can write out of personal experience: for instance, in the bitter winter of 1915–16, which I spent in the trenches, we were far worse off than the French and Germans, with their deep dugouts and supplies of hot food: we had to take the worst of it, in appalling conditions, 'to keep up our *morale*', though in fact we had all been eager volunteers. (After all, didn't Wellington declare he led the scum of the earth?) As for the English being too easy and soft in war, talk to the other side! Once thoroughly engaged, the English are among the hardest and most ruthless peoples who ever went to war. In the Second World War we called up for national service a higher proportion of men *and* women than even the Nazis did. And the final grim decision – stupid and bad, in my opinion – to flatten whole cities, without reference to military targets, thus preparing the world for the atomic doomsday, was an English decision, even if a former German in our service suggested it first. No, the English are not exceptionally kind-hearted at home, and in war they have been hard on themselves and absolutely ruthless defying

'Making Game of Anything'

their enemies. And that great Empire, now fading from memory, wasn't exactly held together by daisy-chains.

But now we move into an area in which Englishness, by which I mean the unique cast and habit of mind I have already described, begins to come into its own, though not entirely free from traces of illusion and self-deception. History shows us how neighbouring nations had power systems that were rational but unreasonable, and so unworkable sooner or later, whereas the English system, though hardly recognized as one, defied the rational in favour of the reasonable, which in spite of various disturbances worked very well. Like power systems elsewhere it worked through a monarchy (or some equivalent) and a ruling aristocracy; but with a very English difference, illogical, inconsistent, seemingly absurd, but for a long time politically and socially reasonable, not intolerable to men of sense.

Let us consider the monarchy first. It is restored after the Civil War and the Protectorate, but without any pretensions to divine rights, with monarchs more or less being tried on as if they were hats. Finally in 1714, with irrationality triumphant, the Elector of Hanover is brought over to become George I. He cannot attend Cabinet meetings because he knows no English; he is a King of England reigning in bewilderment, wondering what his subjects are saying. It seems utterly ridiculous. Yet we know that the stature of this nation is now immensely enlarged in the minds of men of sense and goodwill everywhere, and that for several decades London is the Mecca of the new Enlightenment. Rationality, a logical scheme of things, a clear-cut intellectual system, may have vanished from the English scene, but with this victory of the reasonable the possibility of civilized government, with some guarantee of individual liberty, came closer to the whole Western world. It owes an enormous debt to Englishness.

{17}

When we turn to the second and more important feature, the part played by a ruling aristocracy, we find another odd mixture of apparent absurdity and efficiency, of illusion and self-deception fluttering above basic good sense. And here, so far as major European countries were concerned, the English system was unique. Without Englishness, refusing to be logical and intellectually consistent, it would never have worked at all. What happened was that the English continually manufactured aristocrats while contriving at the same time to venerate the aristocracy. They could bare their heads to members of noble old families that might be neither noble nor old, still having sawdust traces of the workshop about them. Compelled to observe this happening all round him, a typical Frenchman of the same period would feel he was going out of his mind. But then this Frenchman or his successors, rebelling at last against a rigid and over-privileged aristocracy, would rise up, erect the guillotines, sweep everything away, only to make room for Napoleon's mincing machines of French manhood. (I am convinced myself that all really violent revolutions exact a dreadful price: the pendulum swung high comes crashing back, to be stained with blood again.) The English system said in effect: 'We must be governed by aristocrats, so new men who are wealthy, powerful, ambitious and dangerous if ignored must be turned into aristocrats. No more Cromwells and a country parcelled out among major-generals!'

The system worked on a lower level, too, throughout the country. The smaller landowners and most substantial townsmen were brought into local government, and could be widely discovered in mayors' parlours or sitting in judgment on the Bench. This gave England a kind of tough network of political and social institutions and practices not found elsewhere. Strictly speaking it wasn't democratic: the Haves had all the say, the Have-nots had none; and few men are capable of legislating against their own economic interests. And, as we shall see, the system broke down badly when industry developed and the French Revolution terrified the English ruling landed class. Nevertheless, there was always the possibility of democracy here, after various much-needed reforms, as there never was in highly centralized despotic governments ruling their countries through faceless bureaucracies. The English, we might say, *knew* each other, came face to face, even if Sir Tunbelly Clumsy, roaring away on the Bench, showed all over again his prejudice against that impudent fellow, Bill Hodge. With all its weaknesses, the close network held at times when if it had been widely torn there could have been bloodshed and anarchy. There were of course some men who would have welcomed this, having worked out a rational scheme of revolution. But there were never many of them, this not being the English way at all.

Obviously, a society that kept on expanding its aristocracy, to augment

'A Country Girl', by Paul Sandby

and strengthen its ruling *élite*, had to move away from any rigid divisions, from anything like a caste system. So England, as everybody knows, became a country of *classes*. Even today, after so many social changes, the class divisions still exist, though they are not as clearly defined as they used to be. Probably twenty-nine English people out of every thirty even now would be ready to announce which class was theirs. But hazy Englishness, with its dislike of hard definition, has long cast its spell here. Only a foreigner who had spent years in the country could begin to understand what divides one accepted class from another. It is rather as if a regiment could muster on parade, carefully separating its ranks, in what would appear to a visitor to be a dense fog. It is my belief that

{19}

once the English were severely – and then successfully in our time – challenged by other highly industrialized nations, the class system, together with the lingering aristocratic tradition, gravely hindered any rapid development. It has been partly responsible for the so-called malaise of recent years, and, I would say, far more important in its effect than the disappearance of the Empire. A genuine social democracy, of which we had a glimpse during the Second World War, might banish a feeling of staleness, boredom, vague depression, which is now found among so many of the English.

But, while admitting so much, I feel that some ideas about the English class system, coming from outside, stand in need of correction. For instance, when I used to spend a good deal of time in America, people were always harping on 'privilege' in England, apparently unaware of the fact that their own ultra-rich received more deference and were more widely privileged than anybody in England below the rank of royalty. (Somerset Maugham makes the same point at some length in *A Writer's Notebook*.) Another common mistake is that the English class system is imposed from the top, perhaps starting with some dukes and then working down. The truth is, most of the English have an inbuilt sense of class, part of their Englishness. If the upper social orders were suddenly swept away, distinct class differences would remain – and indeed might be sharpened – among the lower orders. I can imagine twenty assorted English in a lifeboat beginning to observe, after the first few hours, their necessary class distinctions. I saw it happen among working women bombed out during the war, when almost immediately they sorted themselves out in terms of microscopic class differences invisible to me. But then it is women – and not only in England – who have the sharper eye for these distinctions.

Yet another mistake has long been made by critics on the outside, protesting and denouncing on behalf of social democracy. They fail to understand that an accepted class system may be easier, more comfortable, even cosier, for most people than what passes for an egalitarian society. Such people, we might say, wear their own shoes and are not for ever trying to squeeze their feet into other people's. And men and women can be truly independent even while acknowledging class distinctions. They know where they stand and are at ease among members of their own class. It is when these obvious distinctions have apparently disappeared and other standards, usually concerned with money, success in business, and economic power, are being applied, that hardly anybody feels at ease. It is harder work keeping up with the Joneses than occasionally having to acknowledge the social superiority of the Earl of Jones. Even in a class society it has to be possible for really exceptional men and women to make their way from one class to another, often going from near the bottom to near the top; and many of the English, past and present, have done this. But most people are not on fire with ambition; they are not wondering day and night how to get on in the world; they want if possible to enjoy a little importance in their own circle; and that is all; for the rest they like to take it easy. This may not raise the gross national product to impressive heights; but they are more likely to find themselves living in a reasonably happy society.

There will be snobbery of course in a class system: the English have been charged with it over and over again. It has never been one of my weaknesses; so I might risk a modest defence of it. First, we must realize that social snobbery, though the most notorious, is only one form of snobbery. There are academic snobs, intellectual snobs, aesthetic snobs, athletic snobs and even discomfort snobs. (These are the people, best avoided, who believe that unless they live uncomfortably, amid disorder and with at least some suggestion of squalor, they are not facing life and accepting reality. Youngish intellectual snobs are often discomfort snobs, too – a horrible combination!) But of course it is the social snobs who have attracted most attention. They have often been taken too heavily and seriously, as for example by Thackeray. (Much to be preferred is the light-comedy manner of E. F. Benson in his *Lucia* novels.) It is absurd to be a desperate social climber, but it is nearly as absurd to be portentous about such a silly pursuit. People must have games to play, and if the Smiths stay up late plotting how to lure the local baronet to their cocktail party, they may be enjoying themselves without doing the rest of us any harm. Social snobbery has lent a sharp flavour to a great deal of excellent English fiction. But it is as well to remember that the most profound and desolating study of such snobbery in all fiction did not come from England but from France, through the genius of Marcel Proust.

One long-lasting feature of English public life, not often found elsewhere, owes something to the class system and something, too, to the lack of rigorous criticism and a sort of lazy-haziness in the public mind. This is the unfailing creation, in one age after another, of apparently important men, ennobled, decorated and beribboned, who have really never done anything in particular. They have just been around and given no trouble. They have never said *No* when they were supposed to say *Yes*. Very often they have been handsome men with an impressive appearance, especially when they have been called upon to take part in some traditional ceremony and wear fancy-dress. (The upper-class English male, as Virginia Woolf, in a sardonic mood, once pointed out, loves parading in fancy-dress.) Up to our own time there was much to be said in favour of these quaint traditional ceremonies, which take place somewhere every other day in English public life. They linked the present to the distant past; they gave both performers and spectators a sense of unbroken continuity; they took history out of textbooks into ancient halls and even into the streets, often complete with trumpets and picturesque costumes. They are now a delight to the tourist trade and colour photography. But traditions and their ceremonies cannot live for ever. Their significance wanes; the life ebbs out of them; and even fond Englishness, which has preserved such things so long, cannot prevent them from appearing foolish and empty to the young of our time. I for one therefore feel that most of this oh-so-English traditional business should be discontinued. England should discover her own living identity, something rather better than a tourist attraction.

I cannot deny that the Englishness I have described, with its unusual balance between consciousness and the unconscious, its refusal to ignore the instinctive and the intuitive, is now being severely challenged. This has happened before and it has survived; but the present challenge cannot be shrugged away. Probably the term *with-it* has already gone out of circulation, for unless we ourselves are *with-it* our vocabulary can be left behind in a few months. Here, of course, we could ask, 'Behind *what*?' Or, for that matter, 'With *what*?' And the answers certainly cannot refer us to Englishness, which takes long and not very short views and always tends to be culturally conservative. It respects age and is cautious and sceptical about youth. *With-it* reverses this. So we have serious newspapers hardly mentioning established artists but concentrating on young rebels who hardly know what they are doing yet. We have apparently responsible directors of public galleries offering space to what seems to many of us to be not *with-it* but a lot of failed experiments or impudent nonsense. When television turns to the arts almost always they represent the extreme *avant-garde*. Critics belonging to the advanced cultural *élite* tell us that only novels about novelists trying to write novels, and not about life in general, are now worth reading. And so it goes on, with the very arts themselves on some fast whirligig of fashion; and whatever this may be, I cannot possibly claim it as another example of Englishness, which, I repeat, is now being severely challenged.

Does this mean that the English public will rid itself of one habit or weakness, well known abroad and always greeted with scorn and derision? This is its fondness for packing concert halls and theatres to applaud old favourite performers, long past their best, singers whose voices have gone, stiff-limbed actors who ought to be back at home nursing their arthritis. The people who do this are not stupid and lacking in taste and judgment, as so many foreigners seem to imagine. They are not applauding cracked voices and stiffened gestures. What is moving them is not continued admiration but affection. That is why I have dragged in this particular example. The English have no monopoly of affection but they have a great deal more of it, both in life and literature, than most other peoples have. Wild consuming love, reckless passion, fanatical devotion – no; but affection, yes indeed! We must not confuse it with sentimentality, which is forced feeling, tears for their own sake, much enjoyed by Victorian slave-driving employers or murderous gangsters thinking about their mothers. Affection flourishes in a region somewhere between love and benevolence on principle. It is warmer than goodwill and more aware of its object, though not in terms of worth, for we can have lasting affection for the unworthy, for even a rogue, so long as he is not callous and cruel, is very much himself and somehow enjoyable. There is always memory playing a part in affection. English literature is suffused by it. There are gleams of it already in the very beginning, at the Tabard Inn at Southwark, along with Chaucer's sly and glinting irony. As for Shakespeare, there is more show of affection, a better understanding of it, in even two or three of his plays than (if we except Chekhov) in the total works of all modern masters of the drama. Some of the English at times have been about as affectionate as an armoured column; but the people in general, the people sweating in galleries and pits to feast on Shakespeare, the people who read Dickens aloud, were never far from affection. In its hazy irrationality, its constant low warmth without fire, it is, I believe, an essential part of Englishness.

Neither this nor much else that belongs to Englishness has been noted by visitors from abroad. A study of their comments, I have discovered, is not rewarding; their impressions are confused and they rarely reveal much insight; to quote all but a very few of them would be to revenge my tedium on the reader. The opinions of the earlier visitors – let us say from the later years of the fifteenth century to the early years of the seventeenth could be roughly summarized as follows.

The English, so they say, have a great opinion of themselves. The highest praise they can give to a foreigner is that he is almost like an Englishman. They are valiant in war and even when at peace at home tend to be pugnacious, arrogant, unruly. Even the common people seem to be proud and seditious. All the English love eating and drinking and making merry. The women, so many of them fair-skinned, handsome, voluptuous, are allowed as much freedom as they want, and so are probably up to no good. Manners are free and easy, unlike those in more civilized countries. There is altogether too much singing, dancing and kissing in public, and with all these goings on a shortage of scholarship, sober and thoughtful travel, civilized social observances, courtly manners.

I think this is a fair summing up, and if we happen to know what was

said later about the English, it seems all very ironical. But we must
remember who made these judgments: not casual travellers, fellows on
holiday, but embassy officials and the like, serious men busy with serious
affairs. Moreover, they came from several countries ravaged by war,
from which Tudor England itself was free, though never free from the
threat of sudden harsh punishment.

Though the saying that the English took their pleasures sadly belongs
to medieval France, it is only during the next phase, beginning in the
later seventeenth century and running through the eighteenth, that the
legend of the sad English begins to haunt foreign visitors. They may
notice other things, from the insolence of the common people to the
unique quality of the London Theatre, but they are dominated by the
idea that the English are morose and melancholy and for ever tempted
to commit suicide. One visitor went back to France to tell his readers
that the London authorities had actually blocked all approaches to the
Thames, because the mere sight of the river might encourage the
citizens to put an end to their mournful lives; and even these precautions,
he added blandly, had little effect. A few attempts are made to explain
this desperate condition of the English – as for example by the London
fogs, too much beef and beer, the spartan education of the young – but
most of these observers have brought the legend with them and are happy
to confirm and enlarge upon it. How much truth was there in it?

Oddly enough, once we forget *The Beggar's Opera* and *Tom Jones* and
take a closer look at the first half of the eighteenth century, we discover

there was a lot of truth in it. There was a deeply neurotic strain in the English, of every class, during all these years. A genuine melancholy, as distinct from a mere affectation of it, overshadowed the country. There was much brooding over Death and the Grave: many of the converted were commanded to think about them every night. Funerals were a favourite spectacle, and there was no better place for a stroll in the evening than the graveyard. Bookshops were filled with mournful verse. And there really were an astonishing number of suicides, far more than in any other country – so many that insurance companies issued policies against it (with strictly limited premiums) and the Church had special prayers against its insidious temptations. But having admitted so much, I must add that the sad-English legend lingered on well into the next century, long after the fashion of melancholy and self-destruction had vanished. One thing that encouraged it was the blank English 'Sabbath' that defeated so many foreign visitors. But there was something else they failed to understand; and here, if only to prove that this is an old question with me, I will quote a passage I wrote forty-five years ago:

We can find many excuses, however, for those foreign visitors, and especially the Frenchmen, who have come so quickly to the conclusion that we are for ever morose and melancholy. England is the land of privacy, and, therefore, the stranger who comes here is at a disadvantage. He sees the high walls, but not the gardens they enclose. He watches Englishmen hurrying silently

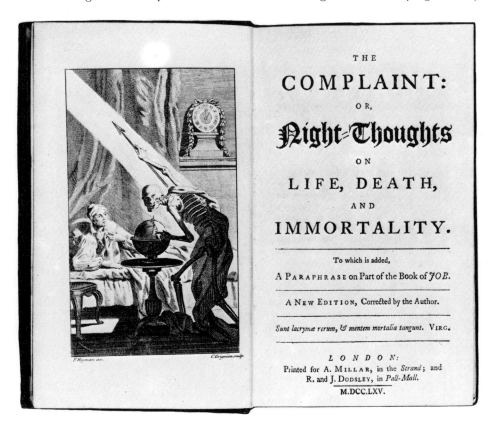

Title page and frontispiece of a best-seller of the eighteenth century, *The Complaint: or, Night-Thoughts on Life, Death and Immortality*, by Edward Young, originally published 1742–5

through the streets to their homes, and does not realize that they are hastening away, out of his sight, only in order that they may unbend at last, turning themselves into persons he would not recognize. . . . A French visitor, finding none of that public gaiety which he has come to associate with a pleasurable life, at once imagines that here is nothing but gloom, a whole nation fog-bound in its wits. . . . He will readily fall into the error of imagining that London is a sad city, just as the travelling Englishman comes too easily to the conclusion that Paris is a very gay city. It is likely that both of them have been misled by surface appearances. . . .

Clearly this was written years before 'swinging London' flaunted a sexy image at a more sedate Paris, far more strictly controlled than it used to be. The points my much-younger self made above, about privacy and hurrying home, were valuable; his argument quite sound. But he had not yet discovered that Englishness which offers us the great clue.

Americans seem to be in the lead among later visitors and critics. They are not remarkable for their insight. Thus a clever American like James Russell Lowell, U.S. Minister in London for several years, can exclaim in a letter home at 'the dullness of the average English mind', possibly not realizing that the Victorian society monopolizing the American Minister would not be regarded by most of the English as enlivening and exciting. He can add in the same letter, 'Let us thank God, dear Charles, that our nerves are nearer the surface, not so deeply embedded in fat or muscle that wit must take a pitchfork to us.' Which is excellent, especially in its reference to nerves being nearer the surface, but all the same he may have been overlooking something. It is not wit but humour that characterizes the English. Some of those beefy, dull-eyed fellows, staring at Lowell as he exercised his wit, may have exchanged among themselves, over a late brandy-and-soda, some remarks about him that were not witty but might be deeply humorous. There was a fair chance that American and French visitors to Victorian London might soon encounter its Podsnaps, but then overlook the fact that Dickens and all his readers were enjoying themselves laughing at Mr Podsnap.

There were – and still are – large numbers of stupid people in England. But living alongside them, easily mistaken for them by lively-minded foreign visitors, are lots of people who seem stupid but aren't. (This was a familiar type in the West Riding, when I grew up there – men who moved slowly and spoke slowly, using the local dialect, apparently almost yokels, but capable of outwitting what they called 'clever Dicks' every time.) Englishness, not based on a rational system capable of supplying rapid questions and answers, can easily suggest stupidity. And sometimes it *is* stupid just because it turns lazy, begins to lose itself in illusions, refuses to accept reality. This is the sullen dark side of the Englishness which, linking intuition and intellect, never governed by the

The plain, practical, down-to-earth John Bull portrayed by Thomas Gainsborough in a characteristically fanciful landscape: Sir Benjamin Truman (1711–80), founder of the famous London brewery

{26}

merely rational, has given so much to the world's literature, science, understanding of politics and the art of living together. So the Englishman who seems so glum and taciturn, offending or bewildering the visitor from abroad who wants to start a talk in the railway carriage, may be coldly arrogant, may be just stupid and oafish. But he might possibly be trying to follow a difficult line of thought, now halted or hurried on by mysterious gusts of feeling, now caught in the light of consciousness or losing itself in the dusk of the unconscious. Hazlitt tells us somewhere about a Frenchwoman who married an Englishman, probably about the middle of the eighteenth century, and when her French friends complained about his long silences she said solemnly, 'He is thinking about Locke and Newton.' Fifty to one he wasn't, and we can lay the same heavy odds against the nearest silent Englishman being deeply engaged comparing the 'Big Bang' and the 'Steady State' theories of the universe. But we could be wrong – and he might even be working out an entirely new theory.

That impressive commentator, Alexis de Tocqueville, visited England in the 1830s, and this is one of his notes:

> The French wish not to have superiors. The English wish to have inferiors. The Frenchman constantly raises his eyes above him with anxiety. The Englishman lowers his beneath him with satisfaction. On both sides there is pride, but it is understood in a different way. . . .

Very neat; very sharp; but based, I suspect, on a comparison between a narrow middle range of the English and a wide range of the French, all grandchildren of the Revolution. Emerson's *English Traits* is still worth reading, though it is rather early travel-book work and far below his best. You can hear Carlyle, a strong influence, rasping away behind Emerson's political-social criticism. (Incidentally, in my re-reading I found a brief passage I must have marked over fifty years ago. He was listening to Wordsworth, and the old poet, suddenly prophetic, 'said of the Newtonian theory, that it might yet be superseded and forgotten'.) Certainly, his final essay ends with almost rapturous praise – e.g. England 'has yielded more able men in five hundred years than any other nation'. But I feel this praise would mean more if it had been erected on a firmer foundation. There is too much plain, practical, down-to-earth John Bull, as if he had met nobody in England except successful farmers, calico exporters and bank managers. Even his essay on English literature begins as if these fellows had written it. And he has been far too strongly influenced by the old French legend, that the English are silent and cold, morose and melancholy, and this lures him into downright silliness: 'Meat and wine produce no effect on them; they are just as cold, quiet, composed, at the end, as at the beginning of

The Ancestor', a caricature of Lord Ribblesdale by Bert Thomas, sums up the time-honoured – if no longer accurate – conception of the English 'Milord'.

dinner.' All the records, memoirs and novels of early Victorian England prove this to be nonsense: he must have been dining at the waxworks.

This chapter must soon give way to the next, so I am leaping over some visitors to mid-Victorian England to join another famous American, who finally settled here – Henry James. He wrote a good deal about England and the English, but the passage I like best comes from one of his earliest pieces:

> The tone of things is somehow heavier than with us; manners and modes are more absolute and positive; they seem to swarm and to thicken the atmosphere about you. Morally and physically it is a denser air than ours. We seem loosely hung together at home as compared with the English, every man of whom is a tight fit in his place. It is not an inferential but a palpable fact that England is a crowded country. . . .

This was well worth saying, especially, to my mind, 'a tight fit in his place'. To make the point that the English live in an old and crowded country requires no great depth of insight, yet many severe or mocking critics of English manners have never taken this into account. A man living in a crowded country may want to armour himself against other people, to keep silent because he needs some time alone with his own thoughts; a session with some inquiring and loquacious visitor is anything but a treat to him. And of course England is far more crowded than it was when Henry James wrote the piece quoted above. But now comes the ironical twist. In recent years, because more and more people have been moved into housing estates, stark towers of flats, accommodation for pensioners, in this new overcrowded England there have been increasing complaints, chiefly from women and the elderly, of desperate *loneliness*. A nice chat would be welcome whether the visitor came from Birmingham, Warwickshire, or Birmingham, Alabama.

André Maurois, who was almost a professional Anglophile, naturally had some pleasant things to say about England and the English; but there was one remark he made that offered him a clue he never accepted. He said rather casually that whenever he returned to England he began to hear about ghosts again. That should have told him something about the English mind, partly existing in the dusk and gathering shadows of the unconscious. As it was, the visitor who came closest to my own idea of Englishness was the Spanish-American philosopher, George Santayana. After lecturing for many years at Harvard he happened to be in England at the outbreak of war in 1914, and so he stayed, in or near Oxford, until 1919. Out of these years came a superb book of essays, *Soliliquies in England*, and if now I begin to ruin the stately march of Santayana's prose, it is because I cannot resist quoting while knowing I must not use up too much space:

The English delight in ghosts: 'Dr John Dee and Edward Kelly making a Dead Person appear in a cemetery' (detail), 1846

. . . I could see clearly that this England was pre-eminently the home of decent happiness and a quiet pleasure in being oneself. I found here the same sort of manliness which I had learned to love in America, yet softer, and not at all obstreperous; a manliness which when refined a little creates the gentleman, since its instinct is to hide its strength for an adequate occasion and for the service of others. . . . Such modesty in strength is entirely absent from the effusive temperament of the Latin, who is cocky and punctilious so long as his conceit holds out, and then utterly humbled and easily corrupted; entirely absent also from the doctrinaire of the German school, in his dense vanity and officiousness, that nothing can put to shame. So much had I come to count on this sort of manliness in the friends of my youth, that without it the most admirable and gifted persons seemed to be hardly *men*: they fell rather into an ambiguous retinue, the camp followers of man, cleverer but meaner than himself – the priests, politicians, actors, pedagogues, and shopkeepers. . . . These self-sufficing Englishmen, in their reserve and decision, seemed to me truly men. . . . The low pressure at which their minds seemed to work showed how little they were alarmed about anything: things would all be managed somehow. They were good company even when they said nothing. . . .

Even while not accepting all these tremendous compliments, we can feel ourselves moving along the right road. I can afford to quote a few passages on the atmosphere and landscape of England, because they will not take us out of our way:

> England is pre-eminently a land of atmosphere. A luminous haze permeates everywhere, softening distances, magnifying perspectives, transfiguring familiar objects, harmonizing the accidental, making beautiful things magical and ugly things picturesque. . . .
>
> In England the classic spectacle of thunderbolts and rainbows appears but seldom; such contrasts are too violent and definite for these tender skies. Here the conflict between light and darkness, like all other conflicts, ends in a compromise; cataclysms are rare, but revolution is perpetual. Everything lingers on and is modified; all is luminous and all is grey. . . .

Later, Santayana asks what it is that governs the Englishman. After replying that it is not intelligence, very seldom passion, and hardly self-interest, he continues shrewdly:

> If we tried to say what governs him is convention, we should have to ask ourselves how it comes about that England is the paradise of individuality, eccentricity, heresy, anomalies. hobbies, and humours. Nowhere do we come oftener upon those two social abortions – the affected and the disaffected. Where else would a man inform you, with a sort of proud challenge, that he lived on nuts, or was in correspondence through a medium with Sir Joshua Reynolds, or had been disgustingly housed when last in prison?

It is a good sharp point, too often ignored by foreign critics who seem to have had more than their share of tailor's dummies among their English acquaintances. Moreover, English prose literature, throughout its history, offers triumphant proof, being itself a 'paradise of individuality, eccentricity, heresy'.

Two brief statements by Santayana take us close to that secret of 'Englishness' with which I began this chapter. The first: *What governs the Englishman is his inner atmosphere, the weather in his soul.* The second, coming later, is very much a companion passage: *The Englishman establishes a sort of satisfaction and equilibrium in his inner man, and from that citadel of rightness he easily measures the value of everything that comes within his moral horizon.* But how does all this come about? I can only repeat – in an abridged version – what I declared at the beginning of this chapter. The barrier between consciousness and the unconscious is not rigidly fixed in the English psyche. The English depend more upon instinct and intuition than other West Europeans do. If this is not the secret of traditional 'Englishness' – and it is convenient and time-saving if I keep on calling it that – then I don't know what is the secret, and ought to be writing some other book. I have not the space to quote other passages from Santayana, who, in spite of the fact that he was a very polite guest, indicated some of the weakness as well as the strength of the English mind – but I have already done this myself. There will have to be more of it in the chapters that follow, where we shall also encounter styles of life and attitudes of mind, belonging to certain classes or groups, that attempt to break away from this Englishness. If, risking tedium, I have hammered too often and too hard at this central theme, it is because from now on we shall do some wandering, sometimes among the English refusing to be English, and must never forget that still existing alongside these various deviations and antics, like a *basso ostinato* when the strings or woodwind are almost crazy, will be Englishness itself.

Finally – the inevitable question: how did we come to acquire this Englishness? I don't know, and I doubt if anybody else does. The mixture of peoples – Celt and Saxon and Dane – may have had something to do with it. (Not the conquering Norman, because it was *he* who changed, like many another conqueror before and after him. Consider the English who settled in Ireland and then became Irish!) Certainly the climate, with its haziness and softening of boundaries and hard edges, must have had a profound effect. Even diet may have played some part. I could add a few more guesses, and so, I imagine, could most of my readers. Let us leave it at that.

Ladies playing cricket in 1890

ENGLISHWOMEN

❀

IN this chapter I want to do two things: first, to offer at least some glimpses of Englishwomen during the last five centuries; secondly, to challenge and banish a spectre that has haunted social critics and satirists for the last hundred and fifty years. This is the idea of the charmless, flat-chested, mannish or absurdly prudish English-woman, either contemptuous or terrified of sex. True, we don't hear very much about her nowadays, certainly not in this country; but I suspect her image still lingers abroad. Even if the type exists here, it is not peculiarly English but can be found everywhere in Europe and America. (What would French novelists have done without their provincial spinsters, at once sour and mischievous and often downright malevolent?) Again, the notion, so widely accepted, that the English find sex frightening or disgusting was entirely based on the opinion and outlook of the Victorian middle class, whose prejudices I have dealt with at some length elsewhere, in *Victoria's Heyday*. As a criticism of the English in general, down the centuries, it is ridiculous, as I hope to prove before I have done with this chapter. It is also incompatible with my basic idea of Englishness – the *Leitmotiv* of this book – which refuses to rationalize sex and sexual love just as it does so many other things. It is the Latin, the chief sneerer, who tends to rationalize sex, keeps it in a compartment, and regards making love as an agreeable afternoon occupation following a good lunch.

Through the sixteenth and seventeenth centuries and into the eighteenth many visitors from abroad were enthusiastic about the appearance and manners of Englishwomen. 'Their women, of any estimation, are the greatest beauties in the world, and as fair as alabaster . . . they are also cheerful and courteous and of good address.' Their freedom, tending to boldness, is noticed, for these Elizabethan wives 'will frequent the taverns or ale-houses for enjoyment . . . and if one woman only is invited, then she will bring three or four other women along and they gaily toast each other . . .'. And again: 'Now the women-folk of England, who have mostly blue-grey eyes and are fair and pretty, have more liberty than in other lands, and know just how to make use of it, for they often stroll out or drive by coach in very gorgeous clothes, and the men must put up with such ways, and may not punish them for it. . . .' As the Venetian Ambassador observed long before, with some disapproval, this was a country in which there was much kissing and dancing and singing and junketing, all very different from the legend of it three centuries later, when all was gloom and melancholy. By the end of the seventeenth century a French traveller, after a stay of three years, could write: 'They pay great Honour to the Women in England, and they enjoy very great and very commendable Liberties: But they have

Mary Fitton (detail), about 1595, from the Circle of George Gower. Born 1578, she was maid of honour to Elizabeth I, 1595; mistress of the Earl of Pembroke by whom she had a child, 1601; later married a Captain Polwhele; at one time considered to be Shakespeare's 'Dark Lady'

neither so much Favour, nor so much Honour, as their graceful Mien, their Genteelness, and so many Charms as they are possess'd might justly challenge' – complimentary if a trifle confused. And even in the later years of the eighteenth century a German pastor, who had settled in London, could write, 'I really believe, that in no country are so many fine women to be met with as in England', but then he reserved most of his praise for the 'more modest, more domestic, more industrious' women of the lower classes, and, like a good German pastor, dismissed most fashionable ladies as idle flippertigibbets, always hurrying from one engagement to another, card-table to card-table.

But this has taken us too far from the Englishwomen we should look at first. These are the women of Tudor and Stuart times. All the evidence we possess tells us that in this period many women of the upper classes, perhaps the majority of them, were a long way removed from being female dummies. Gervase Markham could announce in 1616 that 'our English housewife must be of chaste thought, stout courage, patient, untired, watchful, diligent, witty, pleasant, constant in friendship, full of good neighbourhood, wise in discourse . . .' This is a very large order indeed, a masculine dream of femininity, and we may be sure very few wives fulfilled such an order – or even tried to do so. But undoubtedly the Tudor and Stuart ladies were very different from the pallid shrinking creatures, belonging to the early and mid-Victorian middle classes, accepted abroad as typical Englishwomen. They had minds of their own, and often well-educated minds, like Queen Elizabeth herself. Once the nunneries had gone, it was not easy to ensure that a girl received a good education. The wealthy nobles, of course, could employ resident tutors, but the ordinary country gentlefolk could rarely afford this kind of private tuition; there were only a very few girls' schools; but somehow or other, possibly with the help of maiden aunts, local widows, or clergy-men, most daughters had at least some book-learning. Moreover, apart from books, an impressive amount of useful knowledge, which a conscientious lady of the manor urgently needed, came their way. Many of them, too, had very considerable social accomplishments. It will do us no harm to remember that the Elizabethan gentry, taken strictly as individuals, and not like us the mass heirs of science and technology, far outshone us in their individual accomplishments; and this applies to women just as it does to men.

In the great houses, with their hordes of servants and long-staying guests arriving by the score, we can assume that the huge task of main-taining the household was taken over by professionals. But the wife of a comparatively small landowner had to be responsible for everything herself. She was a caterer who also had to grow and preserve most of the food for her family, guests and servants, with no stores a few miles away,

Lady Jane Grey, proclaimed
Protestant Queen July 1553,
but overthrown by the Catholic
Queen Mary, about 1545,
attributed to Master John

'Conversation Group with Two Ladies and a Dog', by Daniel Gardner

no telephone at her elbow. Nevertheless, even in Tudor times, though she might be a long way from any town, she could not be entirely independent, and there was some shopping to be done, especially for wine and sugar and spices. So we have many instances of husbands, going to London on business, being given shopping lists and strict orders to bring back or have sent off fairly large quantities of the things badly needed at home. Again, most of these country wives not only cultivated a herb garden but also mixed and treated their herbs to compound a fair number of traditional remedies. These were not only used at home. Doctors were still scarce and if they were obliged to travel some distance they were extremely expensive. Very often then the lady of the manor, with her herbal preparations, did a good deal of rough-and-ready physicking for a neighbouring village or two. If this appears to be too barbaric, we should remember that many of these traditional remedies have now been approved by science – even penicillin was anticipated by the use of mould – whereas much of the treatment then by licensed medical practitioners really *was* barbaric, quite horrifying. We can fairly assume than that most of the wives and daughters of country gentlemen in the sixteenth and seventeenth centuries were anything but stupid, idle and irresponsible. It was later, when the eighteenth century began adding its amenities, that so many of them can be found yawning their heads off.

Even a modest household might have a dozen servants, male and female, working indoors and outdoors – after all, it was both a market garden and a small jam-and-pickle factory. The mistress of the house was legally entitled to chastise a servant who was lazy and insolent. A severe beating, bringing real injury, could happen, but so rarely that examples of it soon became notorious. It seems obvious to me that the relations between servants and their employers in the England of these times were far better than they were in the nineteenth century and even in the earlier years of this century. To be given too many orders, to be kept at it from early morning until late at night, to eat cold scrag end of mutton when there was hot roast beef in the dining-room – this was not an easy life. But it was a worse life if, as happened so often later, you ceased to be a *person* in the eyes and minds of your masters and mistresses. Better to have your face slapped now and again than to appear not to have a face, pretending to be a noiseless automaton. Even apart from letters and memoirs, we learn from the old plays how servants were people, turning after much service into free-spoken, cranky, family characters. And there could be many an unoccupied man or lonely woman today who could secretly envy those servants of long ago, busy and bustling in a household where something was always happening.

However, two things happened all too often. Too many children were born and too many children died. So much fertility and mortality ought to have transformed Tudor and Stuart wives into trembling ghosts; but on the whole it does not seem to have done, perhaps because these dames had other responsibilities and accomplishments. Oddly enough, childbirth on a scale that modern women would regard with horror does not appear to have made many of these women, especially the great ladies, seem less sexually desirable. So, for example, the famous Penelope Rich, sister to the Earl of Essex and once Sir Philip Sidney's 'Stella', was still a renowned and courted beauty when she had had about a dozen children. But then it was said that she survived unblemished the dreaded smallpox,

(left) Lucy Hutchinson
(right) Dorothy Osborne

that enemy of women's beauty. A girl could come out of the smallpox sickroom without a trace of her earlier bloom and prettiness. It could be a harsh test of the devotion and constancy of her young lover. Smallpox links two seventeenth-century Englishwomen well known to later generations: the stern Parliamentarian, Lucy Hutchinson, and the charming Royalist, Dorothy Osborne. Here I can quote Macaulay, who delighted in Dorothy Osborne's letters, written to William Temple before they were able to marry, when he had been courting her for years:

> When at last the constancy of the lovers had triumphed over all the obstacles which kinsmen and rivals could oppose to their union, a yet more serious calamity befell them. Poor Mistress Osborne fell ill of the smallpox, and, though she escaped with life, lost all her beauty. To this most severe trial the affection and honour of the lovers of that age was not unfrequently subjected. Our readers probably remember what Mrs Hutchinson tells us of herself. The lofty Cornelia-like spirit of the aged matron seems to melt into a long forgotten softness when she relates how her beloved Colonel 'married her as soon as she could quit the chamber, when the priest and all that saw her were affrighted to look on her. But God,' she adds, with a not ungraceful vanity, 'recompensed his justice and constancy, by restoring her as well as before.' Temple showed on this occasion the same justice and constancy which did so much honour to Colonel Hutchinson. . . .

Both these women, the fiercely loyal and indomitable Lucy, the lively, sensible but tender Dorothy, seem to me to have been made of better metal than their respective husbands, though they were men who played a part in great affairs. It is worth adding a footnote on female education here, for Lucy tells us that about the age of seven she was under instruction by eight tutors.

These two women married the men they were in love with; but a great many girls, especially if they belonged to the nobility and wealthy landed classes, were not so fortunate. It was common for parents to arrange marriages between respective sons and daughters who were still in the nursery; they were really busy uniting families and estates, not individuals. This partly explains – only partly, because there were always fashionable women with a taste for sexual adventures – the numerous, notorious, adulterous, often long-lasting affairs that encouraged speculation and gossip from the years of the Tudors to the Regency. A girl only in her middle teens might be married to one youth when she was already in love with another, whose mistress she became as soon as this was possible, probably bearing his children and often at long last marrying him. These women behaved as normal women, capable of love, want to behave. A society that married off young girls like transferring parcels of land and bank balances should not have pretended to be shocked if they broke 'the sacred vows of marriage'. This was the English busy deceiving

The three illustrations which follow show three different aspects of English womanhood in the eighteenth and nineteenth centuries. Opposite is Thomas Gainsborough's double portrait of the Linley sisters, painted in 1772 with that tenderness which the artist obviously felt for most women and all children, in a mistily sylvan setting. Elizabeth Linley, the elder sister (left), became a celebrated singer and married Richard Brinsley Sheridan, the playwright. Her sister Mary, also a singer, married Richard Tickell, a poet and pamphleteer.

Overleaf is a typical conversation piece, by Arthur Devis (1711–87), of a typical well-to-do provincial family— that of Mr Edward Rookes Leedes, of Royds Hall, in Yorkshire – all of them dressed in their best clothes, and rather absurdly posed against a thoroughly artificial background.

{40}

TEE
TOTAL

themselves, manufacturing cant and humbug. But there can be no doubt that these enormous scandals, providing gossip for all classes, outraged the puritans of the seventeenth century and the various sects and the growing middle class of the eighteenth century, giving the aristocracy a reputation, at once dreadful and fascinating, for depravity and sexual indulgence. And at least in this particular matter I side with the aristocrats. Finally, so far as the Tudor and Stuart eras are concerned, it seems to me we find strong confirmation of the almost rapturous opinion of Englishwomen offered us by foreign visitors, and if necessary we could bring in Shakespeare and his fellow poets as extra witnesses. That legend of the typical Englishwoman – charmless, sexless, mannish or ridiculously prudish – certainly owes nothing to these years.

There is, I feel, some deterioration as we enter the eighteenth century. To illustrate what I have in mind I will take Lady Mary Wortley Montagu, who lived from 1689 to 1762. As a girl she was beautiful, clever, witty. Her father would not allow her to marry the man of her choice, Edward Wortley Montagu (there was disagreement about the marriage settlement) and commanded her to take somebody else; so she ran off and married Montagu by special licence. When Montagu was appointed Ambassador to Turkey, she went with him to Adrianople, where she discovered that people could be successfully inoculated against smallpox, and then to Constantinople, which provided her with the material she used with such skill and sense in her famous letters. But these were not published until after her death. Before she went to Constantinople, and immediately after, she owed her success in society to her looks, wit and charm, and to the enthusiastic friendship of men like Pope, who adored her, and Swift. Then in the 1720s everything began to go wrong. A bitter quarrel with Pope and Swift left her the victim of their formidable power of satire – and often coarse satire. She had no quarrel with her husband or their daughter, who became Lady Bute, but did not make a home with either of them; she had an ambiguous relationship with a Frenchman, Rémond, and lost some of his money, as well as some of her own, in South Sea speculation; and after some years of undignified social and literary squabbling, she did what so many of the English did in that century, she wandered abroad, tried to settle down, then wandered again, chiefly in Italy and France. As with many other expatriates, her loss of looks and style, manners and money, was maliciously reported by English travellers like Horace Walpole. But within a year or two after her death, her reputation was secure as one of the best letter-writers in the English language. These letters, however, belonged to her brilliant young womanhood, a long time ago.

I hope I am not forcing opinion – as well as doing an injustice to Mary Wortley Montagu – if I say I find considerable social significance in the

The idea of the charmless and prudish wife and mother, which so distorted the image of Englishwomen in the nineteenth century, is here amusingly reflected in one of the most popular English art forms of the period, the Staffordshire pottery chimney-piece group.

melancholy contrast between her early life, when she appeared to have everything, and her later life, when she seemed to have lost almost everything – husband, daughter, friends, admirers, a satisfying existence either as a writer, making full use of her talent, or as a wife, mother, hostess. I cannot help feeling that if she had been born much earlier her story would have been very different, much happier. No doubt she had her weaknesses, but it seems to me that the spirit of the age encouraged them.

When we are into the century there are clear signs of this deterioration. Certainly there are the family groups and conversation pieces so characteristic of English eighteenth-century painting; the letters and occasional memoirs of tranquil but busy wives of the country gentlemen; the charm of rural life celebrated by so many poets. But there is something not quite solid, not entirely convincing, in much of this. It is when an enduring and completely satisfying life in the country is on its way out that it is presented with pastoral effects and Arcadian highlights. Easier communications, the spread of fashionable intelligence, with London seeming less remote than it did earlier, created that familiar figure, the bored and resentful manor-house wife, either deserted by a husband who is throwing his money or hers away in Town, or daily disgusted by one who is for ever out hunting and drinking and stumbles to bed in muddy boots. Again, much later, we have the type represented by Sheridan's Lydia Languish, cramming herself with romantic nonsense from the circulating library. Possibly she may have settled down sensibly as Jack Absolute's wife, but it is not unreasonable to be sceptical. And

Mary Wollstonecraft (detail)

Fanny D'Arblay Burney, by
Edward Francis Burney

while there are glimpses of genuine womanhood in Fielding, far more
people were sweating and weeping in Richardson's hothouses.

I feel that the relations between the sexes deteriorated during this age,
and did so on almost all levels. So Englishwomen suffered a defeat, as
they were bound to do. Certainly there were women who insisted upon
asserting their individuality and demanding their rights, from Mary
Wortley Montagu and one or two of her friends early in the century to
the gallant and forthright Mary Wollstonecraft at the end of it. Certainly
the age produced some splendid women, remarkable for both beauty and
character, and while it had more than its share of posturing and scribbling
blue-stockings, it also had its Fanny Burney and finally its incomparable
Jane Austen, though her triumph really belongs to the Regency. But
while admitting this I cannot escape the feeling that what had been right
between Englishmen and their women once – say, up to the Restoration –
had now gone wrong. The English, we might say, were trying to flourish

in the wrong atmosphere. (Though visually they did more than well enough, if we remember their domestic architecture, furniture and decoration, and much of their painting.) They were trying to defy their essential Englishness. The irrational, the instinctive, the intuitive, were to be banished. Believing that he existed in a neat clockwork universe, wound up by the deity and then left to its own tidy devices, the educated Englishman now endeavoured to appear calm, cool, entirely rational, like a Roman of the great age born again to inherit a larger world. But he was playing a part foreign to him. He was obeying rules when he had a natural tendency to ignore or break them. It was as if Shakespeare compelled himself to write like Racine. Where there had been a vague but necessary traffic between the conscious mind and the unconscious, a high barrier was erected or hatches battened down. There must no longer be an open end somewhere in the dark. They were proud to be English but they no longer accepted their heritage of Englishness.

The consequences were inevitable. What they would not accept, what they thought they could safely ignore, took its revenge. When all was light, in rushed the dark invaders. While proud consciousness, bewigged, powdered, smiling in silk and satin, entered by the front door for yet another assembly, the ancient and awesome figures out of the unconscious were waiting at the back door, so that after the musicians had gone home and all the candles had been snuffed out, there could be terrible dreams. Many of the authors in this new Augustan Age were in fact anything but Augustan. Strange rages and fits, melancholy and madness haunted them. (Ironically enough, the man considered to be a gentle lunatic, William Blake, was the sanest of them all.) Many of their readers were as neurotic and secretly moonstruck as they were, and often worse. Behind the show of confident rationality it was an age of eccentrics, of misers and spendthrifts, of brutal sadists and quivering masochists, of occult sects, of Hell-fire Clubs, of being sceptical of everything in public and believing anything in private, of tittering and drinking half the night with wit and fashion, and then reeling home to be devoured again by melancholy and a suicidal despair.

There may be exaggeration here; and I am not deliberately ignoring all those eighteenth-century men who were cheerfully fattening their cattle, hunting or fishing or shooting, adding little temples and bridges to their estates. Because they assumed a complete rationality, making no allowance for the irrational and powerful unconscious drives, many of these men were shockingly aggressive. And this explains not only the brutality of the age but also its failure in sexual relations. It was a failure not confined to narrow classes, to intellectuals, fashionables, rich landowners and sportsmen. The trouble was a deep trouble, penetrating most social levels. So there was a perfervid evangelical movement, with innumerable conversions, often wildly hysterical, to Calvinism and Methodism. Women converts, who were in the majority, were frequently told that they had no hope of salvation unless they were subordinate to men, a John Wesley being in full agreement with a John Milton.

While there must still have been some happy lovers and deeply satisfying marriages, all the evidence I can muster proves that the general relations between the sexes rapidly deteriorated at this time, and that the run-down, losing sight of any sensible standard, lasted, with various modifications, well into the following century. But the eighteenth had its own sexual style. Instead of bringing men and women together as *persons* within a sexual relationship, it set up a barrier between them. The sexes were now at war. (Englishness, which sets the reasonable before the rational, as most women do, could have restored peace, but it had fled the scene.) This was the age when elaborate, cold-hearted seduction occupied a place taken over later by golf and bridge; when middle-aged gentlemen of 'sensibility' bought the services of terrified young girls simply to deflower them; when foolish heiresses were persuaded to elope, not realizing that while marriage was easy, divorce was difficult, almost impossible; when catering for sado-masochism and all its devices became big business; when 'to enjoy' a woman merely meant getting her into bed for a night or two while still regarding her, behind the show of gallantry, as a little idiot; when 'love' lost all tenderness, understanding, personal depth, and was so much lustful conquest for the male, so much bewilderment or cynical calculation for the female.

While the most popular novelist of the period, Samuel Richardson, owed much to his artfully protracted story-telling, it is no accident that his *Pamela* is not really a love story but a triumphant account of how to get the best possible terms for a maidenhead, and that his *Clarissa Harlowe*, sinister behind its pathos, is a saga of sado-masochism. It is equally revealing that Sterne, undoubtedly a genius, can never face sexual love fairly and squarely but prefers lascivious hints and sniggering, likely to repel normal women at most times. It is typical of this age of Don Juanism that London marvelled at the beautiful Mrs Elizabeth Inchbald, who wrote a very successful novel and many stage comedies, because she steadily refused to be seduced. Some of her fellow women writers, of whom the equally successful Hannah More is the best example, retained their honour and chastity, but they were hardly under as much pressure as the supremely attractive Mrs Inchbald.

Possibly the best-known and most widely admired women – at least in London – were a few aristocratic beauties. Strictly speaking, Georgiana, Duchess of Devonshire, was not a beauty, but her combination of grace and charm, lively spirits and good sense, made her irresistible. She was the friend of Charles James Fox and Sheridan, and an enthusiastic Whig,

boldly defying the Court Party, risking much coarse abuse. She could even go canvassing in Long Acre, a rough London neighbourhood, and airily distributed kisses for promises of support. Unlike most duchesses then or ever since, she admired and was devoted to men of talent – altogether an exceptional, splendid lady. When we come down to the next level of fame – notoriety, public interest – it is the eighteenth-century actresses, not its women writers, who claim our attention. Undoubtedly there were more and more women writers, and their readers were multiplied by the circulating libraries, whose patrons were fairly divided between sermons (best-sellers then), heavily moral fables, informative and edifying works, and wildly romantic novels intended for Lydia Languish and her kind. But only research could discover the names of the great majority of these hard-working 'authoresses' – no term I like to use. On the other hand, if we care at all about the Theatre, the names of some eighteenth-century actresses linger in our minds, which

Georgiana, Duchess of Devonshire and her Daughter, by Sir Joshua Reynolds

{50}

continue to hint that they must have been delicious creatures. We have no notion how good they were – and perhaps if they appeared magically before us we might find their tragedy laughable, their comedy pitiful – but I am prepared to believe they were as beautiful and talented as we are told they were, though neither as virtuous nor as wicked as their contemporaries said they were. One point worth making, before I briefly review some of the most famous or notorious, is that these actresses bring us closer than we have been yet, in these pages, to the actual eighteenth-century England and what happened between the sexes there.

Anne Bracegirdle comes first. She was Congreve's leading lady, was reputed to be his mistress, and there were rumours she had been secretly married to him. But unlike most actresses, she kept a close guard over her private life. Her theatrical career was a triumph, especially in comedy (she was a sparkling brunette), and for years it was almost the fashion to fall in love with her. She was not unlike Congreve, apparently cool and careful but also vain and arrogant, and just as he swept out of play-writing after the failure of *The Way of the World*, she left the stage for ever in 1707 because her younger rival, Anne Oldfield, was judged to have played a favourite part better than she had done. Anne Oldfield as a young girl was encouraged to go on the stage by Farquhar (whose early death at about twenty-nine was probably the greatest loss the London Theatre ever sustained) who overheard her reciting at home, in the Mitre Tavern. She began slowly, having had no proper training, but then finally succeeded in a wide variety of parts, her excellent figure, particularly fine eyes and distinctive voice enabling her to play tragedy as well as comedy, although like her audiences she preferred the latter. It was said that towards the end of her career, when she had to endure much pain, managers would pay £50 – a great sum then – for one performance of a favourite comic part. She was a thoroughly conscientious actress, a real professional, and though taken up and petted by fashionable society she was entirely free from the petulant whims and caprices that spoiled so many actresses. Out of pure compassion she rescued the poet Savage and kept him going afterwards with a modest but regular allowance. She left two illegitimate sons, the second by General Charles Churchill, to whom, it was strongly rumoured, she was eventually married. (There were many good reasons, both social and professional, why such marriages were so often not publicly acknowledged.) Pope often sneered at her whereas Fielding thought her ravishing and adorable, and I feel we ought to prefer the latter's verdict.

A very odd career was that of Lavinia Fenton, a London girl, very pretty and engaging, who at eighteen went on the stage in 1726 and left it two years later. She captivated audiences at once, and when in January 1728 she created the part of Polly Peachum in *The Beggar's*

Opera London went wild over her; the print shops were filled with engravings of her portrait; and a 'band of her devoted admirers' escorted her every night from the theatre to her home. But in June she deserted the stage to live with the Duke of Bolton, about twenty-three years older than she was, married but separated from his wife. This seems to have been from the beginning a genuine love affair; they made a devoted pair; and both as an accepted mistress and as a wife-and-duchess – for Bolton married her in 1751 when at last he was free – Lavinia was entirely commendable and much admired for her wit and good sense. But then the wonderful luck ran out, the Duke dying three years after their marriage, she herself only reaching her early fifties, knowing only too well that none of her three sons, being illegitimate, could inherit the title and all that went with it. Often when wandering through Wensleydale, within sight of Bolton Castle, I have remembered Lavinia Fenton, the girl who within eighteen months became the toast of the town and then coolly marched out of it all. Hers must be the strangest meteoric career to be found in the annals of the London stage.

In the sharpest contrast to the lives of the actresses already mentioned is that of George Anne Bellamy, who ought to have been called Georgiana but even her christening went wrong. Though never a steady success in the Theatre for long, she is worth considering because a great deal characteristic of the eighteenth century – not unlike one of its cautionary tales – was packed into her life and career. To begin with, her young mother, though a Quakeress, eloped from her boarding school with Lord Tyrawley, a rather surprising Ambassador at Lisbon. There, just before George Anne was born, she married a master mariner called Bellamy, who promptly vanished. Unlike many noblemen of the period, Tyrawley creditably recognized his illegitimate daughter, made certain she was given an education and made much of her whenever he was in London, introducing her to men like Pope and Lord Chesterfield. But when he went off as Ambassador to Russia she insisted (thereby forfeiting his allowance) upon joining her mother, now comfortably settled in London. George Anne contrived to move in theatrical circles, accepted a few small parts, but fairly soon, with much backing from her father's influential friends, was playing leading tragic roles. Never recognized as a great actress, even so she was successful – and very much the fashion – in some of these parts, owing a great deal to a stormy temperament and, in tragic terms, a piquant appearance – for she was small, a delicate blonde, one of the 'divine creatures' of the time. But now she began to pay heavily for a childhood divided between meeting Lord Chesterfield in Mayfair and trying to cope with Quaker relatives in the country. She was madly vain, arrogant and extravagant, wilful and unreliable, lacking the professional dedication of other leading actresses. She might

George Anne Bellamy,
engraved by Francesco
Bartolozzi after Cotes

have clamped herself into a moral tale against good-looking actresses. She gambled hard, found herself in a maze of debts, ran away with men and then ran away from them, lost her looks, lost her figure, and by the time she was into her forties might have been a whining and cadging old woman. There appeared in 1785 *An Apology for the Life of George Anne Bellamy Written by Herself* (though in fact it was ghosted work), in no fewer than six volumes. Poor George Anne! We could say she became the favourite actress of those determined to write and preach against actresses.

Peg Woffington should not be here – she was an Irishwoman – but she is so well remembered, largely because of Charles Reade's play and novel, that something must be said about her. She had an uncommonly wide range of parts, though her rather harsh voice told against her in tragedy;

she was boldly handsome, occasionally flew into rages, but generally was as professionally conscientious as she was accomplished. The eighteenth century had a fancy for seeing good-looking gallants played by actresses – these were known as 'breeches parts' – and Peg's Sir Harry Wildair was famous. She herself told how she said to Quin, 'I have played the part so often that half the town believes me to be a real man,' only to get the retort, 'Madam, the other half knows you to be a woman,' her sex life being notorious. But like many 'wicked women' she was good-hearted, generous, always ready to help others in need; and when she died, still only in her forties, the whole town mourned her.

At least in comic parts Peg Woffington's great feuding rival was Kitty Clive, who also had an Irish father, but he married an Englishwoman and settled in London, where Kitty was born. Both as a performer and as a woman, Kitty Clive was an odd mixture. She had a good singing voice and was in fact an excellent musician and at the same time had a genius for broad comedy. (The only trouble she gave her managers was in constantly demanding to play in genteel comedy and tragedy, in which her adoring public would have rocked with laughter at her first entrance.) Again, oddly enough, though a full-blooded, high-spirited, 'laughter-loving dame' (as Horace Walpole, a close friend, wrote in his epitaph), once she had separated, quite early, from her barrister-husband, George Clive, she took no lovers and provided nothing for the gossips. Uproariously funny in the theatre, out of it she was a generous-minded sensible woman, and one of the men always glad to be in her company was Dr Johnson, not the easiest man to please. 'Clive, sir,' he told Boswell, 'is a good thing to sit by; she always understands what you say.'

The greatest tragedienne of the era was of course Sarah Siddons. She was a member of a theatrical family, the Kembles, married at eighteen Henry Siddons, an amiable handsome actor without much talent, failed at twenty when Garrick gave her a season at Drury Lane, then played leading parts in the provinces with ever-increasing success. (She often paid return visits to the provincials when London was at her feet.) Her conquest of Drury Lane began in 1782, and soon she was hailed as the greatest tragic actress England – and probably any other country – had ever known. Her majestic power and the force of her pathos could terrify an audience – in those huge theatres, too – and then dissolve it into tears. Critics, including Hazlitt, did not simply praise her – but raved. Bearing five children and losing two of them, constantly rehearsing and travelling, exhausting herself night after night playing angry queens, deserted wives and madwomen, threatened her health, though at the same time it also turned her from an imposing queenly woman into one who was becoming too massive and unwieldy. So she retired from regular seasons fairly

early, but gave occasional performances and recitals for many years. In society she was always respected as well as admired, but she was not personally popular, as a woman, in theatrical circles, where it was felt she was too autocratic, ungenerous to possible rivals, too fond of money and not at all fond of spending it. When a Hazlitt could cry, 'Not less than a goddess, or then a prophetess inspired by the gods!' perhaps we ought to stifle any doubts. But her tremendous Lady Macbeth, her most famous part, launched a tradition of casting that has always seemed to some of us quite wrong. *Our* Lady Macbeth would not be tall, imposing, powerful, but a very feminine little woman, behind her dimples as hard as nails until the final crack-up.

Mary ('Perdita') Robinson can be used as a searchlight on the last quarter of the eighteenth century. Her story, ending not long after she reached forty, might have been the creation of a sensational female novelist of the period. She was born in 1758, was married at sixteen to a man who was supposed to have money and hadn't, spent the next two years encouraging and then discouraging the dishonourable intentions of the town's fashionable rakes, but then found herself sharing her husband's imprisonment for debt. During the nine to ten months in prison she began writing the verse afterwards published in two volumes, thanks to the Duchess of Devonshire. Towards the end of 1776 she made a triumphant appearance at Drury Lane as Juliet, and she then played many different parts there throughout the next three seasons. As far as I can gather she was neither a very good actress nor yet a bad one. What she chiefly had to offer was youthful but already ripe beauty, and we may be sure she had that because all the more important painters of the time insisted upon her sitting for them. She had now fascinated the youthful Prince of Wales (afterwards the Regent), four years younger than she was and still under tutelage. There was some heady correspondence between them, Perdita (her favourite part) to his Florizel. She was offered – and accepted – 'a splendid establishment', with a promise of £20,000 (when the Prince came of age) and cascades of jewels. But within two years Florizel was bored with his Perdita and brutally dismissed her. She never received the £20,000, was deep in debt, and after so much notoriety she could not return to the Theatre. Fox obtained a pension of £500 for her; she tried running an academy in Paris; then went back to England to publish verse and a number of romantic novels. She was a very vain and rather silly woman – she loved to exhibit herself in Hyde Park, riding in a ridiculous chariot in a variety of fancy costumes – but she lacked neither enterprise nor courage. Soon she needed both, a severe illness leaving her partially paralysed. She struggled on, scribbling away, still looking like a fashionable beauty, with liveried servants (covering their arms with white sleeves) lifting her in and out of her carriage. But all that had to go, and it was an impoverished crippled woman, not twenty years away from that bewitching Perdita, who died at Englefield Cottage in 1800.

If I have given so much space to these actresses, it is not because the London Theatre appears to have had a deservedly high reputation, for after all that is not my subject. It is because these exceptional women, whether lucky or unlucky, not only take us closer to the eighteenth-century scene but also in certain instances offer examples of sexual relations far above the average of that time. I feel that men who at first merely wanted to capture and conquer some ravishing toast of the town soon found themselves involved in a real and satisfying relationship with a genuine woman who knew more about life than they did.

We are now in the Regency, which I examined at some length

Mary Robinson ('Perdita'), b
George Romney

elsewhere (in *The Prince of Pleasure and His Regency*) and if I give a summary account of this fascinating period here, it is because I dislike repeating myself. The 'Age of Reason', which in fact it never was, had vanished, and irrationality and romance had been creeping in during the last quarter of the eighteenth century. Our Englishness, though with some modifications and perversions, was back again. And to my mind, no era offers us a more splendid façade than the Regency. It seems to be crowded with exquisite women and superbly handsome and confident men, looking all the better because at last they had escaped from the extravagant and absurd fashions of the eighteenth century. But behind this splendid façade we can discover a brutal era, denied overdue reform, the victim of a savagely repressive government, with a working class throughout the country shockingly overworked, badly fed and housed, with the great landowners and the bigger farmers able to take advantage of the Corn Laws, which condemned the poor to eat adulterated rotten bread that had never known any honest flour. And this at a time when hundreds of acres, charming manor-houses and whole villages were being gambled away every night.

On the lowest level, the life of most women, whether they were in-volved in the industry of the North and the Midlands or were still in the rural areas, was wretched indeed; and, as far as I can judge, much worse than it had been a hundred years earlier. Attractive spirited girls found a way out in domestic service in the great houses, and might find them-selves the petted mistress of rich men (often starting at fourteen), but afterwards drifting into prostitution, especially in London, which then and for many a decade later contained more prostitutes than any other capital city in Europe. There was, however, already a large section of the middle class, inheriting the dissenting and evangelical standards of the eighteenth century, that regarded with disapproval all but 'the good poor', who had to be very virtuous indeed, and condemned to torment in the next life the idle, extravagant, pleasure-seeking, adulterous and 'Sabbath-breaking' aristocracy. It was in this middle class at that time that we discover the origins of the false idea of woman-hood we associate with mid-Victorian England – the wife and mother so pure, so delicate, so wincingly refined, that she was too good for this bold bad world and had to be withdrawn from it. Yet at this earlier time, and from this same class, too, there came a number of women who were already earning a living – and often a good living, too – as professional writers, using their piety and widespread disapproval as material for tracts, cautionary tales and even grisly stories for children.

The Regency was an age of extremes, and as soon as we leave the pious and the disapproving we are in a very different England. It is emphatically not that of the eighteenth century. The relations between

Caroline Norton (seated) and her Sister the Duchess of Devonshire, attributed to Sir Francis Grant. Mrs Norton, a granddaughter of Sheridan and herself a successful writer who had made an early and foolish marriage, was one of the first women to assert her rights to an independent income.

(left) Lady Oxford (detail), by John Hoppner

(right) Emily, Lady Cowper, by J. Cochran after Sir Thomas Lawrence

the sexes, though they might be too often disreputable, were far better than they had been earlier. And indeed, the swing of the pendulum carried society away from the domination of the masculine principle (though male authority would be partly restored later) and, for all the lordly airs of the men, we can discover an assertive feminine principle at work. Country squires might still be ruining parlourmaids, but in fashionable London it was the girls and women who tended to be bold and predatory. Aristocratic young men might see themselves as Don Juans when half the time it was they who were being determinedly seduced. So Lord Byron – who was only professionally a world-weary romantic – was relentlessly pursued by Caroline Lamb, capable of invading his rooms in Albany dressed as a pageboy, was deliberately seduced in these same rooms by young Claire Clairmont, and later was probably taken to bed by the older and vastly experienced Lady Oxford almost before he knew what was happening. Claire's half-sister, Mary Godwin, a very determined girl, made up her mind to have Shelley, though she knew he was still married, probably at sight. To take another famous name at random – that intrepid though not very likeable eccentric, Lady Hester Stanhope, considered very mannish, turned young Bruce, aged twenty when she was well into her thirties, into her lover while on her way towards her Near Eastern fastness. The Regent's wife, Caroline, at least ten years older still, went rollicking round southern Europe and as far as Palestine with the dashing Bergami, originally engaged as a courier. The Regent himself, slack and soft after his first youth, was the prey rather than the regal predator of his succession of ageing mistresses.

Upper-class girls were often married early to men they didn't dislike but were not in love with, but then fell headlong in love with some other man. Then came all the gossip, the scandal, the shaking heads. Yet behind this there might be a relationship, long-lasting, deeply satisfying, beyond the reach of all the disapprovers. Take as an example Emily, Lady Cowper, and Lord Palmerston. A bewitchingly pretty girl, she was married to the handsome, kind but rather dull Earl, to whom she was devoted in a wifely fashion. But she fell in love with Lord Palmerston, who was anything but dull. They became lovers who were often unable to meet for months, Emily nursing her ailing Cowper, frequently abroad at spas, Palmerston rushing from the political arena to the hunt. Cowper died, and then in 1839 the lovers married – when she was fifty-two (but still pretty) and he was fifty-five. There followed nearly thirty years of a wonderfully happy marriage. Intensely devoted to his political career, she became the great political hostess of her time. We are told how, when she was into her seventies and he was a Prime Minister nearing

Lady Hester Stanhope, by C. Hullmandel after R. J. Hamerton

{61}

eighty, she sat through an important debate in the House until three in the morning, and after he had got his majority they were seen fervently embracing in the Ladies' Gallery. Certainly she adored him, but saw herself as a partner in his career and for half a century had made innumerable moves to further it. This point should be made because there is a tendency to assume that happily married, supremely devoted, adoring wives of this period were just so many ninnies. Many of them were nothing of the sort.

Let us take a later instance of a Victorian wife – and it is a bold choice because Emily, wife of Alfred Tennyson, has often been presented to us as the perfect example of the blindly adoring, self-effacing, shrinking Victorian wife. But after their late marriage (Alfred was forty-one and she was thirty-seven) his literary friends, who had not met her before and were ready to be critical, delighted in her. She had a mind and spirit of her own. It was she who encouraged Tennyson to put together the Hallam elegies he had been writing for years in that one big ledger, and suggested as a title *In Memoriam*, which brought him fame at last. It was she who, at the end of one of Carlyle's huge jeremiads, told him firmly, 'That is not sane, Mr Carlyle.' It was to her poor Edward Lear turned whenever he was most deeply depressed. I could go on and on, but by taking this almost notorious example of a false reputation I think I have made my point. I shall soon offer ample proof that Victorian English-women in the main were far removed from cosseted ninnies and dimwits.

The foolish legend owed nothing to the working class or to an upper class that, strictly speaking, was never Victorian at all, if we exclude the later years of the Queen's reign. (But then I take the view that what we call 'Early or Mid' can be considered as being truly Victorian, and that from 1880 the whole scene changed rapidly.) The insipid-angelic legend was largely created by men belonging to the commercial middle class that was increasingly important and influential from the 1840s onwards. They were led to believe that sexuality was entirely masculine, and that even for men – so their doctors were ready to tell them – it was a wasteful and menacing indulgence that demanded restraint. As for women, good women, pure women, fit to be cherished as wives and mothers – never to be confused with bad women, ever on the prowl to ruin a man, physically, financially, morally – these delicate creatures had no sexual appetites and merely endured (as well they might) their husband's rough and brief embraces. These men were not belated puritans. Except in the severest circles, they were not afraid of pleasure in general; they were afraid only of sex. And it is clear to me that it was the men who created this role of the delicate angel in the house, who must be so sheltered and carefully protected. No doubt many women accepted the role, often enlarging it for their own ends, but of course they knew it was so much

masculine nonsense. How can a woman be protected and removed from life when she is the centre of it, often with a succession of pregnancies, births or miscarriages? One might as well try to persuade her she has chocolate sauce in her veins and not the all-too-familiar blood. So, behind the faintings, the squeals of disgust, the prudish outcries, the daily collapse on the sofa, was the myth-making of husbands and dutiful humourless sons.

Ironically enough, this same earlier Victorian age of apparent male domination was devoted to the humour of the hen-pecked. It was the age of such things as Jerrold's *Mrs Caudle's Curtain Lectures*, appearing serially in *Punch*. It was when Dickens could write in *Oliver Twist*:

> 'It was all Mrs Bumble. She *would* do it,' urged Mr Bumble; first looking round the room to ascertain that his partner had left the room.
>
> 'That is no excuse,' replied Mr Brownlow. 'You were present on the occasion of the destruction of these trinkets, and indeed are the more guilty of the two, in the eye of the law; for the law supposes that your wife acts under your direction.'
>
> 'If the law supposes that,' said Mr Bumble, squeezing his hat emphatically in both hands, 'the law is a ass, a idiot. If that's the eye of the law, the law is a bachelor; and the worst I wish the law is, that his eye may be opened by experience – by experience.'

(Incidentally, we can see how Dickens began by offering us pretty cardboard cut-outs as heroines, but before he had done was showing us real girls.) Then a mere glimpse of literary history, well within a single decade, gives us women not to be sheltered and protected. So in 1846 Elizabeth Barrett could suddenly stop being the permanent invalid of

Wimpole Street and run away with Robert Browning. Next year, *Wuthering Heights* was published, reminding us that any attempt to protect Emily Brontë would have been like trying to persuade a lioness into a feather bed. Four years later, Mary Ann Evans, not yet George Eliot, originally from a farm in Warwickshire, became assistant editor of *The Westminster Review* and boarded and occasionally slept with its publisher, Chapman. And we have to ignore a host of women, courageous spinsters or wives with idle or missing husbands and a brood of children to provide for, toiling away at anything publishable, from romances and pious tales to articles on German philosophy and economics and books of popular science.

Some of these women who were wives, genuinely independent and ready to earn their own living, were the victims of marriage laws that were atrociously one-sided. These had been denounced for years by many women and a few liberal-minded men, but it was not until the 1850s that Caroline Norton brought them into the limelight. She was one of the three beautiful granddaughters of Sheridan, the dramatist, and she was a writer, industrious, versatile, fairly successful, even if without original talent. She had made an early and foolish marriage to Norton, who was well connected but a coarse and vindictive fellow and a barrister trying to live without briefs. Having badly lost, in the 1830s, a crim. con. action against his wife and Lord Melbourne (probably a political job to discredit Melbourne), Norton, separated from Caroline, did everything possible to make her life a misery. Not only did he refuse to pay her an allowance but he also claimed, unjustly but quite legally, all her literary earnings. Finally, in 1853, the two had to appear in a

county court, to the joy of the Press and public. Still a beauty and a tempestuous creature, Caroline fiercely denounced her wretch of a husband, who resorted to a very lame letter in *The Times*. Her reply was a pamphlet, *English Laws for Women*, which was followed the next year by her *Letter to the Queen on the Lord Chancellor Cranworth's Marriage and Divorce Bill*, in which she renewed her attack.

Caroline Norton's was the most famous case, but there had been a number of other cases, and there were a great many other protesters, with whom the dashing Mrs Norton was not very popular. It is not easy for women, more critical of one another than men tend to be, to work closely together in a movement. Curiously enough, two women who had boldly asserted their independence and became friends and allies, rejected and severely criticized this movement as such. One was the national heroine of the Crimea, Florence Nightingale, and the other was the leading serious woman journalist of that time, Harriet Martineau. 'I am brutally indifferent to the rights and wrongs of my sex', Miss Nightingale could write to Miss Martineau, perhaps forgetting that her social position as well as her own determination had been an immense help to her. Miss Martineau did not go as far as that, but did feel that the increasing employment of women, making for financial independence, would gradually bring *really competent women* to public positions of authority. But Miss Nightingale was the more obdurate and hostile, and the noble John Stuart Mill himself (to whom the women's movement owed most of all) could not persuade her to sign the first petition to Parliament, in 1866, for women's suffrage.

Another woman's name should be added here, if only because her magnificently dramatic services to a wide variety of radical causes (almost all victorious now) tend to be forgotten, lost in her later, more exotic and fantastic career. Born Annie Wood in 1847, after a fervently religious girlhood she married a conventional, rather stupid clergyman, Frank Besant. She left him after they had had two children, both of whom he contrived to claim, and soon began to disbelieve everything she had believed before. Finally she joined the freethinker Charles Bradlaugh, sharing with him the endless writing and public speaking and all the fuss and abuse and fury of the later 1870s and 1880s. Mrs Besant at this time was an attractive woman, a fluent if not gifted writer, and was developing into a magnificent orator, a wonder among women speakers. At last she broke with Bradlaugh, an enthusiastic individualist, because she was now a socialist; and then, in 1889, after reviewing and meeting Madame Blavatsky, she staggered Shaw and the Fabians by announcing that she was a Theosophist, ready to believe even a great deal more than she had previously disbelieved in. The Star of the East rose for her and eventually she became – reigning for many years, too – a kind of un-

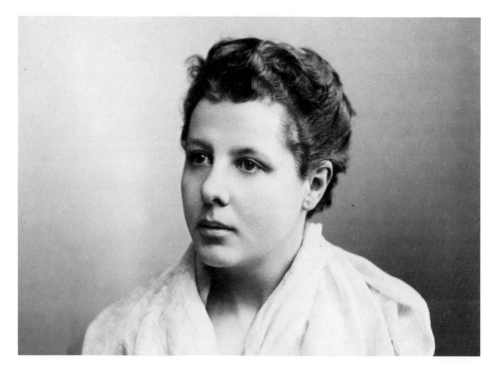

Annie Besant at the age of eighteen

crowned queen in India. Though she was responsible in later life for a good deal of nonsense (fairly harmless, I would say) undoubtedly Annie Besant was a remarkable character, and even if she died as late as 1933, she was also a Victorian Englishwoman.

When we think of these Victorian women in terms of a cosy Dickensian domesticity, there is something we forget. A lot of them, if they wanted to be with their husbands, had to leave those cheery firesides far behind. When the restless and masterful Richard Burton felt it was time to be off again, his immediate command to his adoring wife Isabel was, 'Pack and follow!' – more acceptable to most wives than, 'I'm off. Stay at home and mope.' And there was plenty of packing and following for many Victorian wives. So for example a number of officers' wives found their way to the Crimea, and though they were not in the trenches they endured many hardships in the bases not far away, as we know from Mrs Duberly's *Journal* describing the hard winter in Balaclava. The Indian Mutiny is even more revealing, and every account of it tells how the women and their children were deliberately butchered at Cawnpore and how splendid was their behaviour during the long siege of Lucknow. But then we know – or at least we can guess – how many of their mothers, their sisters or cousins, their daughters, throughout that century had left England for various ends of the earth, taking their parasols, veils, muslin gowns and innumerable petticoats to destinations sweltering in deserts or only recently hacked out of the jungle. Whatever else they were, such Victorian women were no shrinking, fainting, sofa-bound creatures belonging to the idiot-angelic legend. And perhaps they were glad to be well away from it, in spite of their not unreasonable fears of head-hunters, snakes, giant spiders. Perhaps, too, if they had entered their forties, they were happy to be where they could still wear some bright colours and were not condemned to dress in severest black, as if they were going to spend the rest of their lives attending their own funerals. This stupid custom took such a hold and lasted so long that as a small boy I never remember my maternal grandmother, who lived with us, wearing anything but this mournful black, tiny beads and all.

I never knew, at that time, any Englishwomen belonging to the Edwardian upper class, but my reading suggests they were little different – except they had a broader outlook – from the women of the earlier upper classes. But the middle class, if not on the narrowest shop-and-chapel level, had moved a long way from the Victorian middle class and its sexual myths. As for working people – and this I know from my own experience – they could now be divided into two very different groups: one of them, sober and frugal, bent on saving, was too often rigidly prudish and not sexually well adjusted, with the women – certainly in the North – hysterically energetic and house-proud; whereas the other division, closer to English tradition, was improvident, thoughtless, very gregarious, with no nonsense about 'keeping themselves to themselves', and took an easy matriarchal view of sex. However, in more recent years, something like the life-style of this second group has spread and taken over a large proportion of the first group, the matriarchal winning, the patriarchal losing. And although almost instant copulation has its dangers, one great gain – and we have not many to boast about – is an immense improvement in sexual relationships, because on almost all levels they are more personal, with lovers or married couples sharing much more as persons. The old joke about the explosion in the kitchen being the only time Father and Mother were seen going out together has now lost all edge. There was a time when I believed that the average English housewife was inferior in almost every department to house-wives abroad, notably the French and the American, but now I no longer hold this opinion and it is certainly not because I am more tolerant. Englishwomen today have more skills and far more self-confidence than they used to have. They are no longer apologetically behind their men but generally a little ahead. Moreover, a woman may be ahead while accepting the responsibility of a husband, children, a home with its circle of friends, and may not necessarily discover a heightened and deepened quality of life when she wins a seat on the board of an adver-tising agency or a baked beans canning factory.

Finally, we have made too much of the arrival, for good or ill, of our 'permissive society'. So far as there has been one great break-through for Englishwomen, it came years ago, as I for one can testify, during the

First World War, when girls were ploughing, lorry-driving, making munitions, when more independence and the vote itself were already in sight, when a new freedom of manners and the urge of sex, immensely powerful at such times, could not be denied. Strange as it may seem to some readers, English sexual life is far more decent, healthy and honest than it was when I was young, when so much that was cynical and depraved went on behind a high white-washed wall. Perhaps it was the building and whitening of this wall that encouraged a curious notion abroad that the English on the whole were deficient in sexuality, incapable of passionate love. Nothing could be further from the truth. (It is ironical that this idea was mostly fostered by the Latin nations, of all peoples those most likely to make cool rational arrangements to satisfy sexual appetite.) We should remember here that Englishness itself, as we have defined it, must include a strong feeling for and heartfelt appreciation of what is feminine. And after all, it was in England that *Romeo and Juliet* and *Antony and Cleopatra* were written and first applauded; and they were accompanied, then and afterwards, by some of the most exquisite and deeply moving love lyrics the world has ever known. But these were the poets, and, it will be,objected, the bulk of the English have never been poets – indeed, anything but poets. But can so much sweet fruit come out of a sour soil? Haven't the roots gone down to a substratum of widely shared if wordless poetic feeling about the opposite sex?

Like a novelist or dramatist writing about any country he had known from childhood, I could fill pages singling out and deriding certain types of English womanhood – the long-chinned girls, from manor houses and rectories, who would cry in despair, 'Oh Mum-mee!' and then take the dogs for their walk yet again; the Hampstead matrons I remember who sat round the tennis court talking about nothing but schools; the female battleaxes who retired from half-ruining the Empire, because of their ferocious colour prejudice, to suggest that men on strike should be 'put up against a wall'; the vague fluttering hostesses whose conversation, like their cuisine, was too watery and flavourless; the more idiotic young wives of today, bored in their suburbs, who will buy any rubbish so long as they have not to pay for it at once. Yet I say that down the centuries – with some exceptional times already noted or still to be examined – a great mass of the English, from ploughmen to famous commanders, milkmaids to duchesses, have known poetic feeling stirring and deepening what otherwise might be a mere traffic in sensations. Englishwomen from age to age have been able to respond at once to the Englishness in their men. If it wasn't there, then something soon went wrong. When I began this chapter I promised to challenge and banish a spectre – the Englishwoman of popular foreign caricature – that haunted the scene too long. I believe I have challenged it, and now I proceed to banish it.

LORDS AND MASTERS

❀

STATESMEN, politicians, men of action – what kind of men were these who have had power over the English? I want to consider them largely in terms of their Englishness, their acceptance or denial of the national psyche, the English cast and habit of mind. Possibly hardly anybody will agree with my choice of subjects. Readers might like to choose their own men and then test them for Englishness; though I see little chance of this becoming a welcome after-dinner game, unless it should be played very late at night on television. The men of power under review must of course be English: no Scots, Welsh, Irish being admitted.

This means I have to ignore the monarchy. Oddly enough, as far as I can see, the last truly English king was the much-maligned Richard III, the victim of Tudor propaganda, Shakespeare and a succession of actor-managers If this seems absurd, we have only to remember that the Tudors came from Wales, the Stuarts from Scotland, William III from Holland, and the Georges from Germany. When we come to Victoria we find she is mostly German on her father's side and entirely German on her mother's, and that like her father she married a Saxe-Coburg, yet another German. (Germany now defied all competition in the consort export trade.) If blood is our argument, we can say that Victoria's eldest child, at long last Edward VII, must have been just about as German as *Der Ring des Nibelungen*, whereas in fact he turned out to be nothing of the sort, being English on duty, French off duty. And his son, George V, could have been put on show – as indeed he often was – as a typical upper-class Englishman of the sporting kind.

After some hesitation, I decided I could make the best start with a giant – Oliver Cromwell. This hesitation had nothing to do with the genealogy of the Cromwell family. I know that Oliver's great-grandfather was a Welshman called Williams, settling in England and changing his name to flatter his patron, Thomas Cromwell; and I also know that because his mother was a Steward, though her family had been farming in East Anglia for generations, it has been said she was connected, however distantly, with Scotland's royal Stuarts. (As the American comedian, Jimmy Durante, used to cry in mock despair, 'Everybody wants to get inta de act!') Born and bred in East Anglia, like his father and mother before him, Oliver Cromwell was an Englishman. He was indeed very much an Englishman, though one on a gigantic scale. He had a genius for war and government; and he was a huge lump of character that was all Englishness. So the historian S. R. Gardiner could write:

> All the incongruities of human nature are to be traced somewhere or other in Cromwell's career, What is more remarkable is that this union of apparently contradictory forces is precisely that which is to be found in the English people, and has made England what she is in the present day. . . .

Oliver Cromwell, 1657,
miniature painting (enlarged)
by Samuel Cooper

Gardiner's 'present day' was, of course, many years ago, about the time I was born. A few years later, speaking at the Cromwell Tercentenary, Lord Rosebery declared boldly:

> There is one answer I suppose everybody here would give – that the secret of Cromwell's strength rested in his religious faith. I discard that answer, because it would be begging the question. No, my answer is this – that he was a practical mystic, the most formidable and terrible of all combinations. . . .

And there is much more, somewhat inflated – about close communion with the supernatural and the celestial, and with further communion 'on a Sinai of his own' – that belongs to oratory on an important occasion.

Cromwell represents our Englishness on the largest possible scale. Whatever we mean by it – and now I must assume that readers agree with me – he had more of it than anybody else. With him it is not a matter of refusing to ignore the promptings and pressures of the unconscious, as it is with most of the English. Deeply religious, Cromwell when not in action might be said to have moved into the dark of his mind, into its deepest recesses, there to encounter and abase himself before the numinous archetype of the dreadful accusing Jehovah. Easily the most powerful and formidable man of his time – not to be matched now – he would emerge from these adventures of the spirit ready to weep at his weakness and sinfulness. But then he would know how to meet events and what ought to be done next. Quite early, referring to his rapid promotion, he could write, 'I have not sought these things; truly I have been called unto them by the Lord.' It is possible to see him, as of course many people did, as a man who satisfied his lust for power while at the same time, surrounded as he was by zealots and bigots, playing the consummate hypocrite. But the facts of his career, one of the most astonishing in any nation's history, do not seem to me to support this cynical theory. He made some mistakes, of course. He was reluctant to agree that Charles should be executed, and for once overrode his instinctive or intuitive judgment. Like so many Englishmen of power before or since his time, he went wrong in Ireland, establishing there a vast hornet's nest. Though far less fanatically zealous than most of his major-generals and their 'Colonel Fight-the-good-Fight and Captain Smite-them-Hip-and-Thigh', he did adopt at one point the foolish policy of trying to make men virtuous by decree, virtuous, too, in the narrow puritanical sense, regarding any innocent amusement as the devil's work. But where he went wrong once, he acted wisely and promptly a hundred times. And it simply will not do to see him as a man bent on despotism.

A man with so much of our Englishness in him would be incapable of carrying out any long-term coldly rational plan. What came out of him was a warmly intuitive reasonableness, not unlike that of a courageous

{72}

and energetic woman desperately trying to rescue her household. This is obvious as soon as we compare Cromwell with all the factions round him, whether composed of zealous Independents and fanatical Levellers, ineffectual politicians at odds with one another, or embittered Royalists. What Cromwell was trying to do – and he might have succeeded if he had lived longer, for he died in 1658 before he had reached his sixties – was to create an England far closer to ours than the England of the next two centuries. Certainly the people during the Protectorate had to be held on a fairly tight rein, but if they had been allowed to go their way they would have moved in quite different directions, and there would have been war again – or chaos. Again, they detested military government – so creating a tradition that suspected large standing armies and indeed long disliked the idea of a regular army at all – but Cromwell only preferred military government to no government, and wanted to move away from it. People grumbled at the heavier taxes, but we have to pay heavier taxes still without rioting outside the Treasury. There may not have been complete religious toleration, but there was more of it than there had been before or than there was for some time afterwards; and there was less religious persecution in England than in other countries. (Cromwell allowed the Jews to build a synagogue in London – an astonishing step forward.) And, as Macaulay pointed out, 'Justice was

{73}

administered between man and man with an exactness and purity not before known.'

Andrew Marvell (detail), artist unknown

With an energetic and unwavering foreign policy, an army generally held to be invincible, a navy commanded by Blake, Cromwell within a few years raised the influence and prestige of England to a towering height; but this is well known and should surprise nobody. What we tend to forget – when we still remember how the theatres were closed, many pretty customs banished, churches mutilated by fanatical troopers – is what he accomplished at home in his Protectorate, together with what he hoped to accomplish, which might have been a balance between the executive and the legislative we may not have found even now. Though I have never been fond of the puritan style and its Old Testament ranting, not only do I see Oliver Cromwell as a giant but I also accept his extraordinary career as a triumph, the greatest we shall discover, of what we have agreed to call *Englishness*. And we might note

in passing that in 'the public relations' department of his Protectorate
two poets were kept busy – John Milton and Andrew Marvell.

My next subject seems superficially as different from a Cromwell as
one of the latter's russet-coated captains was from a coffee-house wit.
And indeed George Savile, first Marquess of Halifax (1633–95), was
himself a wit, renowned for his brilliant talk, though not a man to be
found at ease in coffee-houses. He was very much a member of the
aristocratic ruling class, and spent the last twenty years of his life moving
in and out of high office. During the confused period when the uncertain
James II overlapped with William of Orange, not yet William III, there
were times when Halifax, if only briefly, controlled the country as a man
might control a restive horse. He was called the 'Trimmer' derisively
because he appeared (like many another public man) to have changed
sides so often. But Halifax wore the badge proudly, wrote about it, and
declared:

Our *Trimmer* is far from Idolatry in other things, in one thing only he cometh near it, his Country is in some degree his Idol; he doth not worship the Sun, because 'tis not peculiar to us, it rambles about the World, and is less kind to us than others; but for the Earth of *England*, tho perhaps inferior to that of many places abroad, to him there is Divinity in it, and he would rather dye, than see a spire of *English* Grass trampled down by a Foreign Trespasser. . . .

Halifax meant this; he was not beating the patriotic drum for effect; he loved his country. If he changed sides, it was not for his own advancement but to keep the realm at peace with itself. And the country must be governed, sensibly too, no matter how loud the party cries are or how many fanatical extremists are thundering away. In an age of fierce bigotry, he was strongly in favour of religious tolerance. He remained in the centre, where sensible government could be carried on, distrusting all movement along extreme positions, and always determined if possible 'to trim the boat'. He is always closer to an experienced and sagacious administrator than he is to any enthusiastic political theorist, but he can be both eloquent and wise about any subject close to his heart, such as England's naval defences.

Halifax seems to me the best example of a type that would appear again and again on the English political scene, the kind of man, almost always belonging to a ruling class, who is more concerned with government itself than he is with the triumphs or disasters of a party. The boat must keep moving securely and therefore should not be rocked. But Halifax differs from his successors in two important particulars. He was in advance of his age, not lagging behind it as so many politicians of this type have been, seeing every demand for reform as a threat to safe government and then becoming repressive. Again, they have mostly been dull men and Halifax was anything but a dull man. Indeed, for a responsible statesman – and this he certainly was – he recklessly indulged his sense of the ridiculous and his lively wit. His writing is dry, aphoristic, weighted with experience: it can still be read with pleasure. His *Character of Charles II* is a little masterpiece of shrewd judgment and sly wit – so, for example:

> . . . He had as little Eagerness to oblige as he had to hurt Men; the Motive of his giving Bounties was rather to make Men less uneasy to him than more easy to themselves; and yet no ill-nature all this while. He could slide away from an asking Face, and guess very well. . . . Ease is seldom got without some pains, but it is yet seldomer kept without them. He thought giving would make Men more easy to him, whereas he might have known it would certainly make them more troublesome. . . .

His *Advice to a Daughter*, for the primary benefit of his own daughter Elizabeth (who became the mother of the celebrated Lord Chesterfield), was reprinted over and over again and during the next seventy-five years was almost required reading. It is austere, cautious, tending to be rather gloomy, but one more personal aside will come home to all the anxious fathers today: 'When my *Fears* prevail, I shrink as if I was struck, at the Prospect of *Danger*, to which a young Woman must be expos'd.' There are other gleams of tenderness, as if a lighted candelabrum had been taken swiftly across a room full of mahogany. Behind his polite and solemn warnings My Lord Halifax undoubtedly loved his daughter. And for all his periwigged urbanity, worldly wisdom touched with cynicism, I feel there was some of our Englishness in Halifax, and that if he was right so often when his colleagues were wrong it was because there was an intuitive quality in his judgment. I feel he brought some imagination to the task of being moderate and reasonable – a rare instance among politicians.

Clearly John Churchill, Duke of Marlborough, cannot be ignored, though I must confess I would be delighted to leave him out, if only because both his character and his career cannot be fairly dealt with in a small space. At one extreme or the other – that is, as a great soldier or a domestic family man – hardly a fault can be found with him. But in the large area between conducting a campaign and sitting quietly at home, he is an ambiguous figure. Even apart from the envy and jealousy he aroused, he attracted from other public men little affection and a great deal of mistrust. But if he 'played both ends against the middle', if he accepted honours and money from one side while secretly corresponding with the other, we must also remember that the last quarter of the seventeenth century was thickly tainted with double-dealing, spying, elaborate perfidy. Already in the army, young John Churchill was handsome, both charming and coolly resourceful. His sister Arabella, a plain girl, had become the mistress of the not very lovable Duke of York, afterwards the completely unlovable James II, who liked his women to be unattractive. So young Churchill arrived at Court, with the Duke his patron. A senior member of Charles II's harem, Barbara, Duchess of Cleveland, took Churchill to bed with her; and the story runs that to avoid being found there by the King he jumped out of the window. Whether as a reward or not, it is certain the Duchess gave him £5000, which he promptly invested. The rumour grew that Churchill was always after money, to keep and not to spend. This grasping and miserly reputation, enlarged by his enemies, haunted him for the rest of his life. Yet, when he could have married an heiress he fell headlong in love with Sarah Jennings, anything but an heiress, and married her.

Though maintained with personal devotion and, especially on his side, lasting tenderness, this was a union of opposites. Sarah was everything her husband was not – wilful and impetuous, and a constant but

impatient and bad-tempered schemer. Her warm friendship with Anne –
and when Anne became Queen they were so close they could use nick-
names – was of great service to Marlborough (as we must now call
Churchill); but then later, when Sarah was supplanted by Mrs Masham
and forced a bitter quarrel on Queen Anne, Marlborough suffered from
the rupture, at a time when he had enemies (including the formidable
Swift) among both parties. He himself was not really a party man; as a
soldier he was in the service of the Crown; but from first to last – and in
this he was consistent – he believed that the Crown must be Protestant
and uphold the Anglican Church. And as a soldier Marlborough was
incomparable, the greatest England has known. He had a sense of

Tapestry showing the
engagement at Wynendael
during Marlborough's siege
of Lille (detail)

grand strategy that was constantly frustrated by slow and unadventurous allies, compelling him to play the diplomat instead of the bold strategist. If, after Blenheim, he had had the freedom of movement that Napoleon later enjoyed, he might have brought down in ruins the huge edifice of power that Louis XIV had erected. Fortunately he was also a superb tactician, one of those commanders whose minds were quickened by battle itself. But unlike so many of them, he cared greatly for his men and was probably the most considerate and humane of all Europe's famous generals. In spite of much frustration he lived for years in a blaze of glory, accumulating, as he loved to do, honours, estates, wealth. But when, after a long time abroad, he returned to London, he found there very few friends and a large number of bitter enemies, ready to accuse him of continuing the war for his own sake and of misusing public funds.

At sixty-one he could refer to his 'great age' though he was to live on for another ten years or so. His only son had died while at Cambridge; he outlived two out of his four daughters; and Sarah, though fiercely devoted to his interests, had to keep adding fuel to her personal quarrels and feuds. Towards the end, when he had more money than he knew what to do with and the Palace of Blenheim was among his many possessions, it was said he would compel himself to walk just to save the shilling a sedan chair might cost him. He was undoubtedly a great man, with a genius for war, but to my mind there is a touch of arid melancholy about his career. Off the battlefield he was too careful, too cautious, too self-seeking, with too much dignity and too little enjoyment and fellow-ship. He is hard to accept as an example of Englishness, of a man aware of the instinctive, the intuitive, the mysterious promptings of the unconscious. Even so, there is a kind of poetry in his unwearied devotion to his Sarah, in his tender patience with her whims and outbursts. Lady Mary Wortley Montagu tells us that Sarah, just to annoy her husband, cut off all her curls. He said nothing, but after his death she discovered he had secretly put the curls away in a cabinet. And whenever the terrible old Duchess of Marlborough, the most notorious termagant in high society, retold the story she never reached this moment of discovery without bursting into tears. Born in the year of the Restoration, she could look back under the reign of George II to that of Charles II, and had lived through some of the most crowded chapters of English history.

Among her bequests was one to William Pitt – 'Upon his merit in the noble defence he has made of the laws of England, and to prevent the ruin of his country.' And indeed, by the middle of the next decade, after a series of disasters in a war that was more German than English, Pitt, who had the whole country with him, could tell the Duke of Devonshire, 'I know I can save this country and that no one else can.' This might seem arrogant – and indeed Pitt *was* arrogant – but it was far from mere boasting. By agreeing at last to share the government with the Duke of Newcastle, a contemptible man but an adroit, untiring and unscrupulous party manager, Pitt took over the House of Commons and the whole conduct of the war. And by 1761, when Pitt was forced out of office by Bute, whose influence on the foolish young George III was profound, England had won a dazzling series of victories, had laid the foundations of the future Empire, and had changed the face of the world.

It can reasonably be argued that Pitt, later Lord Chatham, was the greatest war leader England has ever had, greater even than Lloyd George and Winston Churchill. (True, they had to work on a larger and more complicated scale, but then Lloyd George was never in charge of military operations and Churchill's overall strategy was often faulty.) But Pitt enjoyed some important advantages. In every way he was immensely superior to all the men around him, like an eagle moving among greedy little pigeons. He was scrupulously honest at a time when public funds were regularly being pillaged and most politicians had their price. He owed everything to his own qualities, not to birth, rank,

William Pitt, first Earl of Chatham (detail), Studio of Richard Brompton

wealth. He had a tremendous presence, which awed and then inspired every commander he summoned for questioning. Finally – and this was his most important asset – he was not only the supreme Parliamentary orator of his time but probably of all time. He had the figure and face, the flashing eye, a voice that could tremble with noble feeling or terrify his opponents with its whiplash of invective – and he used all these with superb art. At his best he had only to rise in the House to be complete master of the scene. But he could not be always at his best – far from it. His most pitiless enemy was neither in Westminster nor overseas: it was gout. He began to suffer from it even in boyhood, and in his later years the pain was so intense and continuous that it drove him out of public life for long periods, at times leaving him mentally disturbed. However, he had one consolation denied to so many of his contemporaries: he had made a good marriage and could enjoy the company of his wife and five children, one of whom, the younger William Pitt, became Prime Minister at the age of twenty-four.

William Pitt the Elder, Earl of Chatham, was without a doubt a great

William Pitt the Younger
(detail)

Englishman, but I must venture to suggest that he was not greatly English. I cannot offer him as an example of Englishness in a statesman and man of action. I can imagine him, with the same gifts, the same drive for power and the same energy in making full use of it, the same fervent if narrow patriotism, rising as high in many other nations. He was not essentially an English type. He was too consciously ambitious, preparing himself for a splendid career, from his youth; and even as a young man, we are told, he always arrived late at parties and departed early, to be noticed as someone of importance. While he left his great speeches to chance and the inspiration of the hour – he was a failure with set speeches and never became a good debater – it is safe to say that behind these awesome improvisations were years of practice and rehearsal – of tones, gestures, glances of contempt, glares of fury. As Macaulay suggests, there was a strong, perhaps rather disturbing theatrical element in him. This does not mean he was insincere. An oratorical politician may overplay his part, but even so it may be the right part, as Pitt's almost always was. It brought him, during his great years, immense popularity; he was the people's hero; but I do not see this as the special appeal of Englishness to Englishness. Given the same circumstances, Pitt would have been equally popular in almost every other European country. His successful use of sea-power came from rational not intuitive decisions, but I hesitate to say the same about the attitude he took from first to last to the American Colonies and their settlers. Here, I must admit, there is more than a suggestion of intuition or an instinctive feeling, going deeper than a politician's shrewd judgment – as if there was something in him waiting to greet with joy a republic and a natural aristocracy, without titles, stars and garters, arising out of freedom, honesty and sheer ability. And indeed it was Pitt, so long 'The Great Commoner', who in this scene of conniving inferior noblemen was the real aristocrat. I could go on praising him, but I still cannot accept him as an example of Englishness.

In October 1775, when Lord North's government had made a fool of itself in America, a young Member of Parliament, aged twenty-six, rose to censure it. 'Ministers,' he declared, 'have reason to triumph. Lord Chatham, the King of Prussia, nay, Alexander the Great, never gained more in one campaign than the noble lord has lost – he has lost a whole continent.' This was Charles James Fox, early in his career, which was just as odd and surprising as his character. He was the third son of Henry Fox, Lord Holland, who had made a fortune by being demoted to Paymaster-General. Lord Holland sent Charles, his favourite, to Eton and Oxford but also took him, even in his early teens, to Paris and Spa, where the pair of them sat up late every night gambling. Before Charles had turned twenty his father had bought him a rotten borough and made

Charles James Fox, by Karl Anton Hickel

him an M.P. Yet already Charles had proved himself to be an excellent scholar, with a love of languages and reading that he never lost. So, even by the time he came of age, we can say that Fox combined in himself three different characters – a politician of brilliant promise, a linguist and hard reader, a reckless gambler, sportsman, carouser. And as time went on he did not contract these characters but expanded them: we might say there was more and more of him in different directions. Nor was that all, for while he was black-browed, harsh-voiced, always bulky and later running to fat, he had such natural charm and sweetness of temper that all kinds of people found him irresistible. He was the very opposite of those statesmen and men of action whose ambition was like a cancer eating everything they had worth having. So, for example, for about five years at the turn of the century, though still a member of Parliament, he almost retired from politics. He spent this time in the country with his former mistress, Mrs Armistead, whom he had now secretly married, cheerfully engaged in reading, exchanging long letters, often with scholars, and planning a history of the Revolution of 1688. But the oddest feature of his whole political career was that he passed nearly all of it not in office, except for three very brief periods, but in Opposition. Yet he was a statesman with a great international reputation.

Only on a superficial level can his career be regarded as a failure. On a deeper level he can be seen as one of the most important figures in English political history. Years after he died – in 1806 and still only in his fifties – the liberal humane tradition associated with his name lived on and on. He was no radical, no populist, no demagogue; he was a Whig, leading a party largely composed of wealthy aristocrats, and often having to play the party game, not always very well. But he was a Whig – and a party leader – with a difference. Just as he was a life-enhancing man, he was a life-enhancing politician. His convictions came out of his love of life, not out of a fear and hatred of it. Though prepared to debate an issue with dazzling skill, if that issue was of any real importance then his acceptance or rejection of it came from his depths. As a young man he *knew*, without being told, that the Tories and the Crown (an influence he detested) were wrong about America, and he openly declared it would be far better to abandon the Colonies than try to conquer them. Later he *knew* that if the government had welcomed the French Revolution (in spite of its excesses, which he deplored) instead of declaring war on it, then England, France, Europe, mankind generally, would have gained, there might soon have been less oppression in the world and more liberty. (During the Peace of Amiens Fox risked unpopularity by staying in Paris and having several interviews with Napoleon, then still First Consul. Fox found him 'a young man considerably intoxicated with success' and would certainly have disliked

Horatio Nelson, by Sir William Beechey

{85}

Napoleon as Emperor.) There was something deep-seated, innate, about Fox's desire to denounce severely authoritarian regimes and his lifelong sympathy with the oppressed, from the French peasant to the West Indian slave, from Donegal to the Ganges.

For my part I find more to admire and wonder at, more hope for the future, in Charles James Fox the failure (though as a dying man, briefly in office, he was able to abolish the slave trade) than I do in his successful rival, the younger William Pitt. Fox was the richer, riper, larger character. Lord Erskine said of him, with an unexpected flash of poetry: 'In the most imperfect relics of Fox's speeches *the bones of a giant are to be discovered.*' And he is certainly a prime example of Englishness. Though warmly devoted to his father, the values in his inner world are matriarchal, defiant of or indifferent to rigid masculine ideas of authority. Though there was much talk of his 'indulgence in vicious pleasures', the record, alight with examples of Fox's unselfishness, warm friendliness,

'The Mirror of Patriotism', showing Charles James Fox aping Oliver Cromwell, 1784, by James Sayers

loyalty and wider tolerance, suggests that most of his cold-hearted and unimaginative opponents might have been improved by some indulgence in 'vicious pleasures'. I find Fox's private life revealing as well as rather touching. Knowing that he could easily capture some brilliant heiress, his friends could not understand why he went on and on with Mrs Armistead (finally Mrs Fox), who was older than he was, of humble origin, and clearly destined to put on weight and lose her looks. They missed the point, which was that these two, both of them combining good sense with charm of manner, just went on loving each other and being happy together. And so, we are told, fat and ageing fast, they could be seen going out shopping, keeping an eye open for a cheap set of china. I find here a man who appreciated Woman and understood life. I am ready to applaud everything about him except his passion for gambling, which has always seemed to me idiotic. But a taste for gambling, obeying mysterious 'hunches', is probably one of the weaknesses of Englishness.

It is time we looked at another man of action. Obviously the first choice, in the age of Fox and the younger Pitt, is Nelson. It is to Pitt's eternal credit that he agreed to promote Nelson above many of his senior admirals and sent him off to the Mediterranean, where he fought the decisive Battle of the Nile. This destroyed any chance Napoleon had of invading the East. Nelson had already met the voluptuous and amiable Emma, wife of the British Minister at Naples, Sir William Hamilton. But when he returned in the *Vanguard*, the hero of the Nile, she and her husband led a procession of boats to greet him, and as soon as she came close, aboard the *Vanguard*, she cried, 'Oh God, is it possible!' and fainted in his arms – all in the grand romantic manner. (Emma's favourite term for her own conduct, in her earlier and shadier life, was 'giddy', and though she took pains to transform herself into a presentable Lady Hamilton, the giddy element remained.) Their mutual infatuation – more ingenuous on Nelson's part than on hers – became a genuine love affair, not the less odd and scandalous because Emma's husband, Sir William, genially presided over it. After various antics in and around Naples the three of them returned to London together, set up house there, and were received, not without much sniggering and whispering, by London society. The strangest feature of this relationship, which provided half Europe with gossip, was that while Emma and her lover declared it to be 'pure and platonic', by some suspension of natural causes it produced two children, who were certainly not Sir William's. He died, with Nelson holding his hand; then Nelson was killed at the moment of victory at Trafalgar; and though his grateful country proceeded to erect great monuments in his honour, poor Emma, who with all her faults had made the hero happy, was never provided for as he had wished her to be, and died in obscurity and want.

As the blindly infatuated lover of a woman twice his size and always flaunting her affections, Horatio Nelson was anything but worldly-wise and more than a trifle absurd. But that is where absurdity ends: all the rest of him is shining gold. There is no need to recount his scores of sea-fights, his bravery, his audacity, his wounds. It should be enough to say that when he took command of the Mediterranean Fleet, before Trafalgar, though it had been under Collingwood, who was a fine fighting seaman, the whole Fleet, officers and men, were almost delirious with joy. This was the effect that this small slight man, with his eye-patch and his empty sleeve, with his sensitive face and eager manner, a man quite unlike the traditional grim old seadog, had upon men about to face superior numbers in ships they knew themselves to be inferior to those of the enemy. (It seems to be doubtful if the glorious Royal Navy ever had at any time the better ships: it was usually seamanship and audacity that did the trick.) Like Marlborough on land, Nelson understood grand strategy, and his tactics in battle were brilliant and bold, as Trafalgar proved yet again and for the last time. But something else entered into it, something belonging to the spirit. There was in Nelson a clear flame that set other men alight. The men who served under him did not simply respect him or admire him, they loved him. He had his share of vanity and egoism, no doubt, but there was in him an unfailing store of warmth and sympathy. His men loved him; the country loved him; he was more than a heroic national figure, he was an immensely lovable *person*. He was the opposite of the rigidly masculine type, thick and inflexible; it was as if he had drawn from the sea some magical feminine element to enlarge and deepen his character. In him Englishness is afloat and in action.

The Duke of Wellington should have no place in this gallery. He was an Irishman and not an Englishman. (He was even a Member of the Irish Parliament in his youth.) If I cheat by putting Wellington in here, it is not simply because he provides a sharp contrast to Nelson but for a more important reason that will appear later. He was a great man in his own careful, obstinate, cool fashion, but without the genius for war that Marlborough and Nelson had. And, unlike them, he cared little or nothing for the men under his command, despising most of his officers and dismissing the men as so much 'scum'. (Marmont thought the British infantry the best in Europe.) The troops respected him and obeyed him, and possibly, like the general public, came to admire him, but they and the people never had any affection for him. He himself never asked for any. During the war and after it, he did what he thought to be his duty manfully, never losing his head, but always, it seems to me, without any real insight into, any intuitive perception of, the depth of the issues he had to consider. (And anybody who challenges this should

remember that it was the army under his control for so many years that
finally found itself floundering around in the Crimea.) He had some
formidable qualities, but they are not those belonging to our Englishness.
But then of course he was an Irishman.

There were some ironical consequences, the result of his gigantic
reputation. The Iron Duke's characteristic style and manner began to
be widely copied. He tended to be almost brutally materialistic, avoiding
any high-flown claims, any romantic nonsense, anything above the
immediate recognition of duty. No oratorical flights for him. He was the
masterful and downright figure of masculine authority, displaying no
traces of emotion, poker-faced and laconic in speech – 'Publish and be
damned!' was his style. So I cannot help thinking that before the public
schools created a type, the strong, arrogant, silent Englishman of the
ruling class emerged, controlling his estates or factories at home, going
out to govern the Colonies, and creating a legend abroad. And the irony

here is that what was assumed to be essentially English – or at least so far as England's more important and influential men were concerned – owed its origin to a famous Irishman playing a character part. It seems to me that almost all prominent Irishmen have deliberately played character parts – consider writers like Wilde, Shaw, Yeats, for example – but of course these parts have been widely different. I am not suggesting that Wellington was merely acting; he may have been quite unconsciously living up to his 'Iron Duke' reputation; but I do believe that the legendary upper-class Englishman, poker-faced, laconic, dogmatically staccato, would not have existed without the pattern set by the Duke.

After these resounding names it may seem strange that I should now bring in William Lamb, Viscount Melbourne, who is chiefly remembered as the long-suffering husband of crazy Caroline Lamb and as young Queen Victoria's first – and surely her favourite – Prime Minister. (Lytton Strachey's account of their friendship is one of the best things in his *Queen Victoria*; and Lord David Cecil's biography of Melbourne is at once lively and perceptive.) Melbourne comes in here because while he is an odd and fascinating character, with a lot of Englishness in him,

William Lamb, second
Viscount Melbourne,
by John Partridge

simply as a political figure he can be taken to represent an English type often discovered in the Westminster scene. He was a Whig because he belonged to a Whig family, but he was Tory by temperament. The Whig Party, which finally made him Prime Minister, was a party urgently demanding reform – notably of the franchise and the Corn Laws – but Melbourne did not believe in reform, any kind of reform. There had to be government, and he was willing to take part in it, if only because somebody had to do it, and clever men (and he was clever) had better not step aside for fools. In private he was convinced that things were bad – and always had been – but any change would make them worse. So leave them alone! He was the very opposite of any radical enthusiast, and while he received deputations of eager reformers with his usual charm – he was a great charmer – he got rid of them as soon as possible. Instead of forcing his way into high office, driven by ambition, he might be said to have lounged and joked his way into it. He was an unabashed hedonist, quite free from the usual humbug, and openly loved pleasure and delightful company, especially that of attractive women. And he captivated them simply because he was charming and amusing but also because he saw them as delightful persons and not as so many sexual objects. He refused to swallow pompous political cant, and his famous remark about the Order of the Garter – that he liked it because there was no damned nonsense about merit in it – is typical of his refreshing candour.

However, there was another Melbourne, not to be discovered at Brooks's or at Westminster. To begin with, he read more widely than any other successful English politician I can think of. Moreover, while disclaiming any religious belief, he had a passion for devouring theology, often going back to the Early Fathers. It was as if was driven by an urge in his unconscious to find some secret answer, no matter how ancient, to the painful riddle of life in this world. He could enjoy a good dinner, a party, an intimate talk with a beautiful woman – he was, indeed, a notable enjoyer – but then melancholy would creep in and he would bury himself among his books. He was a political and social charmer who went home to become a lonely and rather desolate figure. As a private person he was considerate, kind, tender-hearted, instantly compassionate, but as a public man, making political judgments, he was airy, flippant, often downright callous – why worry about the children in the mines and factories? He was like a soft hermit crab scuttling back into its borrowed hard shell. He had not been like that in his youth, when he had been an enthusiastic disciple of Fox, when he and Caroline had been entrancingly in love. In the end her whims, folly and madness had taken too much out of him. Something was disjointed, broken, within his personality; his outer world and inner world remained at war. Until he was struck down by paralysis he could still enjoy his pleasures, but any lasting satisfaction (and it might have arrived if he had found the answer to the riddle in one of his folios), and anything like happiness, were denied him. He probably came closest to them during the months when he was instructing and amusing the eager girl-queen, dazzled by the wit and wisdom of her 'adored Lord M.' There was a lot of Englishness in Melbourne, but for a personality of his size and intellect he was not strong enough to make the best of it. Just because it does not wall in the mind with rationality but leaves one end open to the dusk and the dark, Englishness can easily create divided men, fractured characters, even though they are as brilliant and original as Melbourne, apparently sauntering towards the seat of power. His humorous candour, wit and wide learning have not been constantly seen as examples in English political life, but his dangerous philosophy of government – *Let-us-carry-on-with-it-but-change-as-little-as-possible* – has never been long absent from Westminster.

We have seen already that Melbourne's pretty sister, Emily, fell in love with Lord Palmerston and after waiting a long time became his proud and happy wife. Though he had inherited an Irish peerage – and fortunately this meant he could sit in the Commons and not the Lords – Palmerston was English by birth, parentage and education, and indeed it might be said he was the representative Englishman of his time. Just as Fox was hardly ever in office, Palmerston was hardly ever out of office. And, just as Melbourne disliked taking action, Palmerston gloried in it and was unhappy if he had to be patient and passive. He was never much of a party man (except in the social sense), held office as Secretary of War from 1809 to 1828 under Tory governments, joined the Whigs in 1830 and became Foreign Minister – it seemed to the politicians abroad – for ever and ever. This was the time when England, rich and firmly in control of sea-power, was top dog, and Palmerston was just the man to make her behave like a top dog. He was no democrat and cared nothing for any radical reforms at home (though, oddly enough, when he agreed to be Home Secretary in 1853 he did extremely well), but he hated despotic and repressive governments and had a genuine love of reasonable liberty. He was not exactly despotic himself, though he drove his diplomats and officials hard, and was always breezy and affable – very handsome in his youth and then afterwards at least a tall imposing figure, with a long upper lip that easily broadened into a smile or a wide mischievous grin. But he was altogether too self-confident and independent, so that Queen Victoria and Albert detested him, and his ministerial colleagues, who often had no idea what he was up to, never wholeheartedly approved of him and were ready to welcome his downfall. (Moreover, it was generally felt in the House that Palmerston's chatty,

free-and-easy manner lowered its tone.) So who wanted him as Foreign
Minister? Westminster and Windsor Castle knew the answer only too
well: the English public wanted him and cheered every move he made.

There are two reasons for his enormous popularity. The first – and
more obvious – is that the people saw in him a character after their own
heart: 'Pam', and then 'Old Pam', as they called him, who wasn't going
to take any dam' nonsense from any of these fancy foreigners, who was
a sporting gent, too, and not too pious, a bit of a rip if all tales were true.
The second reason is that he was the first English statesman to understand the value of the Press and to make regular use of it. In this way he
got through to the people, who stood solidly behind him, raising an
outcry at once if he was dismissed from office. This partly explains his
long reign as Foreign Minister and the two periods, 1855–8 and 1859–
65, when, astonishingly late in life, he was Prime Minister. But for a total
explanation we must take a closer look at him. His was an odd mixture.
Behind his sporting-squire and man-about-town façade, his hand-

flapping insouciant manner, he was a prodigious worker, the despair of his civil servants, spending unheard-of hours standing at his raised desk, reading or writing and dictating dispatches. Fellow members of cabinets complained that his actions never seemed to proceed from any rational political principles, and that he took appalling risks without even consulting them. This was true, but then, unlike most foreign ministers, he worked almost entirely on instinct and intuition. Moreover, though apparently quite reckless, dealing in thunder and lightning, the instinct or intuition that told him when to move could also tell him when to stop, could slow him up as well as hurry him along. If he seemed unpredictable and maddening to the methodical Prince Consort, that was because he did not understand the level, not rational, not entirely belonging to consciousness, on which his mind, in its Englishness, worked.

So he could make moves his opponents never anticipated, and was always surprising them. A superb example of this was the Don Pacifico affair. Don Pacifico was a shady Portuguese Jew, but having been born in Gibraltar he was a British subject. And that was enough for Palmerston, for when Pacifico claimed damages, probably dubious, against the Greek government and was brushed aside, the high-handed Palmerston ordered a British fleet to enter the Piraeus to capture some Greek ships and their cargoes. This was too much, and Parliament on all sides spent four days attacking Palmerston and demanding his resignation. Then came 'Old Pam's' surprise. He, who had so often been accused of giving the House nothing but airy chit-chat, now marched in and gave it a very long and carefully argued speech, in defence of the principle on which he had acted, closing magnificently with –

> As the Roman, in the days of old, held himself free from indignity when he could say *Civis Romanus sum*, so also a British subject, in whatever land he may be, shall feel confident that the watchful eye and strong arm of England will protect him against injustice and wrong.

The House, the Press, the people, rose and cheered: all possible opposition was swept away. As usual refusing to panic, he knew intuitively when he ought to strike back, then struck with all his force. This was in 1850; he had been born as long ago as 1784; and he had sat in sixteen parliaments and had headed various ministries for close on half a century. He had not the commanding reach of genius that Fox had; his mind had not the range and subtlety of Melbourne's; but as a man of action in politics, carrying the people with him decade after decade, he was their superior. They were unusual men of their time; Palmerston was not, except in his unique relation with the public, and might perhaps be best described as an extraordinary ordinary man. But that meant, as we have seen, that he was governed by his Englishness.

{94}

As soon as Palmerston has vanished from the political scene, we are left staring at Disraeli and Gladstone. But neither need detain us very long. Probably Disraeli's political career, in which a Jewish-dandy-novelist gradually took command of a pack of fox-hunting landowners and almost hypnotized Queen Victoria by the glitter and perfume of his flattery, is the most astonishing and fascinating in English political history. But for all his knowledge of England's social life and his insight into the country's political mind, this impassive Oriental illusionist can have no place here. Neither, I make haste to add, can Gladstone, who declared quite truthfully, as Member for Midlothian, that he had no drop of blood in his veins that was not Scottish. No doubt he was a great and good man, but, in spite of Eton and Christchurch, Oxford, his devotion to the High Anglican Church, his years of conflict and glory at Westminster, he never transformed himself into an English great and good man. From first to last, his temperament, style, manner, were never English, always Scottish. Queen Victoria may never have actually said that he spoke to her as if she were a public meeting, but it is hard not to believe that he spoke to everybody as if he were still addressing a public meeting. He was often accused of being a hypocrite. This seems to me to miss the mark. In his constant prayers for God's help, guidance, forgiveness, I feel sure he was more urgently aware than most men are of his deep sinfulness. But I suspect that it never occurred to him that perhaps he and the Liberal Party were not very important to God. He was not the kind of man who could escape from his ego, take a look at his solemn self – and then laugh. And this, so common among the English, may be a source of weakness or strength; but we may be fairly certain that Gladstone never had anything to do with it. He was no more English than a supper dish of salted porridge.

It is worth pointing out here that both these outstanding political leaders, Gladstone and Disraeli, can be sharply contrasted with the new men arriving to play their part in home affairs or in governing and administrating the gigantic Empire. These were largely the product of the public schools that were deeply influenced by what Arnold had tried to do at Rugby: they were combining a sound education in the Classics with character-building. What the Duke of Wellington's enormous prestige and characteristic style and manner had done earlier, these public schools were doing now. And so strong was their influence that it easily outlasted the Victorian Age and even the Edwardian. While conformity must not be exaggerated, it is safe to declare that now there came into existence, either already belonging to a ruling class or sooner or later being promoted into it, a successful English public-school type. And I propose to consider it fairly, not hooting it at once off the stage.

These men were admirable public servants both at home and abroad.

They were steady; they were reliable; they were honest and decent, doing their best to be loyal to the values they had accepted years before. (Especially in the Colonial Services, the work they did, sometimes enriched by research into local history or a long study of neighbouring flora or fauna, should never be undervalued: it made a contribution in its day to world civilization.) But they had their limitations and weaknesses. Socially and intellectually they were too narrow. They had been brought up not to enjoy but to mistrust and restrict imagination. They wanted to work with – and if possible promote – 'sound' men, and, except occasionally when a war had to be fought, tried to keep well away from 'unsound' fellows. These had either not been to a good school or had been expelled from one. They might be brilliant in their way but had too much imagination, were not dependable, and were ready to be as reckless in their public lives as they had often been in their private lives – drink, sex, all that kind of thing. This prejudice brought English officialdom a certain timidity, stodginess, sameness, a narrow playing-safe Establishment standard, which the people in general instinctively perceived and lamented. What they wanted, among these higher-ups, was an enlivening sign of Englishness.

They were eager to welcome it in General Gordon, though it was in fact blurred by biblical prophecy, brandy and fatalism: his death, so remote, lonely, heroic, caught and fired popular imagination. This brought all the more prestige, I fancy, to his methodical revenger, Kitchener, a hard-driving organization man rather than a great soldier, almost brutally rational when he had to tidy up the mess in South Africa. It was inevitable that he should be given supreme command in Whitehall when war was declared against Germany, and it was inevitable, too, that sooner or later he would be seen to be unequal to the gigantically complicated task. But, even so, Kitchener had had his wonderful moment of insight, for he had swept away complacent official opinion, had declared that the war would not be over in a few months but might last years, and that to win it we did not need a few more divisions of Territorials but a brand-new army of millions. And it is significant that the people, still a long way from the threat of conscription, responded at once, as if intuition had called to intuition, Englishness to Englishness.

An event that occurred just before this war provides us with a valuable note, helping us to understand the psychology of the English in general. Though they may give it a cheer, they do not – or at least *did not* – worship success. Nor, of course, did they admire failure as such. What appealed to their imagination, as if they were so many poetic-tragic dramatists looking for a theme, was a doomed gallantry, a clear flame of heroism extinguished at last by darkness. Amundsen reached the South Pole first

General Gordon, a posthumou replica by Julia, Lady Abercromby of her portrait, 1887

(overleaf) General Kitchener's avenging of General Gordon. The 21st Lancers charging at Omdurman in 1898. Painting by R. Caton Woodville

because his plans and arrangements were far more efficient than Scott's. But if Scott had been equally efficient and had had the luck, too, to return smiling as the first conqueror of the Antarctic, he would have had his immediate rewards but would then have been soon forgotten. But though Scott and his few comrades were beaten to the Pole, together in their terrible misfortune they created a tragic epic, capturing the popular imagination for years and years. And English history is rich in these apparent failures – appalling sieges, desperate last stands, and the rest – that were welcomed and long remembered by the people as triumphs of the spirit.

However, we must return to politics, to the men playing the power game. Joseph Chamberlain, a very ambitious Birmingham business man, succeeded in imposing himself on the public mind, with the help of delighted cartoonists, by taking on a character part, using as 'props' a monocle and an orchid; but though he began as a radical and ended as a Tory, demanding Imperial Preference, he is no example of our Englishness in politics, as the electorate perceived. We begin our own century with two prime ministers who were both Scots: Balfour, who looked very clever and was, but had no intuitive understanding of politics; and Campbell-Bannerman, who looked rather stupid but was in fact a very able politician, only defeated by death. This brings us to Asquith, Premier in 1908–16 over one of the most remarkable cabinets of the last hundred years. But its most remarkable member was of course Lloyd George, whose utter Welshness, giving him energy, radical fervour and ancient Cymric necromancy, puts him outside this book. But had Asquith as much Englishness as Lloyd George had Welshness? The answer must be that he had no Englishness at all in our sense of the term. His was a superbly trained and weighty legal mind, soberly rational, ignoring any pressures or whispers from the unconscious. Good company, and never austere in private, he was monumentally calm and rather cold in public, making no attempt to please crowds and set them cheering, most effective and indeed often very formidable in the House of Commons or calmly taking charge of Cabinet meetings. He was not unlike an eighteenth-century Whig of the nobler sort, though without the magic of a Fox or Burke. And there were times when he suggested some fine old Roman. But perhaps it was his legal training and practice that froze any possible free-ranging and intuitive Englishness out of him. American statesmen have come to politics out of the Law, but at this moment I cannot recall any English statesman – as distinct from clever politicians with their eyes fixed on the Lord Chancellor's Woolsack – who had a legal background.

Leaping like a Gulliver over a mile of Lilliput, I come to the Second World War and to two massive characters who toiled mightily in that

Captain Scott, 1905, by Daniel Albert Wehrschmidt

war. Obviously one of them must be Winston Churchill; and the other, not so obviously to most readers, is Ernest Bevin. I will take the less important man first, while immediately adding that his contribution both to the war and to the welfare of the English people was very important indeed.

Before the war Bevin was a formidable and very successful trade union organizer and leader. After it, in Attlee's government, he was Foreign Secretary, an appointment he never wanted and should never have been given, removing him from the home affairs he understood so well. It was between these two very different passages in his career, when in fact he was Minister of Labour in Churchill's wartime coalition government, that Bevin can be seen as a great Englishman – and in my opinion inspired by his Englishness. He was given a colossal task; he was responsible for the fullest possible use of manpower (which of course included much woman-power); and it is worth remembering that of all the nations engaged in this war Britain called up for National Service the largest proportion of its citizens. This might have resulted – as some American commentators said it must inevitably do – in the creation of a rigid totalitarian society. But it did not. Moreover, thanks to Bevin's powerful personality and his admirable staff, industrial democracy actually gained ground, relations between men and management were more flexible than they had been before the war, and there was more and not less welfare of all kinds. (I take one instance out of many: factories holding any government contracts and employing more than two hundred and fifty people had to provide canteens serving hot food. But no employee was compelled to use them, and if some of the older men still preferred to sit by their machines and munch dry sandwiches, that was their affair. How do I know this – and a great deal more? Because I was responsible for the anonymous official booklet, *Manpower*.) Bevin can be said to have moved forward successfully on two fronts, one for the mobilization of manpower, the other for the improvement of industrial and other agreements and conditions. And while a zealous staff supplied him with figures or went out on inspection, it was the weight, force and insight of Bevin himself that were responsible for this double movement. And I say it was a triumph of Englishness, moving originally from instinct and intuition. I was acquainted with this remarkable man, self-educated, a slow and reluctant reader of official documents, no elaborate rationalizer, more like a tremendous natural force than a quick and clever Minister. He was able to work miracles during the war (not afterwards, when he was in the wrong place and already ailing) because he was a giant-sized Englishman relying on his Englishness.

If Bevin had strong political and social convictions and prejudices, so had Winston Churchill, though his were a long way over on the other

Ernest Bevin, by Thomas Cantrell Dugdale

side. We could put it like this. It was said of Churchill that never in his whole life did he use a bus or the London Underground, whereas Bevin, until he became a Minister, had probably never used anything else. But one huge character can recognize and respect another huge character, especially when they share the same immediate aims, and Churchill, though never inclined to make allowances for his subordinates, allowed Bevin to go his own way. Bevin could attend to manpower while Churchill, in his own commanding fashion, tried to attend to everything else.

Winston Churchill's wartime *persona* was such a mixture of John Bull and his bulldog that we are apt to forget that his mother was an American, Jennie Jerome of New York City. And she was no mere dumb worshipper of her husband, the brilliant if rather unstable Lord Randolph

Churchill. (He died early in 1895 aged forty-six.) She was very much a personality in her own right, a fashionable beauty, very energetic and ready to make full use of her charms and social influence – mostly in London, where she made her home after her husband's death. And indeed Winston saw far more of her than he had done of his father – though he had been closely attached to him – and as a young man with his way to make he owed a great deal to his devoted mother and her pulling of strings on his behalf. His lifelong upper-class English style is obvious; but did this American half of him contribute nothing to his character and career? I think it made an important contribution, often overlooked. It helped to make him responsive always to the new, the untried, the gamble that might pay off, encouraged his contempt for what was routine, conformist, safely mediocre, and added a certain brashness that 'sound' English types avoided and disliked. Even after years of high office in politics he would amuse or annoy Cabinet colleagues by talking too much on too many subjects and bombarding them with memoranda on their own departments. There is an American touch in his refusal at all times to be punctiliously correct, 'to toe the line'. But I must confess that much of this he could have taken from his father. Lord Randolph's career, so brilliant and so suddenly shattered, served Winston in two different ways – first, as a shining example; secondly as a warning. So, for instance, Winston like his father was never really a party man; but unlike his father, who resigned once too often and found the door shut in his face, Winston would go his own way and risk dismissal but avoided resignations.

As a small boy, Winston disliked lessons – and for years was bad at them – but loved playing with his thousand tin soldiers. Later he sought and found adventure, either as a cavalryman or war correspondent, in

Sir Winston Churchill (detail), by Robin Craig Guthrie

Cuba, the North-West Frontier, the Sudan and South Africa. But he had not really a military mind and outlook, which are very different from a boyish love of action and adventure. (Later one of his favourite pastimes was describing, with much eloquence and passion, pieces of grand strategy, global chess, almost always faulty and probably ruinous.) But I intended no sneer when I described his love of action and adventure as *boyish*. It is a compliment to his imagination and spirit. He took this rejuvenating desire into politics, bewildering or alienating men who had forgotten they had ever been boys, and he never lost his love of action and adventure until old age and frailty defeated him. He was frequently accused of being a warmonger, possibly brutal and blood-thirsty at heart. But this was quite wrong. His record in the various high offices he held shows him to have been not only extremely industrious but also unusually humane. (Two out of many examples: as Home Secretary he decided at once for prison reform; as a Minister at the end of the First World War he pressed hard, though not finally successful, for food ships to be sent to Germany.) And then there was something else. To introduce it I shall quote a brief passage from Philip Guedalla's *Portrait* of Churchill and the chapter devoted to Churchill's activities in the First World War:

> . . . He often flew to France; and on one flight when the engine failed above the Channel, he began to wonder how long he would be able to keep afloat and noticed that 'a curious calm' came over him. Someone asked him afterwards whether he had felt afraid of dying. 'No,' he replied, 'I love life, but I don't fear death.' After all he had been fairly near it in his time. . . .

My 'something else' is not concerned with his fearlessness, which nobody ever doubted, but with his 'I love life'. For once, a man who said this meant what he said. He could be too dogmatic and impatient, too egocentric, too apt to plunge into oratory (with echoes of Gibbon) on any and every subject; but behind all this, creating a life-enhancing glow, was his enormous gusto, an unquenchable delight in the variety and fulness of life, not uncommon among artists, but rarely found in Parliament. (Charles James Fox and Palmerston knew it, but Winston Churchill's gusto was greater than theirs.) Finally, at a greater depth in the personality, there was still another something else. And I suggest it was not only a persistent feeling of living in history but also, deep down and not to be brought up and examined, a mysterious sense of destiny.

His whole political career was as dramatic as he was. And it was shot through with irony, something I am not sure he ever did enjoy. Never at heart a party politician, he was a most notable victim of party hostility and its tactics. Out of honest conviction he left the Tories (who then detested him) for the Liberals, and after their triumph in 1906 he took charge of one dazzled ministry after another, ending as First Lord of the Admiralty, confidently taking into the First World War a Royal Navy that 'could have lost the war in an afternoon' – but didn't. He was then brought down at a stroke by the Tories who refused to join Asquith's Coalition unless Churchill went. But later, Lloyd George, a sympathetic friend, made him Minister of Munitions and then Secretary of War. Later still, in the uneasy 1920s, a Tory once more, he shot up again as Chancellor of the Exchequer. But the new Tories, led by very cautious men, were not his style. At thirty-three already a Cabinet Minister, at sixty-three, still in his prime, he was far removed from any ministerial office, and spent much of his time at home, writing hard, painting, laying bricks or hurrying back to the House to drop a few. In the later 1930s, when he was thundering out warnings against Hitler, apart from a small group of Tory friends and admirers the bulk of his party was telling him to shut up and sit down. There was still a considerable number of these mistrustful Tories even in May 1940, when Chamberlain was forced to resign and Churchill became head of an all-party government. (And many of these same men, after some years and victory, almost smothered the grand old man in the chocolate sauce of their adulation.) Then more drama, more irony, for in the summer of 1945, at the height of fortune and fame, Churchill marched his Tory Party, talking more than his share of party political nonsense on the way, into a general election and was disastrously defeated. In 1951 a small majority returned him to 10 Downing Street, but now, a final irony, he was already in his later seventies, and – though he lived to be ninety – he was in fact ageing fast and ought to have resigned before he did in 1955. It is a strange story of ups and downs and ironical twists. But of course we have left out its greatest chapter.

Winston Churchill was back at the Admiralty again during the months of 'the phoney war'. It was his ships that were making the news, and it was his voice on the air, adding trumpets and trombones to the symphony of propaganda, that defied and damned the Nazis. So it was he who was made Premier and also Minister of Defence and given almost unlimited powers to wage war. The man and the hour had met at last, as we shall see when we return to that first glorious year of his leadership. But only idolatry could pretend that his total conduct of the war was beyond the reach of criticism. He was not always right, not always wise. For example, his overall strategy, defying American pressure to concentrate on the invasion of France, was dubious. He was wrong to insist upon 'unconditional surrender'. He should never have allowed Lindemann to persuade him into all-out saturation bombing, an inhumane decision that helped Goebbels to intensify his propaganda. It is my own private belief, not at all tainted with malice, that power itself (though he remained an honourable Parliamentarian), the sheer strain of warmaking on a vast scale, and certain dangerous illnesses, together coarsened to some extent his finer qualities, reducing the magnanimity and generosity for which he had earlier been renowned. He lost the 1945 election because he was no longer in touch with the English people, who still loved him, whereas in 1940 he understood and expressed them perfectly.

This was indeed – to quote a phrase he made famous – his 'finest hour'. In the gathering darkness, when the freedom of Western Europe fell into ruin and despair, all his secret dreams came true. His sense of destiny rose to the surface and blazed up. His enduring boyish delight in action and adventure, his tremendous gusto, his satisfaction in being at last in command of a united nation at war, the odd combination in him of a massive personality and a certain impishness, perhaps even his unusually happy marriage – all these ran together and fused to create a new amalgam, defying every stress, out of which came a towering national figure. Unlike Lloyd George in his great days, Winston was not a natural orator; he had to take a lot of trouble, but it was the right kind of trouble, spicing and sharpening the familiar Gibbon style with his own wit and humour. He offered fearless leadership and at the same time – and indeed through a whirligig of testing times: the sickening fall of France, the threat of invasion, the Battle of Britain, the Blitz, the growing U-boat menace, the gigantic movement of German armies, culminating in the invasion of Russia – he said over the air what the people wanted somebody to say. He not only directed the war, when Britain seemed to be almost alone, but he gave it an inspiring voice.

Disliking austerity himself – as most of the English do – he did whatever he could to protect the people from its coldest ravages. Privileged and aristocratic by birth, upbringing, temperament, he was yet triumphantly able to suggest a common touch. Highly emotional himself – and when I happened to be visiting the House as he made his famous speech about the French Navy, I could plainly see the tears rolling down his cheeks – he was not afraid of appealing to the emotions, sharing them – as most prominent English politicians have been so reluctant to do – with the whole nation. There may have been something of his American inheritance here, as there certainly was in his close relation with President Roosevelt. But for the rest, he was at this time a great Englishman, a war leader of a stature that may have stirred his imagination long before, and a miraculous gift to Britain and what remained of European democracy. And he was a great Englishman whose Englishness at last, in his sixty-sixth year, came thundering and flaming out and astonished the world.

THE UNCOMMON COMMON PEOPLE

❧

IKE many titles trying to be clever, the one above could be misleading. I do not mean by it that I am about to explain uncommon specimens of the English common people. I am trying
to say that while I am concerned here with the English common
people, I believe them to be uncommon – quite different from
common people elsewhere. For a long time they have been chockful of
Englishness. It follows – or it ought to do, now that we are in Chapter 4 –
that I shall not attempt their history but will try to explain them, not in
terms of what they ate, drank, wore, earned, but more or less in terms of
what went on in their minds and what may still be going on there. (There
are of course, many social histories of the English. Offering a well-
documented and substantial one, contained in a single but biggish
volume, I strongly recommend *A History of the English People*, by R. J.
Mitchell and M. D. R. Leys, published by Longmans, Green and Co. in
1950.) Historical events may make an occasional appearance here, but
there will be no chronology, no narrative and indeed no organization of
material at all. This whole chapter will wander around like an old man's
thoughts, out of which, after all, it will be coming. There could be some
laziness and haziness in all this, but even so I can't help wondering if
this isn't the best way to explain the English common people.

Obviously I am now at liberty to start anywhere, and it happens I
have been remembering the middle 1930s. I was told then, not once but
scores of times and always by sternly realistic young intellectuals, that I
must decide between Communism and Fascism, take one or the other.
Any attempt to avoid this decision would be escapist, a retreat from
reality. I replied (I hope with a smile) that I didn't like Communism or
Fascism and didn't agree that I had to choose one or the other. And if that
was just muddling along, then I would muddle along. In this instance I
might be said to have been replying on behalf of the English common
people, who never saw themselves choosing between Communism and

Fascism. (When we consider its strength in so many other countries, Communism failed in England; and Fascism was an utter failure.) Here it may be objected that most of the English, especially 'the workers' then adopted by these young intellectuals, were not thinking at all about politics and economics. The men were far more interested in football, cricket, horse-races, pigeon-fancying and digging in allotments; while their women were wondering how to live decently on far too little money, how to make their winter coats last another two years, and how the Royal Family, various film stars, and Mrs Thompson down the road, were all getting along. This may seem all too trivial, but to my mind it is better than manufacturing fanatics, dangerous idolators, brutal guards for concentration or labour camps. The greatest weakness of this style of

A duel between a Spurs forward and a Chelsea back, September 1913

life was – and possibly still is – that it removes so many people, not necessarily stupid and insensitive, from the challenge, excitement and inspiration of the arts. But then it may be argued that the arts themselves had moved further and further away from the English common people.

The comparative scarcity of fanatics, wild extremists, half-dotty 'true believers', among these people is very important. In spite of some drawbacks, it made ordinary living in England rather pleasanter than it was in many other countries; there was, we might say, more psychological space around people, more room in which to be yourself and go your own way, so long as you did not publicly defy certain lingering traces of the old puritanism. (In my opinion this was never strong in a large section of the working class, as distinct from the carefully respectable lower-middle class.) A quotation I am very fond of might bring us close to the outlook and habit of mind of English working people. It comes from the remarkable *Autobiography* of John Cowper Powys, who describes a close friend and says that he 'combined scepticism of everything with credulity about everything', and this, Powys adds, is the true Shakespearean way to regard life. Certainly we can find this irrational but not unreasonable combination in Shakespeare; we can also find something like it – and well into the past, too – among England's common people. Naturally there have been exceptions, notably the type of working man who severely educates himself out of such irrationality and becomes narrowly sententious and logic-chopping. (It is a type even more familiar in Scotland.) But most of the English people have never found it hard to be both sceptical and credulous, ready to believe in marvels and equally ready to take a sharp look at them. We discover more than a touch of this if we go back as far as Cromwell and his advice to the troops: 'Put your trust in God, my boys, and keep your powder dry' – a mixture of faith and shrewd self-reliance.

I seem to recall recurring scenes in French popular novels and films, if they were concerned with rural or small-town life, that may help me to make a point here. In these scenes the local schoolmaster, a severe rationalist, possibly an avowed atheist, confronts the local *curé*, a rather simple soul who believes almost everything, except of course in the school-master's cynical scepticism or disbelief. Now while it would be possible to discover these two opposed types among English people, no popular novelist or film producer here would think it worth while creating scenes out of their disagreement. The long war between what have been called the Red and the Black would not be familiar to English readers and film audiences. As I have already suggested, the English tend to combine in themselves both scepticism and credulity. They are neither fervent devotees of any established form of religion nor yet entirely irreligious. (There is a great deal of Englishness in this, for while it is reasonable it is not strictly rational, and because it does not determinedly disregard the unconscious it cannot escape the feeling that life is a mystery.) It is important to remember that the two great popular movements in the England of the last hundred and fifty years were not religious movements. The first of these was Chartism, which was apparently defeated, though

'Grand National Finish', 1843 (detail), by William Tasker

in fact only one of its famous six points, the unreasonable demand for annual parliaments, was finally seen to be unacceptable. The other and later movement, less dramatic, slower but surer, was concerned with the growth and immense development of Trades Unionism and the Labour Party. Clearly neither of these was a religious movement. (The Oxford Movement was, but then it never captured the common people.) On the other hand, I would argue that an enduring desire to obtain *for other people* better material conditions is basically religious.

We have read and heard much, perhaps too much, about tradition in England's Establishment and upper-class life. But it seems to me that tradition has been more important among the common people, passing it down not through picturesque ceremonies and various rather empty rituals but by way of talk at the fireside or the pub. Such talk can take in quite a length of social history; grandparents retelling to children what their own grandparents told them when they were children.

Let us take first a rather imposing example of popular tradition. Historians, who delight in contradicting earlier historians, now tell us that the Wars of the Roses did not greatly affect the ordinary life of the country, that we must no longer imagine their being waged against a background of general disorder and ruin. But I am still convinced that that is how Shakespeare saw them, thanks to his boyhood, to tales round the fire, and a lasting local tradition. After all, he was grown-up before the Battle of Bosworth was a century old, and rural tradition could easily outlast a century. And I feel sure that it was not simply his own temperament nor the desire to please a Tudor Queen that made him praise a stable hierarchical government and denounce disorder and any threat of anarchy; the force of tradition among the common people must have played its part. We can take another example, also literary but from the eighteenth century. No doubt the English Romantic Movement owed something to Germany and Johann Gottfried von Herder, but I think it owed still more to English rural traditions, which knew nothing about literary fashion and the Enlightenment but perhaps still remembered the *Secret Commonwealth of Elves, Faunes and Fairies*.

Now we come to our own day, when we have been able to discover the weight and influence of tradition, still in terms of ordinary working people, even on our television screens. To illustrate this, let us imagine a conflict between the Union of Reservoir-keepers and the Ministry that employs them. The Union has demanded an immediate increase of fifteen per cent on wages and an extra week's holiday. After some show of resistance the Ministry offers three days more holiday and a wages increase of ten per cent. This is not good enough; the Union renews its demand; and it now threatens to take 'industrial action'. There is a strike: reservoirs must look after themselves. Up to this point perhaps

'Street Scene: Painting 1935', by L. S. Lowry

{112}

only the general secretary of the Union has been seen on television, but now a number of its ordinary members are interviewed. Three or four out of five of these men behave in an odd fashion. They appear to generate far more emotion than the situation calls for, and far more than their own Union officials. They are strangely aggressive or bitter, as if their employers were trying to take the very bread out of their mouths. And I am convinced that this over-reaction comes from tradition, from what their fathers and mothers, grandfathers and grandmothers, have told them, from a time when men worked far too long for too little and went on strike out of sheer desperation. In these unexpected and indeed uncalled-for aggressive or bitter tones we are catching echoes from the past, listening to some melancholy chapters of English history. Perhaps, after all, it is the working class that has the longest memory, recalling grim reminiscences from childhood and the fireside, and while never mentioning *tradition* is most deeply affected by it.

To understand something of what has happened to the English common people we must dive into history. We need to take a look at three revolutions: the English Revolution of 1688, then the French Revolution, and finally the Industrial Revolution. Although to a Macaulay the English Revolution was the greatest event in human history, in its *direct* influence upon the lives of the common people – as distinct from those of the various classes above them – it is the least important of these three revolutions. But a note or two on the unhappy reign of James II, who combined Catholic fanaticism with obstinacy and cruelty, can be set down here. It was largely the common people of the South West who, untrained, untried, were swept into Monmouth's crazy rebellion, scattered and hunted down by the royal regular soldiers, then afterwards shouted down and condemned in the Bloody Assizes of the half-mad Jeffreys. It left a tale of horror, of evil screaming its head off, retold over and over again among the farms and moors of the South West. Again, because the Edict of Nantes had been revoked, a large number of Huguenots, to escape the dreadful persecution, arrived in England, decent skilled men and merchants for the most part, representing an English gain and a serious French loss. Meanwhile, James II maintained what amounted to a Catholic regular army of 30,000 men on Hounslow Heath, like a musket primed and pointed at London.

Though comparatively well behaved, Cromwell's highly professional army, ruling England through its major-generals, had been heartily disliked by the people, who were to mistrust and dislike standing armies of regular troops for a long time. Though these same people would be able to provide generation after generation of recruits to famous infantry regiments, not especially spirited in attack but matchless in any stubborn defence, they were never military-minded. If necessary their young

The English soldier, as depicted by George Stubbs. Detail from his painting of men of the 10th Light Dragoons, 1793 men could go marching to wars and fight hard, but the English people as a whole had no affection nor respect for the style of life created by armies. It seemed to them either tyrannical or ridiculous, and in this they were the exact opposite of the Germans, who, during the later part of the nineteenth century and right up to 1918, tended to behave even in civilian life as if they were still in the army. The English, including most of their officers, spent as little time as possible in uniform and were always glad to be out of it. They could never take seriously a solemn, official bloodthirstiness. So, during the First World War – and here I write out of first-hand experience – when it was mistakenly decided to send around huffing and puffing senior officers to talk about 'the Spirit of the Bayonet' they were greeted with open derision. Here again, tradition was at work, and it was a decidedly unmilitary tradition.

Fortunately, the English Revolution of 1688 was unmilitary too, for James II bolted to France and William of Orange took his place without blood being shed in England. The Revolution established a constitutional monarchy and the supreme authority of Parliament, abolished many abuses (including, seven years later, Press censorship) and finally banished the idea that one religious sect could savagely persecute any other religious sect. So far, so good; and clearly the common people shared some of its benefits. But it was not really their Revolution; it belonged to Parliament (whose Members they did not choose), to the lawyers and the bishops. From the point of view of the English common people the Revolution brought in an era that denied any further and very urgent reforms, an era that was oligarchic and not genuinely democratic, and one for which the common people, by the end of the eighteenth century, were to pay a very heavy price. Apart from the evangelical movement led by the Wesleys that produced the various Methodist churches, the triumphant ascendancy of the Anglican Church throughout this period cut it off from a great many of the common people, who saw it as part of the Establishment, the friend of the land-owners and the wealthier employers and, always with some exceptions, indifferent to the people's needs and cares. But to understand the heavy price that had to be paid later, we must turn from the English to the French Revolution.

The first few years of the French Revolution, from 1789, were welcomed by a large section of the English, including most of the common people and the Whig gentlemen led by Fox. France, it was felt, was more or less going the same way that England had gone. Two events changed the picture. One was the Reign of Terror that began in 1793, when even Fox declared there was no 'shadow of excuse for this horrid massacre'. So far as the news of it reached them, the majority of the English people were horrified, too, and so were ready to support any war against the French.

The second event was the astonishing success of the new improvised French armies against the regular armies of reactionary governments, which learned with dismay that Paris was promising to assist any rebellion of their subjects. Pitt's Tory government behaved as if it were equally panic-stricken, apparently believing that there were not only these successful revolutionary armies abroad but that also in England there were innumerable republicans and 'Jacobins' (as they were often called), a potential 'Reign of Terrorists'. It is possible that Pitt and his friends believed what they wanted to believe; what is certain is that though they must have known they had most of the people, now fervently patriotic, solidly behind them, they proceeded hastily to destroy any popular political life the country might have had, one precious liberty after another vanishing. Habeas corpus was suspended quite early; radical societies were suppressed; public meetings were forbidden; any outspoken reformer might be accused of high treason and kept in prison without trial; and the Combination Acts declared all associations of wage-earners illegal. In short, the common people were being called upon to defend a country that was busy robbing them of all their rights.

It is true that there was more rural poverty, more vagabondage and destitution, in the eighteenth century (when common lands were being gobbled up by the enclosure movement) than we imagine when we are under the spell of its artists. Even so, to my mind, the period covering the French and Napoleonic Wars, 1793–1802, 1803–14 (or 1815 if we remember Waterloo), and the remaining years of the Regency, was a very bad time indeed for the English common people. No doubt many of them were glad and proud to be defying and then defeating 'Old Boney'. They had certainly nothing else to be glad and proud about. The government headed by Lord Liverpool in 1812, with Castlereagh as Foreign Secretary, and Sidmouth as Home Secretary, was even worse than previous Tory governments, even more determined to make the rich richer and the poor poorer. If this seems too steep a statement, consider first the Corn Laws, not to be repealed for many a long year, which protected the home market for wheat, no matter how high the price rose, by proportionately increasing the tariff against imported wheat, so supporting the landowners and wealthier farmers at the expense of everybody not so fortunate. Moreover, when there was peace at last, income tax was abolished, and to compensate the exchequer there were heavy duties on tea, sugar and soap, that the poor had to pay. Smallholders, with no wheat to sell, and farm labourers were in a desperate situation, often compelled to feed their families on bread and butter and potatoes and strong tea; and all too frequently the potatoes would be half-rotten and the darkish bread made out of adulterated flour. No wonder so many of them took themselves and their wives and children to work in the mines and foundries and new factories. Finally, if a man out of sheer desperation stole a piece of meat or a few shillings, he might be hanged or transported to New South Wales in appalling convict ships or lashed into unconsciousness. The laws protecting all forms of property were dreadfully harsh; and it has been said that in no other European country were there so many offences on the statute book that demanded the death penalty.

Reform was urgent but all roads to it were blocked. It was dangerous to belong to any radical association, any movement of protest. Enthusiastic public meetings were regarded as menacing riots, 'Jacobinism' preparing for fire and slaughter. Like all severely oppressive governments, this one employed secret agents to spy on its own people; and there can be little doubt that between 1816 and 1820 a few of the more artful of these spies wormed their way into radical movements and then acted as *agents provocateurs*, deliberately urging reckless courses of action that would excuse calling in the cavalry and more arrests. But when the worst happened – and disaster was inevitably on its way – there was not even this excuse. The immense crowd that assembled in St Peter's Fields, Manchester, on 16 August 1819, looked forward to some stirring radical oratory, but it was in a holiday mood, a lot of the men bringing their wives and families. No weapons, only a number of banners, were to be seen. The regular troops stationed in Manchester, the 15th Hussars, were called to the scene, but it was the squadrons of local yeomanry, probably summoned by magistrates who lost their heads, that charged into the crowd, trampling people down and even using their sabres. There were nearly six hundred wounded or badly hurt, with over a hundred women among them, and at least eleven deaths. And this – as it was soon bitterly called – was Peterloo.

If Manchester had been in some other country it might have gone up in flames that night. And indeed if there had been a revolution at this time, when the war was over and yet conditions were worse than ever, no compassionate observer could have blamed the common people. Why was there no concerted action that even suggested a possible revolution? I believe there is no simple direct answer. Of course there were small radical groups, especially in the industrial districts, where there was fiery late-night talk about weapons; and in some instances actual weapons, probably none of them the newest and deadliest, were handed round in secret. But the common people in general were not members of these groups. In point of fact, the radical leaders were for the most part from the middle classes. (But then most revolutions have been plotted and then set alight by rebels from the educated middle class.) Whether they were in the country or in the new industrial towns, the people must have been intensely aware of their wretched plight, the men knowing

The rigour of the law, 1824.
The execution of John
Thurtell who was found guilty
of the murder of William
Weare

they could expect no reform from a Parliament that did not represent them, their wives wondering in despair how to feed and clothe their children. What then kept these people from open furious rebellion? Were they overawed by the squadrons of hussars and dragoons, never stationed too far away? Possibly, though they had never been a people that lacked courage. Were they patient simply because they were so thick, stupid, bovine? Some of them, no doubt, certainly were. But I feel there was something else that made it impossible for them to join a huge violent uprising, to stage a revolution like the one the French had staged. And that something else was their Englishness.

Let us see how this works out. There seem to me to be two main types of revolutionaries. The first is both intellectual and fanatical. He accepts quite early a doctrine and all its dogma of revolution, may refine it and enlarge it as time goes on, as Lenin did his Marxism; but he is ready if necessary to spend a lifetime waiting to put theory into practice: he is essentially the professional revolutionary. The other type begins by being fairly rational, perhaps attends a few meetings of fellow Marxists or Syndicalists or Anarchists, where he talks more and louder than anybody else; but then something happens (and it might be the increasing suppression of inner doubt) and he explodes into irrationality, commits himself and his group to violent action – buildings must be blown up or burned down, bourgeoisie must be rounded up, imprisoned or executed, with all Rubicons crossed.

I hope I have said enough about Englishness now to make it clear that such a habit of mind, aware if only hazily of unconscious contents or pressures, constantly relying on what is instinctive or intuitive, would not produce either the fanatical rationality or the sudden break-through of wild irrationality. Englishness would tend to brood, to grope about slowly for some reasonable balance between fear and hope, between doubt and faith. It is significant that the revolutionary creeds that promise *to change everything at once* have made far fewer converts in England than they have in every major European country. It is significant, too, that any demands for complete equality, for equal pay all round, for any egalitarian whims and fancies, have never been pressed by the English common people, only by a few middle-class intellectuals. Talk to any trade union leader about money, and very soon the term *differentials* will be heard. This would have annoyed George Bernard Shaw, a great egalitarian *in theory*, but then he was an Irish middle-class intellectual and about as far removed from the average English working man as one decent human being, using the same language, can be from another decent human being.

However, let us have no jumping to large conclusions at this point. I am not suggesting that the Englishness of the people keeps them right about everything. I think they have been right to reject any idea of a sudden and probably violent revolution, partly no doubt because I have never favoured any such idea myself. But Englishness has its shadow side. It can be foolish as well as wise. As I pointed out originally, too often it encourages a cosy self-deception. The English people have sometimes been lazily satisfied when they ought to have been vigilant. They have assumed a gradual but steady approach to better times when in fact regress has taken over from progress. (One Press trick that fools them is to label the comparative few who are being vigilant on their behalf as busy-bodying 'do-gooders'. After all, who wants 'do-badders'?) Again, Englishness does not work in situations that cry out for rational consideration, for some application of logic, when a slow-moving hazy reasonableness simply will not meet the challenge of events which demand immediate sharp decisions. In our time this weakness, together with the force of tradition on both sides, has played havoc with English industrial relations, haunted by a class system that has vanished from the scene in most other industrial countries. Again, I would say that the English people as a whole are politically alive and active only on rare occasions – for example, in 1906, when they swept the Liberals into power,

Liberal and Labour leaders:
(left) Herbert Henry Asquith,
Viscount Oxford and Asquith

(right) Clement Attlee, first
Earl Attlee

and in 1945 when they did the same for Labour – and that at most other times either they feel the other chaps should have a turn, or their wandering attention is caught by some cheap electioneering trick that would never fool them if they were politically alert. In some countries the cafés are crowded with men arguing about politics all day and half the night. England is not one of those countries, except, I repeat, on very rare occasions. In its pubs, either the customers are not arguing at all or they are deeply involved in some interminable and complicated discussion about anything and everything except politics. But somewhere behind this nonsense – and ten to one it *is* largely nonsense – there remains, waiting to emerge at the right moment, a tolerant, rarely unkind, live-and-let-live reasonableness, that makes the English common people uncommon.

We come now to the third and most important of our revolutions, the Industrial Revolution. It is difficult for a man in his later seventies to recall exactly what he was taught in his earlier teens, but I seem to remember being given a completely wrong impression of the Industrial Revolution. For example, I was left with the odd notion that it all happened at once: as if Lancashire farms and cottages suddenly vanished in a grim transformation scene that revealed, beneath a pall of smoke, hundreds of factories and their tall chimneys and a corrugated wilderness of back-to-back houses; as if one year there was talk about the harvest, and the next year there was already 'trouble at t'mill'. Now I realize that the Industrial Revolution really took place in slow motion, beginning in

a semi-rural style, with no enormous buildings and great steam engines, and then gradually expanding, putting up bigger and bigger mills and warehouses and creating whole new towns. These were quite different from the old market towns, and even today, when industrial areas have established their own amenities, this difference is easily detectable. These Lancashire and West Riding towns, creations of the Industrial Revolution, might be described as dormitory extensions of the mills and warehouses, looking as if the steam engines had planned them to increase their owners' profits.

Again, I was taught that England easily led the way, becoming so rich and powerful, because it possessed the natural resources for mechanization, notably iron and coal. But in fact England had no monopoly of such resources; there was plenty of coal and iron elsewhere. Now I know – though other people had to discover it for me – there is no simple explanation. Even the country gentlemen and the large-scale farmers, who vastly improved English agriculture throughout the eighteenth century, played their part. So did the medical men, who brought down the death-rate and enlarged the number of potential industrial workers. Even more important were the new men who realized what mechanization and large-scale production might do for them. For the most part they were North Countrymen, energetic, ambitious, hard-driving, making their way out of austere Nonconformist communities. After a generation or two of successful mill-owning, finding themselves esteemed in Manchester and Liverpool but ignored in Westminster and Mayfair, they became formidable opponents of the political and social Establishment.

But, most important of all, the men indispensable to the Industrial Revolution were the inventors, the creative men, who kept on arriving from many different backgrounds throughout the eighteenth century, transforming the production of iron, the application of steam-power, the processes of textile manufacture, mining and transport. (We must not be surprised to discover that most of them made very little money out of their inventions, for it is men who think about *money* who pile it up.) I feel that Englishness was at work here, and indeed down to our own time. The English are an inventive people – though less enterprising in later industrial stages than other people in exploiting inventions – but not, in my opinion, simply because they were and are uniquely mechanical-minded. After all, England was never busy manufacturing watches, cuckoo clocks and the like, and the most ingenious mechanical devices, from musical boxes to impressive automata, belonged to the Continent. So I feel we cannot ignore Englishness. Clearly a man actually at work on a spinning jenny or a power loom – or, for that matter, a jet engine or a television system – would have to be severely rational, quite logical, to succeed. But it is more than likely, I think, that his original conception and its possible future use would have come to him in the hazier atmosphere of Englishness, with its open end, its brooding, its feeling for a larger time-scale. I cannot prove this, but then there is hardly anything that seems to me deeply significant that I can prove. However, I certainly cannot accept the common idea that the English have been so inventive because they have always been so practical. It is not the inventors but the men who have made money out of them who have been so practical. But haven't these men been English too? Not especially English: the type is well known everywhere.

Finally, I was taught – and some recent historians are still at it – that the Industrial Revolution was altogether and without any doubt a triumph for England and a colossal boon to its common people. But it seems to me possible, without being sentimental or cranky, to bring in a few doubts, too often ignored. To do this we must take a much wider view, which will have to include the England of this century, when somehow things began to go wrong, when instead of leading the field we were overtaken by more than one of our commercial competitors and then more recently have fallen well behind – suffering, it is suggested, from some strange malaise. But is it strange? Perhaps we are suffering from that triumphant early start in the Industrial Revolution. This may seem far-fetched, but I think I have a case to support the conclusion. To begin with, I must add that our early start was only triumphant commercially, *and not psychologically*. Once industry was booming, the men responsible for its expansion still felt they could never be challenged. Because the aristocratic tradition outlasted the downright socially democratic Manchester outlook, grandsons of the original successful mill-owners and merchants were sent to public schools, to Oxford and Cambridge, and too often fell in love with the country-house style of life, probably the most seductive of all styles of life. So time, attention and money too often went elsewhere, not back into business. As soon as England's industry and merchandising were seriously challenged, by foreign competition that was thoroughly professional and up to date, they began to seem rather amateurish and old-fashioned. Even English inventiveness, which still existed, frequently provided no new asset because the inventions had to be taken abroad to be properly adopted and exploited. (Many English manufacturers to this day refuse a new and original design, because if they are doing badly they say they cannot afford it, and if they are doing nicely they say they do not need it.) Of course, the tremendous long start, together with the resources and growing needs of the great Empire, kept things going; so England was still right up there, still imposingly rich and powerful. But somewhere behind the grand façade the rot was setting in, quietly, unnoticed except by a few cranky pessimists.

Obviously the common people, once called 'the operatives', later 'the work force', were involved in all this. No doubt, as we are told, the early start of the Industrial Revolution provided them – and soon their growing families – with work, food and shelter when they might have been wandering in search of Poor Relief. But, even so, they went into the mills and foundries and mines at a bad time. While a few employers tried to co-operate with their employees, the majority, driving hard, wanted the maximum amount of work for the minimum amount of pay. Generally they behaved – and there is plenty of evidence for this – as if their 'operatives' were their enemies, rather as if they had found these people in an occupied country. Men who could weep with their families in the evening over the deaths of Little Nell or Paul Dombey could clamp their workpeople into the most appalling conditions. It is true there was a gradual improvement, carried through among outraged cries that trade would be ruined. But seeds had been deeply sown – and here let us remember the force of tradition among the working class – that would grow only to bear Dead Sea fruit. Moreover, while the early employers were simply hard bargainers and did not see themselves as belonging to a different social class, those who came afterwards, because their education and backgrounds had changed completely, could not help regarding themselves as members of a different social class. The result was that the class system complicated and bedevilled the relations between employers and employed. Workers must not be paid too much, otherwise they 'would not know their place'. So I can well remember the satirical (ill-natured rather than humorous) Press comments on the rumours that some miners were actually buying pianos – what next! And even now, as I write this, so long a time after the Industrial Revolution, the nation is still trying to cope with its 'industrial relations'.

Again, because this Revolution developed so early and then so rapidly, at a rough-and-ready time, it showed a face that was far too grim and ugly. There were now two Englands, entirely different in appearance, manners, styles of life, as various early and mid-Victorian novelists were eager to point out. The common people lived in both Englands, but the industrial English and the old rural English, taken on a broad basis, hardly ever set eyes on each other. It was difficult for them to believe they all belonged to one nation. In the smoke-blackened regions, extending north from the West Midlands, ordinary people referred to 'Down South' as if it were a foreign country, and were still doing it when I was a youngster in the West Riding. (In spite of all the more recent changes, this feeling of being different from 'Southerners' still lingers in the North.) During the first half of the nineteenth century – and occasionally rather later – foreign visitors cried out in horror at the sight of industrial England, as if smouldering sections of Hell had been brought to the surface. Any horror would have been justified during the earlier years of industrialization, before any urgently necessary reforms had been introduced, when ill-nourished families, living in packed hovels, had been worked to death. But, when we reach the 1850s, I suggest that life in the industrial towns was not as hellish as the visitor, catching a glimpse of them through a train window, imagined it to be. It looked ugly enough, not offering the eye and mind even a hint of grace and charm; but the people behind those dark curtains of smoke, though they were still worked too hard and were paid too little, were no longer pallid creatures existing in utter despair.

I have referred to the 1850s, not because I happen to have written a book about them but because it was then that Dickens, writing in a hurry to provide a serial for his *Household Words*, brought out his *Hard Times*. Now Dickens – a genius but a 'Southerner', we must remember – really did not know enough about industrial England, certainly not at that time. If he had lived, even if only for a week or two, in Coketown, he would not have found it necessary to bring in a travelling circus to represent skills, odd characters, warm human relationships, because he could have found them all in Coketown. And how do *I* know? How can I be so sure? Because I was born and brought up in a Yorkshire version of Coketown, and there as a boy I listened to grandparents and great-aunts whose memories went back into mid-Victorian industrial England, and some of those memories were as good as a circus. Certainly the hard-working people deserved something better than that blanket of smoke, the giant forest of mill chimneys, the factories like black fortresses, the rows and rows of wretched little houses 'back o't mill'; but nobody must tell me that the people were defeated by them, and so incapable of producing courageous and independent, odd and richly humorous characters. I know better: these were my people. They were the full-flavoured fruit of trees that had known dark days and bitter winds. And if my word cannot be accepted, then I will make a final point on this subject. Many people now take a nostalgic interest in the old music halls and their great nights that vanished long ago. Well, the original talent that blazed in the old music halls came almost entirely either from the industrial North or the East End of London, both crowded with 'shockingly under-privileged' people who could somehow rise above it, answer back and, whenever they had the chance, enjoy themselves – something the highly privileged often fail to do.

If I return briefly to 1813 this does not mean, as we shall see, that I have abandoned all hope of considering the industrial workers of our own time. It was in 1813 at York that there was a mass trial of 'Luddites', when at least a dozen of them were hanged and scores were sentenced to transportation. The 'Luddites' were a mixed lot, all rebellious but for various reasons; and some men joined what was really a vague general movement, extending from the Midlands to Yorkshire and Lancashire, not because they shared the actual trade grievances but because they were enthusiastic 'Jacobins' and hoped to organize a violent insurrection. (There is little doubt that some of these apparent firebrands were in fact *agents provocateurs* working for a government that needed an excuse to condemn the whole movement.) The particular 'Luddites' that interest me, men for whom nobody has ever had a good word, were the handloom weavers in the textile trade of Yorkshire and Lancashire. It was they who went out at night with big hammers to smash any new power looms, so obvious a threat to their own cottage industry. They were denounced then – and have been ever since – as stupid, short-sighted enemies of sensible mechanization and progress; and indeed the term 'Luddite' is still used as one of reproach or abuse. But I think some of this reproach or abuse has been stupid and short-sighted. I am not saying that the men were right to smash these new machines. But I do suggest that if we ask ourselves why the men did this, running a terrible risk, we might learn something important about the English common people and their attitude towards industry.

The handloom weavers, doing piece-work at home, were paid very low rates indeed; they could have earned rather more and would not have had to work so long, looking after the machines they wanted to smash. Probably they were the victims of habit, custom, an obstinate conservatism. But I think there was something more deep-seated than mere foolish prejudice, something that belonged to their Englishness. They did not want their lives and their work to be geared to machines. They might have to work at home for abominable long hours, sometimes exhausting themselves to earn a few more shillings, but even so they were to some extent their own masters. No machines dictated how and when they should work. They were men, not cogs, and if a beautiful afternoon called them to the moors or the trout streams, then off they could go. And I say that something of this protest by the 'Luddites', so universally condemned, lingers yet among English working people, appealing to the Englishness that still survives in these very different days. Anybody who considers this far-fetched should answer the following questions. How is it that in England men who work more or less at their own speed and in their own fashion may earn comparatively low wages, but they rarely do any protesting and demonstrating? Why is it that there is most trouble where the hours are reasonable and the wages comparatively high, in those industries, like the manufacturing of cars, in which the men have to adapt themselves to the rhythm and relentless demands of machines? Can it be a coincidence that high-pressure plants of the American type, with their time-and-motion studies and computerized policies, almost invariably run into trouble when they are established in England? And is it not possible that England, for all its inventiveness, never heads the league in up-to-the-minute Admass industry because there is still something in the English that mistrusts and dislikes it? Long ago they led the way, but now that it has gone so far, arriving at the frontier of some steel-and-concrete robotland, secretly they long to loiter, and even call a halt, before the grass has all gone.

With the exception of those who can take a pride in what they are doing, English workers, engaged more or less in mass production, are often accused of being lazy and sourly aggressive – 'bloody-minded'. And generally they cannot explain themselves, which makes them seem all the more difficult and awkward. They are probably always silent about their deep feeling of unease, their underlying disappointment at the way life seems to be going, so clutch at any excuse to be belligerent – the tea break isn't right or the foreman shouldn't have talked like that to Old Fred. I believe that behind this disappointment, this unease, is their Englishness. Because it lies partly open to the unconscious, because it refuses to allow rationality to block the instinctive and the intuitive, Englishness is in a position – though it may never find words for it – to give the whole sad game away. For what is wrong with any highly industrialized and technologically advanced society is that it asks men and women to accept secondary satisfactions in place of primary satisfactions. The latter seem to respond to deep-seated desires that are part of our psychological inheritance. Perhaps we want certain things to happen because they have happened to our ancestors through hundreds and hundred of generations. Secondary satisfactions may seem delightful, but if people – and this applies to both sexes – still feel dissatisfied on a deeper level, then they will be haunted by a sense of frustration. Labour-saving devices may please a woman, but if she finds it impossible to root herself and her family, if she is continually being moved around, if there are always miles of concrete between her and any grass, flowers and trees, she will feel frustrated. Cars and television sets are excellent things, but if a man has no chance to exhibit a little skill of his own, hasn't a bit of importance somewhere, isn't really recognized *as a man*, then he will feel that life is disappointing and frustrating. For the new secondary satisfactions cannot really take the place of the old primary satisfactions. And the very Englishness of the English leaves them more vulnerable, more constantly aware of these feelings – hence the 'bloody-mindedness' of so many workers. They may not know it but really they are telling us that our kind of civilization lacks juice and nourishment.

It would be splendid if I could now announce that the English common people were finding more and more nourishment in the arts. Probably some of its youngsters are, for much is done both in school and in adult education to encourage them, but the people as a whole are not enthusiastic patrons of the arts. There may have been some loss instead of a gain. For example, it is impossible to hear what happened to Dickens on his later provincial reading tours without realizing that a mass of ordinary people had been reading him with delight for many years. True, we cannot provide such people with a Dickens now, but even if we could, I do not believe he would have the same rapturous reception. Most of the old magic of novel-reading has gone. No doubt something has been transferred from fiction in book form to the very popular serials on television and radio, which win continued interest and curiosity but, except among children, rarely become magical. It is true that there are occasional television productions of dramatic masterpieces, from *Hamlet* to *The*

Cherry Orchard, that are excellent from every point of view. (In some instances, Shakespeare comes off better than he does on the stage.) But, without having any figures to guide me, I cannot help suspecting that the proportion of ordinary working people who enjoy such productions is very small indeed. And most of their favourite programmes are no great treat to anybody who demands some taste and intelligence from the TV screen.

Long before radio and television caught and held a mass audience in England, outside the cities, where fine new playhouses had been built, the Theatre had gone into a decline as widely popular entertainment. We are apt to forget how many playhouses there were at one time in England. Roughly from the middle of the eighteenth century until about the middle of the nineteenth, there were whole 'circuits', where a touring company would play a number of neighbouring 'dates' all settled in advance, that

{129}

vanished long ago, hardly leaving any trace behind them. We can read how actors, afterwards famous, captured audiences in towns that have not seen professional players for the last hundred years. There would, of course, be melodrama and rough farces, but there would also be some of the fine old comedies – and Shakespeare, almost always Shakespeare. The middle classes would attend these theatres, but so, too, would working people. After the decline of the old 'circuits', when playhouses, probably small, but genuine theatres, rather mysteriously disappeared, it was the larger theatres in the cities that dominated the provincial scene. They never housed stock companies, but many touring actor-managers brought a reasonable repertory of productions. But these actor-managers, with Henry Irving at the head of them, died or retired; and just before, during and after the First World War, there were successful actor-managers of a new type – like Gerald du Maurier – who hated touring and depended entirely on their West End runs. Meanwhile, the provincial working class had drifted away from the Theatre, preferring variety shows and then cinemas.

However, there still lingered, well away from the cities, some very modest and thoroughly traditional forms of touring. For example, in the middle 1920s, when I was living in an Oxfordshire village, I was able to spend several nights – delighting in every moment of them – with what must have been about the last of the old 'barn-storming' companies. They offered a different programme every night – though somebody always wore the crimson waistcoat that suggested the dressiest character

Theatre Royal and Empire, Nottingham, about 1904

A performance at a country barn theatre; perhaps the Witches' scene from *Macbeth*, 1788, by W. H. Pyne after John Wright

— and they followed tradition in presenting not only a serious play, usually very melodramatic, but also a farcical sketch. I soon discovered that they were able to exist on a hundred (at the most) sixpences in villages because the company was really a travelling family, with an oldish Dad playing aged characters and Mum taking the money, with daughters and their husbands, sons and their wives, dividing all the other characters between them. After several nights, I came to the conclusion that they were not working from printed texts and that the whole repertoire was based on oral tradition, one generation teaching the next. To me the performances were at once terrible and wonderful, as if a more modest and rather run-down Crummles was somewhere in the background. For their part the village audiences seemed to enjoy everything offered them, and I suspect they were having a much better time

'Strolling Actresses in a Barn',
1738, by William Hogarth

than they would have had attending to du Maurier at Wyndham's
Theatre. Now, after nearly fifty years, I have seen on television some
youngish players, their beards bristling with enthusiasm, who on a
minute subsidy from the Arts Council are cheerfully invading pubs and
schoolrooms to present their own little acts, not unlike the farcical
sketches I once saw in an Oxfordshire barn.

But though provincial cities and larger towns have now seen theatres
built, instead of being torn down, with decent stock or repertory companies supported to some extent by the local authorities, such evidence
as I possess – and I make no firm claim for it – suggests that working
people are not falling in love again with the Theatre. The middle-aged
prefer their television programmes, their bingo halls, and the clubs that
can afford to pay astonishingly high salaries to their performers. The

young people, I imagine, go in search of the more daring new films and an ear-battering from their favourite pop groups. (There is irony here: the pop singers who offer themselves as simple folk rebels have all too often been created by astute agents and managers and are enmeshed in a web of limited companies; and while crying out against our age are making the fullest possible use of its electronic equipment.) If the extremely wealthy big trade unions ever invest any of their funds in the arts, no account of their subsidies has ever reached me. Not that I blame them; I am sure their members make no such demands. A great artist, with a tremendous international reputation, like Henry Moore, may have come from a working-class background in the West Riding, but the number of people around there who enjoy his work must be very small indeed. During the last twenty years an ever-increasing range of painters, writers, musicians, actors, have come out of the industrial North to find success in London, belonging – and making no bones about it – to working people. But only a tiny minority of those people have kept up with the artists, unless of course they have been writing or acting for television.

Henry Moore at work in his studio which he converted from a stable

However, we can make a distinction between *the arts* (a somewhat chilly term though it ought not to be) and *art*. We can find art of a varying sort in many diffcrent activities and places. So, for example, it can be discovered in sport and games, and that is where so many of the English common people – certainly the male half of them – have found it and loved it. To enlarge on this, I propose to quote something I wrote in 1927:

> Thirty-five thousand men and boys have just seen what most of them call *t'United* play Bolton Wanderers. Many of them should never have been there at all. . . . When some mills are only working half the week and others not at all, a shilling is a respectable sum of money. It would puzzle an economist to discover where all these shillings came from. But if he lived in Bruddersford, though he might still wonder where they came from, he would certainly understand why they were produced. To say that these men paid their shillings to watch twenty-two hirelings kick a ball is merely to say that a violin is wood and catgut, that *Hamlet* is so much paper and ink. For a shilling the Bruddersford A.F.C. offered you Conflict and Art; it turned you into a critic, happy in your judgment of fine points, ready in a second to estimate the worth of a well-judged pass, a run down the touch line, a lightning shot, a clearance kick by back or goalkeeper; it turned you into a partisan, holding your breath when the ball came sailing into your own goalmouth, ecstatic when your forwards raced away towards the opposite goal, elated, downcast, bitter, triumphant by turns at the fortunes of your side, watching a ball shape Iliads and Odysseys for you; and what is more, it turned you into a member of a new community, all brothers together for an hour and a half, for not only had you escaped from the clanking machinery of this lesser life . . . there you were, cheering together, thumping one another on the shoulders, swopping judgments like lords of the earth, having pushed your way through a turnstile into another and altogether more splendid kind of life, hurtling with Conflict and yet passionate and beautiful in its Art. Moreover, it offered you more than a shilling's worth of material for talk during the rest of the week. A man who had missed the last home match of t'United had to enter social life on tiptoe in Bruddersford.

The game here, of course, is association football. (Rugby enthusiasts can easily adapt the quotation to their own game.) Together with lawn tennis, another English invention, it has gone out and conquered the world.

It costs a great deal more than a shilling to see a first-class football match now, and the really important grounds on really important occasions may take in 70,000 spectators before being compelled to close their gates. (Indeed, to some matches only ticket-holders are admitted.) The finances of a First Division club today – the value of the 'gates', the enormous transfer fees, the salaries and bonuses paid to the players – would make a club chairman or manager of 1927 think he had wandered into the Arabian Nights. But while big money and publicity may heighten both individual and team skills, now very impressive, I think they tend to destroy innocence, on the playing area and among the spectators. I played the game before 1914 and occasionally, as a soldier, during the war, and for a few years after the war I regularly attended, and often reported, First Division matches. And while in my time the game might be rough, it was rarely vicious. There is even a certain viciousness among the spectators, now so young and so devoted to singing rather dreary choruses, and they make me feel that they are so ruthlessly partisan that any enjoyment of good football escapes them. Superior training, skill, tactics, may have improved the game, but I must confess I dislike the endless passing back to the goalkeeper and regret the vanished sight of a whole forward line of five, making use of quick short passes, weaving its way towards the goal.

The other great English game, cricket, has gone down just as certainly as association football has come up. It has not only lost favour as a mass-spectator sport, but – unless I am hopelessly biased – it has also declined as a display of skill. (I may be peering through a mist of nostalgia, but I cannot help feeling that two or three of the great Yorkshire sides of the past would have been more than a match for any of the Test teams I have seen during the last twenty years.) In spite of the recent jazzed-up one-day matches, cricket to be fully appreciated demands leisure, some sunny warm days, and an understanding of its finer points – and as it depends more than any other ball game on varying conditions, on the state of the pitch, on weather and wind and light, it multiplies its fine points. Though it is often considered a 'gentlemanly game', an idea supported by its leisurely progress and breaks for lunch, tea, cool drinks on the field, we must remember that many of its greatest performers came from the industrial North, which also supplied, until our own time, large numbers of its most knowledgeable and keenest spectators. But even while we mourn the decline of this very English and, at its best, very subtle game, we must also remember that it is still being played every fine Saturday in hundreds and hundreds of small towns and villages.

This brings me – and not before time, too – to the common people of rural England, who have been neglected so far here. They might be said to have been neglected in a much broader sense, in an altogether wider scene. While they have often been praised, though always niggardly rewarded, during the last two hundred years they have probably lost more than they have gained. (Unless of course pure air and a variety of jobs to do count as a permanent gain.) I have not in mind now the yeoman farmer, a very English type always of considerable importance to the country, but the humble smallholder and the farm labourers. In most Continental countries there was a great gap between such people and the aristocrats and owners of large estates. In England there were members of intermediate classes – characteristic of the English – who could close this gap. But I have sometimes wondered if this was really a good thing. The humbler rural English ceased to form a peasantry. I have no particular tenderness for peasants, but the fact remains that in many different countries they have been able to live in a special world of their own, at ease with their own customs, manners, clothes, food, drink, songs and dances. The same folk in England lost all this and were never quite able to replace it with anything else, remaining uneasily on the far edge of the greater world, wondering about emigration, domestic service for their daughters, the army or the police or a job in industry for one or two of their sons. It is during the years since the end of the Second World War that a change has taken place, with more mechanization, better transport, the invasion of the country by city commuters or weekenders, and, perhaps above all, the spread and growing influence of radio and television. But even so, something has been lost, for this represents the townsman moving further and further

Group of agricultural labourers, about 1870

out, and not the countryman enjoying his own style of life, his own culture, as he did long, long ago.

Now I may be wrong about what follows; I have done no research, and anyhow there could be no statistics; it is simply something I have noticed over the years. However, Englishness comes into it, so I propose to risk making the point. Let us say that a middle-aged manual worker, perhaps engaged in heavy industry, arrives home at the end of the day. He stands no nonsense from anybody. He is ready for a meal, and the meal must be ready for him. He has done his work and his wife has to have done hers, which indeed she has, as she immediately starts to wait upon him. If for any reason he is a bit out of temper, then there it is, and wife and family – if any – had better just keep quiet for the time being. Apparently we are observing a patriarchal scene. Dad dominates it. But this may be a superficial judgment. If we knew much more about these people, we might find that it is Mum and not Dad who has the stronger and more lasting influence, and that, assuming there is a family, it is a family existing in something like a matriarchy, with the patriarchal style a mere façade. I have noticed this over and over again among working-class families, and even the young men who have left home to be successful, perhaps in one of the arts, keep mentioning Mum not Dad in their interviews. Young working men who get into trouble with the police are usually inclined to bring Mum into the picture. And lads who have joined one of the services seem to have their mothers on their minds, not their fathers. Indeed, the free-and-easy style of life and the absence of any severe standards, now to be found in a very large section of the working class, suggest a matriarchy. So, as the world of industry is entirely dominated by the masculine principle, then clashes are inevitable.

If I think the English common people are uncommon, this is not because I consider them to be better than people in other countries who are more or less on the same financial and social level. As I have tried to show, they have their own peculiar weaknesses as well as their own particular virtues. Naturally I am more at ease with them because after all they are my own people. During my lifetime I am certain they were at their best in the Second World War, especially in 1940 after Dunkirk, when so many of them worked until they were ready to drop from exhaustion. It was not fear that drove them on; I never saw any signs of panic among them. They felt we were alone and must now depend upon ourselves. So they were inspired – for the first time – by a sense of a great common purpose, and indeed during those months, perhaps those years, they were themselves a great people. It cannot be a mere coincidence that it was at this time that there was an unusually eager popular demand for books, good music and drama, a new hunger of the spirit. From 1940 to 1945, it was a privilege to share a country with such people.

ENGLISHNESS IN THE ARTS

✿

THIS chapter is quite informal and very personal. There can be
no awards for general artistic merit here. What I shall be looking for are evidences of *Englishness*, and of course the artists in
question must necessarily be English. To take the first examples that come to mind: two painters of our age whose
work I have long admired for various good reasons are Sickert and William
Nicholson. But Nicholson's masterly painting does not to my mind
suggest Englishness. Sickert's does, but he was born in Munich of a
Danish father, so cannot be included.

To begin with, why not a leap into what in this book represents the
far distant past, the Elizabethan Age? I have in mind Nicholas Hilliard,
the Exeter man who became goldsmith and chief 'limner' for Queen
Elizabeth. He was, of course, a painter of portrait-miniatures, fashionable because they could be worn, often set with jewels, or easily sent as a
gift from one person to another. Hilliard's pupil and later his successful
rival was Isaac Oliver, probably of French extraction and never himself
using the Englished version of his name. I find his portraiture sharper
and more realistic than Hilliard's, yet there is something in Hilliard that
is lacking in Oliver, and that something is all-important here because
I believe it to be Englishness. Consider Hilliard's portrait-miniature that
almost everybody knows, that of the unknown youth leaning against a
tree among roses. It might be a Shakespearean sonnet in paint. Un-
requited love, desire not gratified, suffering perhaps largely imaginary,
one or other of them has stretched him on a rack – though it could be a
rack of roses – and his elongation offers us a smiling verdict on youth, for
on first sight we notice the legs, often so busy but now at rest, then the
richly clothed upper body and the giant dandy's ruff, and last of all the
head, probably used least of all, and a long way from us. It is as if
Hilliard anticipated Bacon's famous yet still surprising dictum: *There is
no excellent beauty that hath not some strangeness in the proportion.* It is his

'A Young Man Leaning
against a Tree among Roses'.
Miniature painted about 1588
by Nicholas Hilliard

young men – at least to my mind – who are best, almost always with a suggestion of promise and wonder about them: it was an age of such young men. On the other hand, his women, though several of them were renowned beauties, are disappointing, curiously charmless, as if he was secretly trying to please his royal patron, apt to welcome handsome young men more than she did any ravishing ladies. But at his best, in addition to his superb technique, Hilliard has the open-ended quality, beyond realism, for which I am beginning to search.

But now, taking a huge leap forward, what are we to make of William Hogarth, today recognized as a masterly and highly original painter? English, very English? Of course he was! Quite so; but we must remember what I am looking for. He cannot claim my definition of Englishness simply because of his technical achievements – his serpentine line, his mastery of composition, and the rest of it – nor even because of his superb sense of character. There has to be something else, taking us towards depth psychology, revealing his inner world. How and where is it to be found? Well, on the way we may note in passing that there is in this genuine moralist and satirist a fairly constant suggestion of the erotic. But we cannot stop there, even if it should prove the pressure and influence of the unconscious. Where I finally arrive is at an impression that has made me wonder for some time. He makes me feel that I am in a theatre – and here I don't exclude some of his conversation pieces and portraits – staring at the illuminated stage. I am not thinking now of his early interest in the Theatre, which incidentally seems to have had a greater influence on the England of the eighteenth century than at any other time before or since, though that interest may have come to move him on a deeper level. Nor am I suggesting that his painted fables and parables are marked by a mere theatricality. No, what he makes me feel is that in this life, to which there must be a deeper and more enduring reality, we are condemned to play our scenes of comedy and tragedy as if on a lighted stage, while our more essential selves stare, laugh or cry, seemingly helpless, in the darkened auditorium. (The fact that eighteenth-century playhouses were not lit in this more recent fashion is beside the point: my image stands.) And this to my mind is proof enough that Hogarth's most characteristic work came out of his Englishness.

There has lately been a rage for the horsy and eccentric North Countryman, George Stubbs, now equally attractive to sporting men and animal lovers and to aesthetes who admire his draughtsmanship and composition. I find more than a touch of Englishness in Stubbs, and readers who don't might ask themselves, for instance, in what world his lion-and-horse series is supposed to be taking place. It seems to me, though I cannot pretend to have made a close or even a fairly wide

The erotic element in William Hogarth's painting and the curiously theatrical character of his composition are both evident in this detail of one of his satirical series of paintings, *Marriage à la Mode*, scene ii, 1743.

study of Stubbs's work, that even in his hunting and general rural scenes, over and above the sharp observation and rhythmical composition, there is something that does not belong to naturalism, a strange element coming out of that lion-and-horse world and some recess of George Stubbs's odd but strong personality.

Though it may not be obvious at once, there is a lot of Englishness in Gainsborough, whereas I find little or none of it in the justly eminent Joshua Reynolds, the charming Romney or that dashing prodigy, Thomas Lawrence. Any expert, presenting Gainsborough, will produce what is almost a roll-call of artists who influenced him – Ruisdael, Van Dyck, Rubens, Watteau, Murillo and many another. But while the influences may be there, Gainsborough, though constantly making changes and experimenting (sharing with Turner a love of mixing his media), was a great original in his art and very much his own man outside his work. He was touchy and rather quarrelsome yet generous-minded, tender-hearted. He became the favourite painter of the Court and the aristocracy, but cared little for high society. He had a passion for music and delighted in the Theatre, yet ignored literature, detested writers and read as little as possible. His letters are lively reading, but I think they hide rather than reveal the essential Thomas Gainsborough, who is only to be discovered in the best of his art. When Sir Joshua Reynolds told the Artists' Club that Gainsborough was 'the first landscape-painter in Europe', Richard Wilson (a master of landscape who must be ignored here because he was a Welshman) retorted sharply that in his opinion Gainsborough was the greatest contemporary portrait-painter in Europe. This exchange of opinions, though hardly impersonal, can be taken as a tribute to Gainsborough's astonishing versatility. But I cannot help feeling that the essential Gainsborough, not at all times but when at his best, was trying to create something that cannot be divided into portraiture and landscape, a special and memorable Gainsborough world, neither entirely natural nor artificial, in which elegance can merge into innocence, human character relate to distant foliage and vague clouds.

Though Gainsborough did most of his painting in Bath and London, the countryman stays on in him, and even his most fashionable portraits seem to suggest we are all *still in the country*. But it is special country, not unreal but not entirely removed from Arcadia, and to this he brings the same tenderness he feels for most women and all children. He is not the usual romantic idealist; he was a robust character deeply concerned with the technique of his art; but almost all the time he was painting the outer world partly in the lights and shadows of his own inner world. He was, we might say, always trying to *take us somewhere*, not anywhere fantastic but to a special Gainsborough place, with its own magic. When he was dying and brought Reynolds, with whom he had quarrelled, to his bedside, he whispered, 'We are all going to heaven, and Van Dyck is of the party.' If he could no longer paint out of his Englishness, he could whisper it.

Now we arrive at the art form that England has made her own – watercolour. It began to attract so many painters, not so much at first because it is peculiarly suitable for the hazy English landscape, but simply because artists on tour, whether at home or abroad, found pen-and-wash or watercolours in general easier to carry and then apply rapidly than oils. It was in fact the watercolour that took painters out of the studio to work face to face with Nature. But a few of them arrived on the scene with their own individual vision of how it should be recorded. The brought not only paints, brushes, paper, but also commanding temperaments. They took the Alps or the ruins of Rome into their inner worlds. This is Englishness at work in them.

One of these men was Francis Towne, so early (born *c.* 1740) and yet so surprisingly modern, imposing design and a sense of mass, though often through rather thin pen-and-wash, together with a dreamlike feeling of utter stillness on his varied subjects. In his admirable *English Water-colours* Laurence Binyon devoted space he badly needed and even his frontispiece in colour, 'The Source of the Aveiron', to Towne. This was in 1933, and yet even a few years later I was able to buy two landscapes, one Italian, the other English, for a very modest price indeed and

'A Mountain Landscape Study', by John Varley

I still have them. By the way, I am not 'a collector' and have never pretended to be. I haven't enough money to be one kind of collector, and I've never had sufficient time and patience to be the other kind. But I can bear witness to the surprisingly late discovery of this pioneer of the watercolour, not simply as a topographical record but as a highly personal art form.

Thomas Rowlandson deserves a brief paragraph in passing. He was never as savagely effective a caricaturist and cartoonist as Gillray, and it is probable he would never have ventured into this noisy arena if he had not had to make good his gambling losses. He added nothing to the technique of watercolour, being content to use a reed pen and then light washes and tintings. While so many of his drawings show us a zest for a fat amplitude of life – as well as a trick of raising skirts to show us some woman's jolly legs – there was nothing coarse about him, strictly considered as an artist. Almost always there is a delicate poetry in his glimpses of the countryside or of woods melting into Arden or some frontier of Arcady. A smack of Englishness here, I would say.

I can discover it, too, in John Varley, though one of his romantic compositions I happen to possess is too dark for successful reproduction. But the man who brought watercolour into its own, turning its 'drawings' into 'paintings' was Girtin, who if he had lived longer – he died at twenty-seven – might have become a giant like his friend Turner. Once he was free of architectural drawing and the like, he insisted upon using big brushes on rougher paper and breaking the tradition of standard shadowing. And when he broke out at last – Englishness taking over – he really broke out, and it is not merely because I know the scene so well that I regard his 'View on the Wharfe, Farnley' as one of the supreme masterpieces of the great English School of watercolour.

John Sell Cotman, the greatest of the Norfolk men, began splendidly, going to London in his teens and working alongside Girtin for a time. His famous 'Greta Bridge' seems at first a triumph of a smooth and placid naturalism, but there is in it a subjective element that removes it from

Stonehenge, about 1835, by John Constable

the familiar portfolios of the contemporary topographical watercolours – it is the bridge in a more harmonious world than the one we know. Probably a manic-depressive type, Cotman soon ran out of luck or careful judgment – that is, in his life rather than his work. The last thing he wanted to be was a drawing master, and so, returning to East Anglia that is what he became. It was as if a race-horse volunteered for farm work. But on his well-earned holidays, often visiting the Normandy coast, he sometimes painted boldly to satisfy his Englishness. I have lived happily now for a good many years with one of these works – a 'Landscape in Blue'. Readers may judge for themselves what this wonderfully gifted drawing-master-on-holiday could do.

It would be as absurd to discover Englishness in Turner as it would be to discover salt water in the sea. If we include his watercolours, especially those of his later years, he seems to me the greatest artist, English or not English, that the nineteenth century can show us: a poet in paint of the very elements themselves, taking the watercolour as far as it can go, into its final home – as a memorable dream of light and air, Prospero's conclusion haunting him as he stared at his paper and took out his brushes.

John Constable might be best described, outside his art, as a nobly patient and unaffected man, but when in 1829 (he was born in 1776) he was elected to the Academy and told by its President, Lawrence, that he ought to consider himself fortunate, he lost his patience and was bitter for once: 'It has been delayed too long, and I cannot impart it.' A grieving widower, the father of a large family, already suffering from neglect of his work, Constable faced some unhappy last years before his

(left) William Blake at Hampstead, about 1825, by John Linnell

(right) Self-portrait, by Samuel Palmer

'Carrying Corn' (detail), 1854, by Ford Madox Brown

death in 1837. Yet in his work he must have been one of the happiest of our painters. He carried in his inner world, long after his boyhood and youth had gone, the freshness, sparkle and glow of the Suffolk scenes he had known so well. We are not cameras; we don't simply observe; what we have known and what we feel help to create the scene before our eyes. So it was with Constable, a great original who loved the English landscape and its skies and, breaking through the brown-shadow-and-monotonous-green convention, saw everything freshly with the delighted eye of love. In his highly finished big Academy jobs – though there are some splendid exceptions – he tended to retreat some way towards conventional standards. But both in his small oil sketches, done quickly on the spot, and the larger studies still not intended for customers, he could satisfy the true demands of mind and eye, put in what ought to go in, leave out what was best left out. So he created Impressionism – long before it was thought of – for his own and our love and

{147}

delight. What needed an aesthetic theory and a manifesto later in Paris came out of him through memory and feeling, instinct and intuition. I call this Englishness.

Now what about Blake? The answer is – a very reluctant answer too, because I love the man – that I can't allow him in here. As an artist he exists somewhere on the far side of Englishness, his face turned away from us, towards some interior region of mythology and symbolism. He is the exact opposite of those artists who must be ruled out, however masterly their technique, because their work does not suggest any traffic with the unconscious, any irrational and intuitive element. Instead of having too little, Blake has altogether *too much*. This may or may not give him the bold splendour of genius, but it certainly leaves him outside Englishness as I have defined it.

On the other hand, Blake's disciple, Samuel Palmer, cannot be ruled out. What he saw and painted in and around Shoreham, in excitement rising to ecstasy in his twenties, may be far removed from anything we can see – and let alone paint – even if we spent the next ten years hanging around the Kentish countryside. But that is our misfortune – and indeed it overtook the painter himself – but young Sam Palmer, however great his excitement, was keeping his eyes open and not shutting them to discover images rising from the unconscious. So we must grant him Englishness, of an unusual ecstatic sort, which few painters over a century later could begin to recapture.

It seems to me that the innumerable acres of Victorian painting, for all the skill displayed, will yield to us here a very meagre harvest. Anticipating objections, I make the following points. Only *English* artists can be considered: a limitation easily overlooked. Then a picture may illustrate imaginative literature without being itself pictorially imaginative. And indeed I would say that a desire to fasten on to the Bible, Shakespeare or Arthurian legends is almost always a bad sign, even though it may have been gratified just to attract customers. Finally, allegory, as distinct from symbolism, does not belong to Englishness; it suggests a rather calculating rational mind gingerly letting itself out on parole; it does not trust imagination.

For example, Holman Hunt, who lived to enjoy a tremendous reputation among the general public, was very much the allegorical painter. However, his early masterpiece, painted at twenty-four, 'The Hireling Shepherd', can be regarded as a complete defeat of allegory. Hunt was a stern moralist and deeply concerned about the Church. Its divisions were weakening it. 'The Hireling Shepherd' was designed to illustrate this melancholy situation. A close examination of the picture can be translated into a warning sermon, with the shepherd (the faulty Church) neglecting his flock (souls), and the sheep making for the corn; the pet

'The Hireling Shepherd', 1852, by William Holman Hunt

{148}

lamb and the apples, the death's-head moth the shepherd is displaying, even the little cask of booze at his belt, all having their ecclesiastical or moralistic meaning. But does the picture make us think about the state of the Church in 1850–1? Not at all. For my part I have always felt strongly its strangeness, its *heat*, its *sensuality*. It is as if some burning underside of Hunt's puritanism, some erotic dream on a hot afternoon, took over the painting, making it appeal from imagination to imagination.

There is nothing so ironical or so fascinating in the work of a better painter, Ford Madox Brown, but he has his magical moments – as for example the superb little landscape, 'Carrying Corn' (in the Tate Gallery), painted in 1854 and so owing nothing to French Impressionism.

Philip Wilson Steer was a large placid man, often falling asleep when theories of art were being discussed. Yet while still in his twenties his work was so violently denounced that he nearly abandoned his career as a painter. I find a pleasing Englishness in him, but not so much in his large Order of Merit performances as in his early painting at Walberswick and the translucent watercolours of his last years. Mention of this surprising late development of Steer's strengthens my decision not to include artists still alive as I write. (Or living composers in my next section.) I realize that with this reservation – and the further reservation that they must have been English – I am left with an odd mixed bag, and I apologize if readers discover some shocking omissions.

I have no doubt whatever about the triumphant Englishness in the later work of Paul Nash, who took his stand somewhere along the frontier between consciousness and the unconscious: his ill-health and comparatively early death must have robbed us of some masterpieces. James Pryde, though a likely candidate at a first glance, I must reject, for there is something consciously theatrical in his determined romanticism. But there are traces of Englishness in both Henry Lamb, who could translate his almost impudently humorous temperament into paint, and Edward Wadsworth, whose meticulous bits of machinery often seem to be remaining in some strange world, probably existing long after our technological age has withered away.

Nevinson was a very successful war artist – his severely Cubist manner giving force to his subjects – and his work has been welcomed by many famous galleries. I cannot pretend to know it all, but what I have seen appears to me to miss the mark I am looking for. Is it there, writ large, in Stanley Spencer? Critics we must respect have hailed him, more or less, as the most strikingly original, creatively imaginative, deeply religious English painter of this age. And who am I to say they are overestimating him, just because the sight of the resurrections, even when

'Oxenbridge Pond', 1928, by Paul Nash

{151}

they are happening at Cookham, leaves me cold? But is this display of
opening graves and crosses necessarily very imaginative? Was Spencer
really so deeply religious that he was compelled to paint as he did, often
in a manner so curiously repellent? In his life as well as his art, did he not
cultivate strangeness rather than allow his unconscious to move him
towards it, which, after all, is what happens with Englishness?

Many English painters today, of course, are well beyond the boundaries of representation. To indicate some pleasing exceptions would be
to break my own rule. Personally I regret that not enough seems to be
done in that fascinating area that lies between representation and
abstraction – what might be called late de Staël territory. It offers great
opportunities to Englishness. Possibly I am now too old and stupid to
enjoy, so to speak, private emotions expressed to me in what seems an
entirely private language. I need bridges between me and the artists
that appear to have been blown up long ago. Whether there is Englishness in all this – and, if so, how long it declares and shapes itself – I am
simply not competent to decide. Finally, when we come to the really
wild performers, while I have long tried to enjoy the arts, I cannot begin
now to appreciate the anti-arts by anti-artists – enough is enough!

Here is a personal note to end this section. Knowing what I was up to,
a friend sent me Pevsner's book, *The Englishness of English Art*. However,
I deliberately set it aside, unread, until I had written this section,
feeling I had to blunder along in my own way, which I have done, out

of reach of any perceptive expert. Now I find that although there may be a little overlapping here and there, the fact remains that Pevsner and Priestley are not writing about the same kind of Englishness. Roughly speaking, while he looks at it from outside, I look at it from inside – which, being English, and old at that – I am compelled to do.

2.

The subject of this section is Englishness (my sort) in Music, and it promises all kinds of trouble. For example, I know about writing and I have some amateurish experience with painting, but though I have listened to serious music for about sixty-five years and have known many distinguished musicians I have never attempted musical composition and have no idea what happens in a composer's mind. I realize that this is a highly technical and very complicated art. When it is strongest I assume that it comes from a combination of a technique that is almost mathematical with emotions of every colour and force, reaching from despair to ecstatic joy, and with all manner of ideas. I feel I can risk the statement that quite pleasing music, which most of us have enjoyed from time to time, can be written out of technical mastery and a calculation of effect, being in fact entirely a product of the conscious mind. But I am sure that great music cannot be created in this fashion. Irrational elements, emerging from the unconscious, must be fused into such music.

Now this easy relationship between the conscious mind and the unconscious, and this refusal to be bounded by rationality, are characteristic of Englishness. It is reasonable to suppose then that a well-trained and ambitious English composer, who has accepted his Englishness, should be well on his way towards creating great music. But history denies this. The nation is deservedly famous for its literature and, with those who understand the medium, its watercolours, but not for its great composers. In any world league of these England occupies a very modest place. Now why is this?

Clearly I have run into the trouble I anticipated. Most nineteenth-century Germans would have rushed me out of it by telling me that the English are not a musical people, that England is the land without music. But this is simply not true. In fact the later sixteenth century and the early seventeenth saw Germans visiting England to listen to music. Even back in the fifteenth century Dunstable enjoyed a European reputation for his church music, and nearly two centuries later Dowland's songs and airs for the lute were widely printed and performed abroad. We know how Elizabethan and Jacobean gentry, in their country houses, had a passion rather than a mere taste for singing madrigals, quite

The three illustrations that follow are examples of the art form that England has made her own – watercolour

(opposite) 'Landscape in Blue', by John Sell Cotman

(overleaf) 'Cascade at Rydal Mount', by Francis Towne

{154}

difficult to perform; and though these were originally imported from Italy an English 'sea-change' went to work on them, inspired by men like Morley. And before we leave the seventeenth century, we should consider not merely the ravishing quality of Purcell's best work but the sheer amount of music, of all kinds, and most of it performed, that he produced during his short life – c. 1659 to 1695. Such a supply suggests an eager demand, together with an ample number of singers and instrumentalists, at least at Court and in London. Where Italy and Germany had the advantage, which they retained for a long time, was that instead of having one great overshadowing Court and capital they had dozens, with opera-houses and orchestras flourishing all over the place.

Here I propose a brief halt. When Purcell – the most glorious member of a whole family of musicians – frankly admitted his debt to Italian masters, he went on to express his desire 'to bring the seriousness and gravity of that sort of Musick into vogue and reputation among our countrymen'. There was more than a suggestion at this time and a little later, both at home and abroad, that music passing through the English mind tended towards 'gravity', a certain melancholy. Has this haunted us ever since? Do we unwittingly deepen and darken ancient tunes that once were airy and sprightly? I cannot help thinking here about 'Greensleeves', once that 'merry song' probably heard in so many taverns, now sounding like some love-sick lament, a tune deep-sunk in melancholy, making us ready to weep over some fading spectral glimpse of a might-have-been Merry England. But even in this, wasn't Shakespeare anticipating us, for in so many of his songs, needing no music to create the mood, we find a half-smiling melancholy, more than a hint of that nostalgia which would sigh its way into English music three centuries later.

Among my memories of life in the West Riding before the First World War a firm place is occupied by Handel's *Messiah*. It ought to be performed at or just before Christmas; but so keen was the rivalry between local chapels, all hoping to get their *Messiah* in first, that it came earlier and earlier, long before Christmas. I mention this to illustrate how complete and long-lasting was the hold that Handel and his magnificent oratorio, dating back to 1742, had on the English people, especially in the North, the home of choral singing. (I remember the year when the Bradford Old Choral Society went abroad for once, to compete with mere foreigners, and swept the board of awards.) But then Handel, a composer who knew exactly what he was doing, must have been aware of the value, to performers and audiences alike, of an existing tradition of English choral singing. England may have been very backward indeed in the creation of symphonies and concertos, but a nation so eagerly vocal can hardly be described as being pathetically unmusical.

'Vignette, with Mackerel in the Foreground', 1820–30, by Joseph Mallord William Turner

And if London, after Handel, produced no great music, it could heartily welcome such music, and if necessary, as the record shows, was ready to commission work from famous composers when their own Central Europe was leaving them stranded. Certainly London was comparatively rich, and unravaged by war, but among its citizens there must have been persons anything but indifferent to great music.

The eighteenth-century English delighted in the Theatre and entertainment in general. It is this rather than any passion for music that explains the popularity of ballad opera, which usually offered as much

Manuscript in the composer's own hand of part of 'Mr Cowley's Complaint', by Henry Purcell

Frederick Ranalow and Sylvia Nelis singing 'Without disguise, heaving sighs' in the 1920 revival of *The Beggar's Opera*, at the Lyric Theatre, Hammersmith

spoken dialogue as it did songs and dances. The earlier ballad operas had no original scores, only popular tunes arranged and adapted to fulfil their needs; it was those that came later which had scores specially composed for them. The supreme triumph in this form of mixed entertainment belongs, of course, to *The Beggar's Opera*, first produced in 1728, with John Gay supplying the words, the satire and wit, and Pepusch (a German, oddly enough) collecting and adapting the tunes – though there were many rearrangements of the score for revivals later. It appears to have been revived five times in the eighteenth century, three in the nineteenth, and then had its most successful revival of them all in 1920 at the Lyric Theatre, Hammersmith, where it ran for 1,463 performances. Later revivals came from producers who considered Nigel Playfair's Hammersmith version too stylized and pretty-pretty, both visually and musically. For my part I take the unfashionable view that Playfair and his colleagues, Lovat Fraser and Austin, were right and their contemptuous detractors were wrong. It seems to me that the satire and fundamental irony that Gay brought to the piece (after taking a hint from Swift) are more sharply pointed when everything in it looks and sounds so charming. It is a fault common among producers now to use a severe realism with operas and old plays when more is lost than gained by it.

{161}

England was still busy with oratorios and ballad operas of little merit when music's Romantic Movement turned fiery suns and strange moons into sound. To this feast of new great music English composers did not contribute even the smallest savoury. Creative Englishness went into poetry, prose and astonishing watercolours. But why not into music? Because – as the legend had it – this nation was unmusical? Or because these islanders were too proud, too stiff, too reserved and emotionally starved, to be capable of composing music really worth hearing? (It was never argued, I think, that they were incapable of singing or playing such music – or indeed of enjoying it.) We can dismiss the 'unmusical' legend because it simply does not fit the facts. The second charge – of being too proud, too stiff and so forth – was absurd if applied to the nation as a whole; but an important foreign musician, visiting London, might easily come to this wrong conclusion just because he would be meeting its high society, an Establishment England that had trained itself out of Englishness. However, it is odd that a nation that was probably far more aural-minded than visual-minded should produce a giant like Turner and yet out of all its music-making could offer the world only dwarf composers. We could of course brutally cut short any further discussion by simply declaring that there happened to be musical geniuses around in Central Europe and Italy and, later, in Russia, and none in England. But I cannot resist poking about a little longer, if only to air my own prejudices.

For example, I suggest that the musical climate of Victorian England was unfavourable to bold and original composition. It had plenty of ideas, as we know, but its musicians were not living among those ideas: they were usually in church, playing the organ or training the choir: quiet gentlemanly fellows, most of them. They were not sitting up late among groups fanatically devoted to music and all excited. Too often they existed in a kind of permanent English Sunday. So did many of the critics, who favoured a rather sweet or flavourless anthem-style solemnity. When at last something like genius flashed out, they never recognized it – and kept on failing to recognize it even into our century.

Read the article on English music in the eleventh edition of the *Encyclopaedia Britannica*. Arthur Sullivan is the test case here. In that article his work with Gilbert is never mentioned at all, yet we know now it was by far the most important work he ever did. When he felt he was taking a holiday from serious responsible music – anthems, cantatas, overtures and the rest – Sullivan jumped from plodding talent into mastery, his impudent comic-opera gaiety touched with genius. Only occasionally, when he wants to stop the nonsense and be solemn, do we seem to be back in the organ loft. Elsewhere he sparkles away, astonishingly versatile, and having a good deal of private fun with what he learned

Frederick Delius, 1929, by
Ernest Procter

ERNEST PROCTER '29

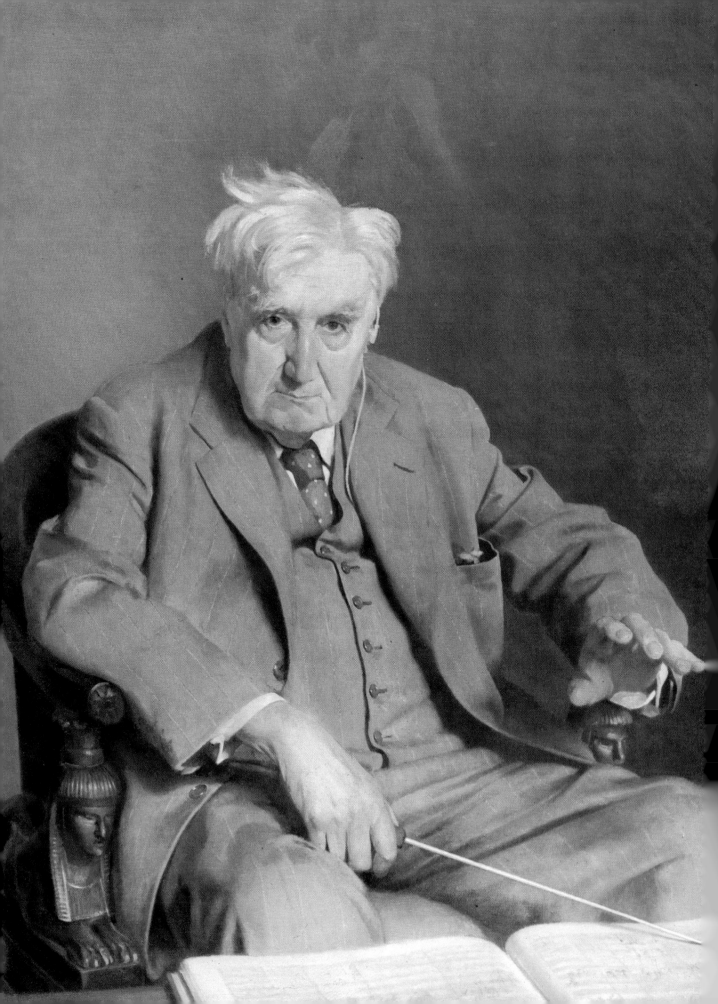

at the Leipzig Conservatorium. Not only has he worn better than his librettist, Gilbert, but, to my ear, he outlasts Johann Strauss (the *Fledermaus* one) and even his master on the lighter side, Offenbach. He added champagne to the tea and muddy port of Victorian music, and only the public, never the critics and musicologists, recognized his gift. And as soon as he let rip and had fun there was Englishness in Sullivan.

There was even more – and of a larger and weightier sort – in Elgar. Unlike younger English composers, of whom Butterworth was a tragic example (he was killed in the First World War), Elgar made no use of folk music, yet he is all Englishness – and in certain passages like the end of the adagio in the First Symphony or the moments of bitter regret in the Cello Concerto, he seems to some of us to suggest a heartbreaking Englishness. He began as an outsider, a self-made provincial musician a long way from the musical Establishment; but after some success and a marriage (to a social superior) he achieved a *persona*, more or less that of a squire off to the races, acting as a carapace to the sensitive quivering artist. *But* – and here is the point – there is no *persona* in his music. He put all of himself into it. If he wanted to be cheerfully loud and vulgar, then he had a go. This made him vulnerable to the stupidest kind of criticism, the hostile-negative kind that considers artists on their lowest instead of their highest level.

Again, we have often been told that Elgar is 'typically Edwardian'. But this is really a shallow comment on his *persona* and is ignoring his serious music, which goes against the spirit of his age and is filled with sudden anger – the brass suddenly raging against the strings and wood-wind – and dubieties and bewilderment and regrets and a nostalgia not for youth and the Malvern hills but for some world we have all lost. Here his Englishness, so open to the unconscious, so defiant of rationality, calls to our Englishness, which may explain why conductors like Boult and Barbirolli can interpret him while eminent foreign conductors, when at last they do decide to include some Elgar, seem to be baffled by his characteristic rhythms and cadences and often miss the whole shape and flow of him. He is of course intensely individual, so he bores the musicologists, who always want a composer to lead them to another composer, to hurry them on, as if the arts were all on their way to some unknown destination. This may be good for their trade, but for the rest of us it isn't better to travel than to arrive – perhaps at Elgar.

I am taking these composers in the order of their birth-dates, so Frederick Delius comes next. An Englishman? Well, perhaps I am bending the rules a little, his parents being German exiles, but after all he was born and brought up in Bradford, so any fellow Bradfordian, like me, considers him English. From every point of view he is an oddity. In the first part of his life, bobbing about from Bradford to Florida to

Ralph Vaughan Williams, 1958–61, by Sir Gerald Kelly

Leipzig to Paris, he seems to have been a hail-fellow-well-met extrovert; and then in the second part, paralysed, then blind, at Grez-sur-Loing, he achieved an aristocratic, laconic and ultra-fastidious *persona*. Again, after comparatively little formal musical education, he was able to use unusually large orchestras to create his own particular sound. Again, while at a first hearing he seems the vaguest and most shapeless of all well-known composers, he can soon establish himself after a few bars, and, as Cardus pointed out years ago, he gains in strength after repeated hearings. Finally, most of his work does not suggest to me a nature-poet in music, nor anybody close to the natural scene (the fair has long-vanished from *Brigg Fair*). What it does suggest – at least to my mind – is the curious homesickness of a man who was never at home anywhere. As I wrote a few years ago: 'Just as so many artists, moving towards an early death, have worked prodigiously in feverish haste, as if their unconscious knew they had so little time, so possibly Delius in every creative mood felt a faint foreshadowing of those years of paralysis and blindness that were waiting for him.' His general Englishness has often been noted; but he had my kind as well.

Had Ralph Vaughan Williams? Not, I feel, to the same degree as Elgar and Delius. His general and national Englishness is obvious, of course, if only because he was so strongly influenced by folk song, and I gather (from people who know more about musical structure than I do) by Elizabethan polyphony. He was himself a splendidly large and

(left) Edward Elgar
(right) Arthur Sullivan

admirable person, and he wrote, while showing great versatility, much splendidly large and admirable music; not afraid, as many of his English contemporaries were, of tackling symphony after symphony, even if some of them were not very symphonic symphonies. The fact that André Previn, a fine conductor with a background entirely different from that of Vaughan Williams, should have expressed his personal enthusiasm for this work should make the rest of us, not responsible for programmes and recordings by great orchestras, hesitate before pronouncing our own judgments. It is more than likely that I have not listened long enough to Vaughan Williams, but, in spite of his 'mystical' passages, up to now he has never – or at most only very rarely – made me feel that what emerged from his unconscious is capturing my imagination, as if I were receiving a special if secret Vaughan Williams verdict on this life: on this level he is not saying anything. But this could be my fault, not his.

Arnold Bax cannot be ignored, but I will admit at once that although I was not unacquainted with him personally, somehow I never had the chance of hearing a large majority of his works, which include no fewer than seven symphonies. He was an odd fish. Born, brought up, musically educated, in London, a tremendously gifted technician (he could give an account on the piano of a full score *at sight*), Bax was a romantic who never looked like one, a wilful introvert who insisted upon going his own way, which might lead him to some remote Irish village or an inn in rural Sussex. Both in works for full orchestra and in his chamber music, even in my limited knowledge of them, he can be over-complicated or indecisive but also capable of passages startlingly beautiful. There was Englishness in him, even if it suggested a deliberate Celtic Englishness.

Thank Heaven I have debarred myself from examining English composers still alive and hard at work! There are a great many of them, with an ever-widening range, from the harshly cerebral – not, to my mind, good examples of Englishness – to latter-day experimental romantics. Indeed, this style today is full of noises, and not without *sounds and sweet airs, that give delight, and hurt not.*

3

It seems to me quite impossible to offer here, in terms of my 'Englishness', any examination of English Literature in general. To be worth doing at all, any such examination would take up far more space than I have at my disposal – and indeed would wreck the whole construction of this book. Moreover, it would be covering ground that has been covered over and over again. A large number of the critics and literary historians concerned have in fact done my work for me, even though nothing like my Englishness may ever have been mentioned. But the idea of it lurks behind all those discussions of the classical and the romantic, of the influence of the unconscious, of deeply subjective writing as against naturalistic objective writing, of private or public literary creation; and so forth, on and on. Finally, we have to remember that Englishness in writing can take innumerable and widely different forms, just because it leaves itself open to the unconscious. Rational thought and formal accepted images are not without variety, but they shrivel at once if we compare them with the wild and astounding diversity of dreams. And though, for example, the English Romantic poets have certain things in common, arising from their Englishness, it is obvious that as artists and as individuals they are all dissimilar, all great originals. Sheer lack of space would prevent my examining Wordsworth, Coleridge, Shelley and Keats in turn; if I must choose one of them – as I feel I must – let us take Wordsworth as one great example of Englishness in poetry.

When we are not reading or remembering Wordsworth at his best, as the poet of magical moments, we are too apt to see him, as so many of his London acquaintances did, in terms of his middle or old age – prosy, complacently portentous, self-centred, humourless, almost one of those large Lake District sheep. We should force ourselves to recollect his childhood, when he was the most wilful and difficult member of his family, at once obstinate and fiery-tempered, and then his young man-hood, when he was still determined to go his own way, to think his own thoughts, to cherish his own feelings at whatever level they might arrive. In the 1790s, before he met Coleridge (with each young poet acting as catalyst to the other), he had been torn between conflicting loyalties and emotions. He had rapturously welcomed the French Revolution but had begun to find its excesses and violence detestable. And then there was a further conflict, even more deep-seated, for the Revolution adopted the narrowest creed of the eighteenth-century Enlightenment and solemnly ushered in an age of reason, which was so much arid and bigoted rationalism. All this was entirely alien to Wordsworth's temperament and habit of mind, and it explains the savage bitterness of his poems condemning 'Philosophy' and 'Science'. The final result of all this turmoil was a hardening of his sense of purpose and a heightening and strengthening of the Englishness in him. He would now avoid easy rational conclusions, would encourage his old habit (from boyhood) of long brooding in solitude, would wait to hear those 'promptings' that suggest to us that the unconscious has been broached by consciousness.

It will be remembered that when he and Coleridge decided on a joint publication it was agreed that Coleridge should be responsible for the supernatural department, Wordsworth accepting 'the things of every day' but giving them 'the charm of novelty'. Nothing was said yet about poetic diction. It was in his preface to the second edition of *Lyrical*

William Wordsworth, 1818, by Benjamin Robert Haydon

Ballads that Wordsworth argued that the poet should use the language of real life. This is a position difficult to defend. (Real life has many languages: Billingsgate has one, Parliament another, and so forth.) It would have been better if Wordsworth had simply dismissed the faded rubber-stamp diction of late eighteenth-century versifiers. It would have been better still if he had said nothing, leaving his poetry to carry the argument by example. As it was, his theory was not accepted by the periodical reviewers (they cared nothing about poetry anyhow) and his examples of it in practice chiefly delighted the parodists, who did not leave him alone for many years. The truth is there are few signs of Wordsworth the great poet in most of these over-simple and rather silly rustic verses, composed to illustrate a theory. All too often the poet is too stiffly distant from the folk he is writing about. He was no Burns who had gone boozing and wenching with his fellow ploughmen. Only now and then – as with his vague Lucy – does he suddenly catch fire and offer us poetry:

> The stars of midnight shall be dear
> To her; and she shall lean her ear
>   In many a secret place
> Where rivulets dance their wayward round,
> And beauty born of murmuring sound
>   Shall pass into her face.

And all is magical.

The secret of Wordsworth's greatness has nothing to do with his feeling (not especially strong) for ordinary working folk. And in my personal opinion it has little to do with his moralizing tone, his insistence upon dutifulness, plain living and high thinking, even his famous special relationship with Nature. (Which clearly did not apply to Nature as she reveals herself, let us say, in India or round the Amazon, ready to offer us not only rabbits and sheep but also sharks and tigers.) Moreover, while he may take us close to the actual scene of this life, he takes us no closer than some other poets had done or were to do. Wordsworth's secret, when we consider him as a great poet, is that he not only takes us into the scene but at his best he also takes us clean through it, into some magical realm. His poetry as a whole might be compared to a long day's walk in greyish weather. It is dull and we are beginning to feel we have had enough of it – but then as we turn a corner where is an unexpected and superb flash of beauty: the walk and the day are transformed; we are never going to forget them. At these inspired moments, Wordsworth is able to take a simple and unadorned phrase, giving it extraordinary light and depth, leaving us bewitched by it. There can be no doubt that as he went on his solitary walks, day after day, Wordsworth was in search of such moments, when the familiar mountains and the few bare trees and the grass would seem to be lit up from within, and simple words in some new magical arrangement would rise into consciousness.

This is how Englishness worked for one of our great original poets. (Other poets, other methods.) Out of long brooding over the natural scene there could come – though only at certain times: in later life hardly at all – a wide acceptance of unconscious contents by consciousness, together with a temporary loss of the ego – incidentally, very strong in Wordsworth. Where other poets might find their consciousness invaded by fantastic beings, mythological or archetypal images, or by weird landscapes from the inner world, Wordsworth's enlarged mind is almost always deeply concerned with humanity itself, arriving at –

> That blessed mood,
> In which the burthen of the mystery,
> In which the heavy and the weary weight
> Of all this unintelligible world,
> Is lightened. . . .

If Wordsworth's 'healing power' has been so rightly praised, it is because at his best he can restore to us those times when, the conscious mind having been quietened and slowed down, we relate ourselves to the natural scene through our unconscious, seem to lose the ego and our separateness, return to the enchanted unity that we knew in childhood. Of such heart-easing times, Wordsworth at his height is the prophet and the bard. Moreover, it is the genuine *participation mystique* he discovers and celebrates. He is not merely indulging in the sentimental nostalgia for childhood common among so many English writers. He is at war with all narrowly rational, reductionist life-shrinking ideas and attitudes of mind; he is trudging his thirty miles a day to catch a beatific glimpse of Nature as the symbol of God, of another life for us when we are ready to receive it; and it is not only in one of his greatest poems that he is searching for *Intimations of Immortality*. But though his essential poetry, as distinct from his routine verse-making, can be reduced to quite a small volume, it would contain more than these moments of communion charged with the necromantic power of the unconscious, for on a level nearer home he can be apparently quite simple in language and structure and yet strangely haunting, as if what is said so easily comes from some depth of ancient incantation so that it remains with us all our lives:

> The silence that is in the starry sky,
> The sleep that is among the lonely hills.

So here we have one poet's Englishness. And we have had – and indeed still have – many, many poets.

ENGLISHNESS IN HUMOUR AND HOBBIES

❀

MANY foreigners – and any count must include a large number of Americans – seriously believe that the English have little or no humour. This may seem wildly idiotic until we remember that some English, who have been carefully educated and socially trained to avoid Englishness, such as leading politicians, diplomats and senior officials, are precisely those best known to foreigners. Am I suggesting then that Englishness, as I conceive it, develops and then sustains a keen sense of the ridiculous? I am – and most emphatically. It is an essential part of the package, as I hope to show. But how could this legend of the humourless English grow when the nation's literature is so rich in humour? The answer is that it could not if people did not insist upon removing writers from the soil that nourished them. It is the right soil that produces the fine flower, the juiciest fruit. Shakespeare was a popular Elizabethan dramatist, among other things, and not, as some Germans used to think, really more German than English. There would have been no Dickens, as we know him, if there had not been a huge crowd of ordinary Victorian English eager to laugh and weep with him. (To understand how an intellectual Englishman, entirely without Englishness, could miss the mark, read Leslie Stephen's account of Dickens in the *Dictionary of National Biography* – a disaster.) Of course, it is quite possible that many thoughtful people abroad are well acquainted with English humour but do not find it very laughable, merely a rather mysterious alien drollery. That I can understand, for it is very much a national humour, engendered, I believe, by Englishness. And this surely is one good reason why I must give an account of it here.

The humour belonging to Englishness is not childish – far from it – but the peculiar quality and form of this humour have some roots in childhood. If as children we had some imagination and were not fixed in resentment, spite and hate, as some unfortunate children are if they

For sheer energy, inventiveness and fecundity Charles Dickens is the master in English humour. An unfamiliar portrait, painted in 1855 by Ary Scheffer

Henry IV

Sir John
Falstaff

Ralph Richardson

grow up in a bad atmosphere, we begin to be humorists at an early age. This is probably true of children belonging to many different countries, but there they have no Englishness to develop and encourage a particular attitude of mind. On the other hand, there are plenty of English youngsters who are drilled into humourlessness, and many of them are the kind of people who thank God they have a sense of humour when in fact they have none. But, if conditions are favourable, we start to create comic characters in our childhood. We find our raw material in rather odd adult friends of the family, always turning up, or in those ancient relatives, great-aunts and the like, who regularly assemble at Christmas. We must not hate them; we must have a certain wondering affection for them; we must rejoice in the way in which they are so tremendously themselves and yet suggest actors consistently playing funny parts; and then, either in our private thoughts or in family gossip, we expand or contract these droll figures at will, in a rough-and-ready juvenile fashion. We have then put a foot on the road that leads to the masters of English humour in our literature. In them the links with childhood remain, as they do indeed with Englishness in general. Severely adult persons, who for one reason or other have completely cut themselves off from their childhood, who cannot remember what it was to be a child, may laugh at jokes, often immoderately, but they have lost the leaven of humour and all too often are solemnly successful or embittered power-mongers.

There are good reasons why Englishness creates a climate in which true humour can flower. It is, so to speak, open-ended, avoiding closed rational systems that encourage men to believe they know everything about everything. (This makes for pride, at once the enemy and victim of humour.) Being open-ended, it has at times to move dubiously – and indeed humbly – in a mystery. Having a much larger outlook, even if it may be hazy, it is quicker than other types of mind to perceive incongruity, fanatical claims to certainty that are monstrously out of proportion, and so are ridiculous. (But am I not more or less doing the same thing at this moment? Yes, I am, but I am also aware of it, and so I can grin at myself.) It is true that severely intellectual and arrogant dogmatists can turn on their opponents, and, using sharp wit and irony, can make them look ridiculous. It is an advantage to a satirist if he is based on a rigid set of values and opinions. But, strictly speaking, a satirist is not a humorist: they are different kinds of men. The satirist is using ridicule as a weapon, as a means to an end. The humorist is enjoying a state of mind, and hopes we will enjoy it, too. Falstaff is often witty and satirical, his victims being the enemies of humour, but fundamentally he is not only a humorist but a supreme commander in the humorous way of life, possibly the only great man in literature who wants us to enjoy

Ralph Richardson as 'Falstaff' in Shakespeare's *Henry IV*, with the Old Vic Company at the New Theatre, London, in 1945. Costume design by Roger Furse

{175}

him and ourselves. (Actors who go waddling around with a load of padding, with a lot of hearty business, gulping cold tea out of pewter tankards, miss this commanding great-man aspect of Falstaff – the only exception I remember being Ralph Richardson, whose every look suggested a generalissimo of drollery.)

That larger if hazy outlook of Englishness brings its humorists tolerance and a smiling acceptance of all manner of people. However absurd they may seem, they are human beings, who live, feel the sun's warmth, then die, sharing the mystery with us. Outside his tragic or sardonic moods, Shakespeare is the supreme master of this tolerant acceptance, often touched with affection. So with a speech or two he can light up a face and a figure – Feeble, the woman's tailor, let us say – that we remember for ever, comic and yet revealing our naked and bewildered common humanity. Justice Shallow and his cousins Slender and Silence are compact of silliness, old silliness or young silliness; yet they all have their individual differences and are alive. (And actors should accept them as they find them, and not invent unnecessary comic business, as if they could improve on Shakespeare.) Dogberry is an ignorant pompous ass, a type we would hastily avoid in real life, but we have just enough of him to give him a droll and lasting reality. Clearly we could multiply examples, but we might note in passing that, with the exception of the great commander, Falstaff, and the lesser figure, Sir Toby Belch, Shakespeare's genuinely comic characters are all very serious persons with no intention whatever of being funny. (This is the secret of farce and all broad comedy, and is too often missed.) When they are not ironic commentators, his professional clowns, like Touchstone, are tedious or irritating. But then I think Shakespeare did not *enjoy* them as he did his solemn asses and pontificating dolts. The true humorist has to enjoy people. Ben Jonson could construct massively effective comedies – better to see performed than to read – but they are not warm and alight with humour because he tended to despise most people, clamped his characters into their parts, never allowed them – as Shakespeare did – their own life.

Thomas Love Peacock, a highly original writer too often ignored or misunderstood, shows us the difference between satire and humour. He is frequently described as a satirist, chiefly because he assembles companies of wild idealists, romantic posturers and pseudo-philosophical cranks, sets them talking, and laughs at them. But Peacock is really a humorist, not a satirist, even though he handles a few types, notably economists, quite roughly. He enjoys his idealogues and crackpots and even has some affection for them. (After all, he was a close friend of Shelley.) We might say that the convivial atmosphere in which they exist, for ever passing the bottle, represents his enjoyment and affection.

When Shelley wrote of Peacock: 'His fine wit / Makes such a wound, the knife is lost in it' his reference to the lost knife marks the transition from Peacock the satirist to the more fundamental Peacock, the humorist. Whenever his satire is closely examined, we find it turning into humour.

The fact that the loaded dinner table is nearly always there, with everybody, even the gloomiest pessimists, tucking in and passing the bottle, is an essential part of the humour. In this atmosphere his characters have to declare themselves, so his caricature of Byron, Mr Cypress, has to remark, 'Sir, I have quarrelled with my wife, and a man who has quarrelled with his wife is absolved from all duty to his country', and then has to paraphrase his affected lamentations from *Childe Harold* into sharp Peacockian prose, delivered over a bottle, making them ridiculous. This, like a hundred other passages, is satire melting into pure humour. The part played by his young women, though always small, is important, if only because they are sensible and good-humoured, unlike the daft men, who are, however, all happily boozing. I have another reason for singling out Peacock. Some later writers have tried to imitate him but have all missed the mark, simply because they have all been satirists – and rather sour satirists at that – and not humorists, ready to enjoy and indulge their characters. So, for example, the early novels of Aldous Huxley are extremely clever, but show about as much affection for their people as the encyclopedia that Huxley carried on his travels.

The humour of Englishness, then, arises from a certain outlook, a certain attitude of mind, which in turn encourages tolerance, indulgence, expansiveness and some degree of affection. I would not greatly modify what I wrote forty-five years ago in my book, *English Humour*, long out of print:

In order to be a humorist, you must have a needle eye for the incongruities, the pretensions, the inconsistencies, all the idiocies and antics of this life, but you must also have – strange and contradictory as it may seem – an unusual quickness and warmth of feeling, an instant affection for all that is lovable. . . .

I would agree with my younger self in keeping out Swift, whose flashes of humour are only the glinting of his two-handed sword. But the point I wished to make here is that the humour of Englishness, within my definition, still allows considerable variety. It is like sherry, which can range between the extremely dry and a heavy dessert wine, but is still sherry. When we consider our most famous comic characters, another point to remember is that they have been expanded outside our time. They exist in something like the 'Great Dream Time' of the Australian Aborigines, of which we seem to have glimpses in our childhood. It is idle to complain, as some critics have done, that these tremendous drolls

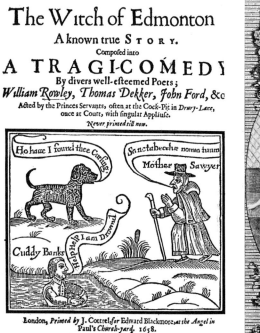

never change, as we ourselves are compelled to do: they have been taken beyond change and mutability, into some mythological realm. (Perhaps they share some of it with fiction's most popular private detectives.) But in the most richly creative humour there is a kind of poetry. It is no accident that the literature of the English has been equally enriched by lyrics and comics.

Shakespeare's sunniest moods turn his contemporaries into rushlights; but even so there is true humour to be found, for example, in Dekker and Middleton and the earlier plays of Beaumont and Fletcher. The Restoration comedies are mostly wit, impudence and rough stuff, but real humour arrived when Farquhar took comedy out of London into the provinces and fresh air. But – alas! – like Goldsmith and Sheridan later, he was an Irishman, and if I mention him it is only to add, for my own satisfaction, that in *The Beaux' Stratagem* he was as good as they were, and had he lived longer – he never reached thirty – he might have been a great deal better. There are some touches of genuine humour in Foote's farces, especially in his *Mayor of Garratt*, with its solemn militia officers in a phantom campaign somewhere between Hounslow and Brentford. But it is two great novelists who restore rich humour to the eighteenth century – Fielding and Sterne.

Fielding was a master of grave irony, in a manner owing much to Cervantes. This is best seen in the construction of his novels, especially in *Tom Jones*, which nobody should judge by the popular film bearing that name. Like many another eighteenth-century novelist, he was fond of rough-house scenes and tavern scuffles, which he would describe at

(left) *The Witch of Edmonton*, by divers well-esteemed poets: William Rowley, Thomas Dekker, John Ford, etc. 1658

(right) 'Parson Adams protecting Betty the Chambermaid from the Fury of Mrs Tow-woufe', detail of an illustration to the 1793 Cooke edition of *The Adventures of Joseph Andrews and his friend Mr Abraham Adams*, by Henry Fielding

{178}

length and tiresomely in a solemn mock-epic style. There is some excellent humour in *Tom Jones*, but it was in the earlier *Joseph Andrews* that he created his humorous masterpiece – in the character of Parson Adams. Fielding has an enormous affection for his little country parson – so brave and foolish, so naïve and innocently self-deceiving, so good at heart – and Fielding's ironic humour only plays around him like summer lightning. While Fielding was a moralist himself, he realized that a great deal of formal eighteenth-century morality was a lot of humbug, and that even the men who preached it were constantly deceiving themselves. So, for example, after Parson Adams has eagerly agreed with a gentleman who denounced vanity as the worst of passions, we read:

> Adams now began to fumble in his pockets, and soon cried out, 'Oh la! I have it not about me!' Upon this the gentleman asking him what he was searching for, he said he searched after a sermon, which he thought his masterpiece, against vanity. 'Fie upon it, fie upon it,' cries he, 'why do I ever leave that sermon out of my pocket? I wish it was within five miles; I would willingly fetch it to read it to you.' The gentleman answered there was no need, for he was cured of the passion. 'And for that very reason,' quoth Adams, 'I would read it, for I am confident you would admire it; indeed, I have never been a greater enemy to any passion than that silly one of vanity. . . .'

Readers who are enjoying that little scene for the first time – and it is one of many involving Parson Adams – should try Henry Fielding, refusing to be daunted by his ponderous narrative style. He can blend ironic invention and comment with humour as few other novelists have contrived to do.

Laurence Sterne's mother was of Irish origin and he was born in County Tipperary, but only because his father, an English army officer, happened to be stationed there. He was educated in England and spent the rest of his life here, first as an odd kind of Yorkshire vicar and later as a literary celebrity, thanks to his *Tristram Shandy*. In spite of the silly tricks he and his printer played in it, and some determined whimsicalities that do not quite come off, it is a work of humorous genius. As an entirely original humorous vision of this life I doubt if any writer in any literature has beaten it at its own whimsical game. What I said earlier about the humorist combining the needle eye and the instant affection fits Sterne perfectly. (Later novelists owe him a great debt because he showed them how to make the fullest use of minute details of talk and behaviour.) While much of his humour depends on his close observation of every scene between members of the Shandy household, together with his droll asides, it has as its basis something that has been worrying writers today and is even the subject of whole series of solemn lectures, namely the difficulty of communication. The Shandy household

(left) The frontispiece by
William Hogarth to Vol. IV
of the 1761 edition of *The Life
and Opinions and Tristram
Shandy*, by Laurence Sterne

(right) Laurence Sterne
(detail), by Sir Joshua
Reynolds

consists of people who are fond of one another but find satisfying communication impossible. So, for example, Mr Shandy, the narrator's
father, an eccentric amateur philosopher who loves disputation, feels as
frustrated as an enthusiastic pianist would feel if he lived always among
tone-deaf people:

> It was a consuming vexation to my father, that my mother never asked the
> meaning of a thing she did not understand.
>
> That she is not a woman of science, my father would say – is her misfortune
> – but she might ask a question.
>
> My mother never did. In short, she went out of the world at last without
> knowing whether it turned round or stood still. My father had officiously
> told her above a thousand times which way it was, but she always forgot. . . .

Mr Shandy's brother, Uncle Toby, can be even more irritating, for there
are moments when it looks as if a satisfying dispute might arise, but then
Uncle Toby recollects some military instance and sends for Corporal
Trim – and both these retired soldiers are superbly drawn – to confirm
his recollection. And so it goes on in Shandy Hall, with hardly anybody
understanding what other people are saying. This would be intolerable
– and some grim writers since Sterne have proved this – if Sterne's
characters did not exist in an atmosphere of personal concern and
affection. This is Sterne's secret, as it is, though often to a lesser extent,
with all true humorists, not to be confused with mere funny men.

As far back as Shakespeare's time Middleton had made his Mayor of
Queenborough cry, 'O, the clowns that I have seen in my time! . . . Here
was a merry world, my masters!' Possibly these clowns were all energetic

funny men, considerably removed from the renowned comic actors who arrived in the eighteenth century. Some, like Foote, had a natural wit, even if they were not deeply humorous:

> When his friend, Sir Francis Blake Delavel, died, Foote was so overcome that he saw nobody for three days. On the fourth day, his treasurer called to see him on urgent business, and Foote, still tearful, inquired when Sir Francis was to be buried. 'Not till the later end of next week, sir,' the treasurer replied, 'as I hear the surgeons intend first to dissect his head.' 'And what will they get there?' Foote cried, his face still wet with tears. 'I'm sure I have known Frank these five and twenty years, and I could never find anything in it.'

But it was not until the Regency that famous comic actors like Liston and Munden had admiring critics of the first order, namely, Hazlitt and Charles Lamb. Readers must take Hazlitt on Liston for granted here, but I must make room for a quotation from Lamb's appreciation of Munden, his favourite, whose humour Lamb caught and then enriched by passing it through his own wild imagination:

> Can any man *wonder*, like him? Can any man *see ghosts*, like him? Or fight with *his own shadow* – 'SESSA' – as he does in that strangely-neglected thing, the *Cobbler of Preston* – where his alterations from the Cobbler to the Magnifico, and from the Magnifico to the Cobbler, keep the brain of the spectator in as wild a ferment, as if some Arabian Night were being acted before him. Who like him can throw, or ever attempted to throw, a preternatural interest

'Mr Liston's Principal Characters'

over the commonest daily-life objects. . . ? The gusto of Munden antiquates and ennobles what it touches. His pots and his ladles are as grand and primal as the seething-pots and hooks seen in old prophetic vision. A tub of butter, contemplated by him, amounts to a Platonic idea. He understands a leg of mutton in its quiddity. He stands wonderingly, amid the commonplace materials of life, like primeval man with the sun and stars about him.

This is like a magical tall tree of humour arising out of a forest of it. And indeed I consider Lamb to be the greatest humorist of his age, and if I do not enlarge upon him here, it is because he will appear again in the next chapter.

There is of course plenty of humour in Jane Austen; but it is cool feminine humour, generally resisting the temptation to indulge, to expand, her comic characters, not letting them rip as male humorists tend to do. But she is fairly expansive with Mr Collins in *Pride and Prejudice*, and it might almost be said that he took charge of her, that by expressing him so richly his snobbery and toadyism rise to an innocent grand passion, so that there is a kind of poetry in his wonder and delight at Lady Catherine's invitation to dinner: he is probably the only poetical character in Jane Austen. Like many another poetical character, it could never occur to him for a moment that he might be ridiculous, so he is in deadly earnest when he discusses with Mr Bennet the little flattering things, like so many sugared almonds, he offers his patroness:

'These are the little things that please her Ladyship, and it is a sort of attention which I feel myself peculiarly bound to pay.'

'You judge very properly,' said Mr. Bennet, 'and it is happy for you that you possess the talent of flattering with delicacy. May I ask whether these pleasing attentions proceed from the impulse of the moment, or are the result of previous study?' 'They arise chiefly from what is passing at the time, and though I sometimes amuse myself with suggesting and arranging such little elegant compliments as may be adapted to ordinary occasions, I always wish to give them as unstudied an air as possible.'

We cannot understand how Mr Bennet, supposed to be a connoisseur of the absurd, should ever have tired of this innocently happy and solemn simpleton. For the rest, Jane Austen's humour plays round people who are excited about everything, like Miss Bates, and people who refuse to be excited about anything, like Mr Woodhouse and Lady Bertram. All remain a joy for ever.

Books and periodicals multiplied so fast in the nineteenth century that an increasing crop of funny men was inevitable, especially as there were always flippant or satirical weeklies needing contributors, with *Punch* at the head of them. (It began as a rather ferocious radical weekly, and then gradually became more and more respectable until at last it was snobbishly conservative.) Some amusing scenes can be discovered among the

Mr Munden as 'Sir
Francis Gripe', 1791, by
Thornthwaite after De Wilde

minor novelists, of whom Albert Smith was the type, largely influenced by the tremendous early success of Dickens. We will ignore Dickens for the time being, to take a look at the important Victorian novelists, to discover how much genuine humour there is in them. Thackeray has an excellent sense of fun and is able to create several droll characters, but neither by temperament nor inclination is he a humorist. His early contributions to *Fraser's* and *Punch* have always seemed to me gritty, too savage, generally repulsive. His most fervent admirer, Trollope, was capable of a few comic scenes – as, for example, the startling invasion of the Proudie reception by Bertie Stanhope and his sister, the Signora, in *Barchester Towers* – but when he sets aside his usual sobriety he is always in danger of being merely facetious. On the other hand, that delightful woman, Mrs Gaskell, has a very real sense of humour, which she fully exploits in *Cranford*, in which the reminiscent manner allows her to be sentimental while offering us a gallery of droll innocents, sharply observed by the feminine eye. Both George Eliot, in her earlier work, and then Thomas Hardy, much later, offer us genuine humour with their rural folk, often muddle-headed, their rustic wits and philosophers. But the bent of their minds was not humorous. George Meredith has perhaps the most showy and sparkling intelligence to be found in all English fiction, but he is always determined to be witty, using wit as a weapon, and is never really a humorist.

Now we can no longer ignore Dickens. His mind had not the breadth and depth of Shakespeare's, and he lacks the poet's marvellous power of being able to create a memorable figure, half-comic, half-pathetic, in a brief speech or two. But for sheer energy, inventiveness, fecundity in humour, Dickens cannot be beaten, and for every one of Shakespeare's comic characters he offers us at least twenty. And he makes it look so easy that many critics (though not lately) have waved him away, telling us not to mistake this gross caricaturing for real creativeness. To such critics we could apply the final words of Mrs Sapsea's astonishing epitaph: 'Stranger, pause. And ask thyself this question. Canst thou do likewise? If not, with a blush retire.' And indeed neither those critics nor any of their friends and readers could do likewise. It demands not only Dickens's extraordinary creative force but also his peculiar cast of mind. To begin with, he creates a whole world of his own, to nourish the host of fantastic droll creatures that form a great part of its population. (There are, of course, other important elements in Dickens, but here our subject is humour.) It is a world that restores us, at least in part, to our childhood, and I suspect that people who have completely forgotten their childhood rarely appreciate the humour of Dickens: they feel that it is all overdone, just as they would feel that most poetry is overdone, 'a bit much' as people say. But then there is also a lot of *youth* in Dickens's humour. When we are young and high-spirited, laughing in a group about silly people we all know, we begin to pile up extravagances, so going a little way towards the creation of Dickens's comic characters.

It is a waste of time elaborately comparing him with, say, Thackeray, George Eliot or Trollope. Though he is hardly aware of it himself, he is not trying to do what they are doing; he is not reporting on this world but busy excitedly exploring his own world. I have thought for some time that his novels – even reaching as far as *Our Mutual Friend* – might be best considered as grotesque prose poems. And as such they represent a huge explosion of Englishness, with the barrier between the unconscious and conciousness in tatters. If this seems far-fetched, then observe the profound difference between Dickens writing as a journalist and Dickens in the full roaring tide of creation.

It may be argued that Dickens contradicts my theory that there must be affection in the humour of Englishness. After all, he can create comic characters out of downright villains or detestable humbugs, for whom he

'Restoration of mutual confidence between Mr and Mrs Micawber', an illustration by Phiz (Hablot Knight Browne) to *David Copperfield*, by Charles Dickens, 1850

Restoration of mutual confidence between Mr and Mrs Micawber.

cannot possibly feel any affection. As a man and a responsible citizen, certainly not; but as a creator, peopling his own world, he can enjoy such dubious characters, even doting on them. Indeed, his own tremendous enjoyment of the scene can infect us. But there is something else, perhaps the key to him as a great humorist. It is what he is able to do with these characters once he has thought of them.

Let us take the first example that comes to mind (and there could be scores of them) – the Micawbers. Any experienced novelist or playwright might imagine a seedy penniless clerk with a taste for pompous rhetoric, and then his devoted wife, astonishingly logical but daft. But what would he or she do with them? Dickens's genius for absurdity shows us what can be done with them, giving us exact accounts of what they say and how they behave, and piling one memorable piece of drollery on top of another; and doing it not once, for this pair, but doing it over and over again, with essential differences, in what looks like a whole country of the ridiculous. And doing it, too – even though he himself could be a hard man if he felt like it – in an atmosphere suffused with a warm humanity, the creation of a man who longed intensely for happiness – and never had it except when he was working well. Can we wonder if Dickens conquered the world as no English writer since Shakespeare has ever done?

Dickens came close to writing sheer jovial nonsense at times. But here he was outdone by other Victorians, especially by those who were not professional funny men but turned to pure nonsense as a holiday or as a temporary relief from the pressure of existence. But I feel there has been too much surprise over the fact that the Victorian Age should be so famous (in England, not abroad, where it is all mystifying) for its nonsense. People forget that although it was an age of low spirits – tormenting religious doubts, iron-bound economics, gloomy respectability and the rest – it was also an age of high spirits, proof of which can be discovered in many Victorian memoirs. Of course it is possible to take a sudden jump from low to high spirits, as I fancy that Edward Lear (not a happy man) occasionally did. But one reason why the Victorians could produce and enjoy sheer nonsense is that they had far more confidence in themselves and their age than we have had since. There is in this nonsense a large element of what we have learned to call surrealism, but the difference is that while the Victorians were having fun with it, our surrealists seem at once solemn and neurotic, patients of Dr Freud. True, an odd mournful strain can creep into Lear's wildest lyrics –

> Far and few, far and few,
> Are the lands where the Jumblies live

and in Lewis Carroll's crazy dreamland – especially in the much under-

Self-portrait of Charles Keene, perhaps the finest draughtsman and most richly humorous of all *Punch* artists

(overleaf) 'The Meet at the Fox and Hounds', watercolour drawing by Thomas Rowlandson

rated *Hunting of the Snark* – there can be an unexpected touch of the sinister. I enjoyed both these masters of nonsense when I was very young, and still enjoy them, with Carroll leading now, in my old age, when I sometimes wonder if his Humpty Dumpty was not a prefiguration of some recent arrogant literary critics and the Walrus and the Carpenter a pair of successful modern politicians. W. S. Gilbert, though a superb provider of libretti, is below their rank in the kingdom of nonsense, where he is perhaps the Solicitor-General. There is a lot of efficient hard work in his comic operas, but only in one particular of them does he reach inspired absurdity, and that is in the ideas that originate them – the curious gentility of the sailors in *Pinafore*, the tender hearts of the *Pirates of Penzance*, the astonishing but triumphant conjunction of fairyland and the House of Lords in *Iolanthe*, the committee of ghosts in *Ruddigore* passing resolutions in the matter of the daily crime. Here, like Carroll and Lear, he represents Englishness going wild.

I am leaving behind a number of successful Victorian funny men – and the B's alone would give us Barham, whose *Ingoldsby Legends* could be described as very witty but rather gritty, and Burnand, whose earliest drollery, *Happy Thoughts*, is his best – because I want to welcome an astonishing piece of Englishness in humour, born like me in 1894. I call it astonishing because of its unexpected authorship, well removed from the Society of Authors, for *The Diary of a Nobody* was written by the comedian, George Grossmith, and his younger brother, Weedon. It first appeared in *Punch*, and other contributors, such as the successful and ingenious Anstey, never came near it. The innocent Mr Pooter's confessions are not simply laughable, though there is some gorgeous fooling in them, but contrive to touch the heart: he remains one of England's memorable and lovable fools. If there are readers still unacquainted with Mr Pooter and his family, with Cumming and Gowing, with Burwin-Fosselton of the Holloway Comedians, and Mr Padge, who never says anything but 'That's right' and yet contrives to be a tremendous character, they should buy or borrow *The Diary of a Nobody*. It is a little masterpiece of true humour, which I believe would have delighted Shakespeare and Sterne, Lamb and Dickens; but in a few years, if we go on as we are doing, it may no longer be understood, either in its drollery or its suggestion of a sort of tenderness.

We must make room here for the black-and-white artists, the illustrators and *Punch* men, of the Victorian Age. We can begin with 'Phiz' (Hablot Knight Browne) who illustrated so many of the earlier Dickens novels. I can remember how surprised I was when I learnt that Browne was a friend and constant companion of Dickens, who gave him careful instructions. Until then I had imagined that Dickens was the victim of Browne, because the illustrations, in which so many characters were

Programme illustrations by Alice Havers for *H.M.S. Pinafore* and *Iolanthe*, by Gilbert and Sullivan

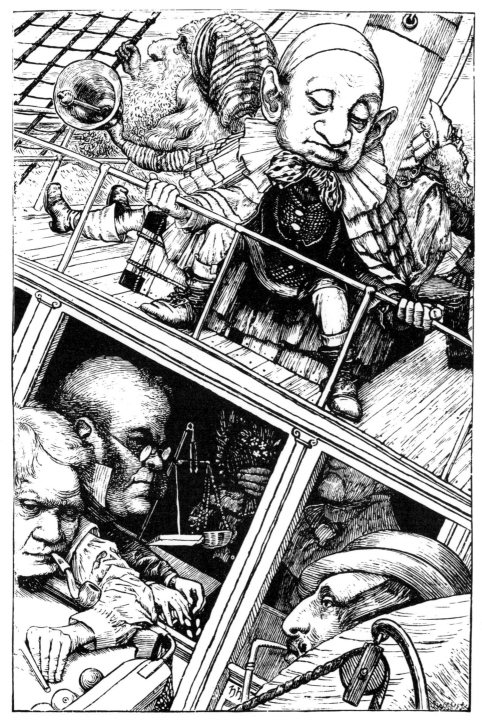

'He had wholly forgotten his
name', illustration by Swain
after Henry Holliday to *The
Hunting of the Snark*, by Lewis
Carroll, 1876

either enormously fat or grotesquely thin, and so many scenes suggested
a riot in elfland, greatly exaggerated the element of caricature in the text.
In my youth I used to stare with amazement at these drawings of mad
marionettes, gnomes and monsters. Cruikshank, a stronger character
than Browne, also went to work in the same cramped grotesque world,
but brought it closer to horror, with a sinister touch of his own, so that he
was very much at home with Oliver Twist. He was even more at home

with the grimmer German fairy-tales. Both Cruikshank and Browne were not entirely ineffective but, I have always felt, unpleasing artists.

Of the famous *Punch* men, John Leech was pleasing enough, and there was a suggestion of real Englishness in his kindly humour, but perhaps because he did so many hunting pictures and jokes (I am prejudiced against hunting) I have always thought him overrated. Nor do I admire, as a comic artist, a later *Punch* celebrity, du Maurier, who provided its readers with so many elongated aristocratic personages and favourite satirical characters like Sir Gorgius Midas and Mrs Ponsonby de Tomkyns The jokes are there but not any essential drollery in the drawings.

My men are Charles Keene and Phil May. They have much in common. They were both extremely fine draughtsmen; they found their humour among the lower orders and were not interested, either as artists or men, in high society; both died too young, Keene after a long illness, Phil May from too much amiable roistering. Keene was no bohemian but quiet and very hard-working, for ever smoking his large pipe, and in addition to his *Punch* drawings he did a good deal of clever sensitive illustrating. He had real humour both in his outlook and in his perceptive and economic draughtsmanship. So had Phil May, and

'I looked like Marat in the bath, Madame Tussaud's', from *The Diary of a Nobody*, by George Grossmith and Weedon Grossmith, 1892 'April 29, Sunday . . . I had got a chill, and decided to have a bath as hot as I could bear it. Bath ready – could scarcely bear it so hot. I persevered, and got in; very hot, but very acceptable. I lay still for some time.

On moving my hand above the surface of the water I experienced the greatest fright I ever received in the whole course of my life; for imagine my horror on first thought was that I had ruptured an artery and was bleeding to death, and should be discovered, later on, looking like a second Marat, as I remember seeing him in Madame Tussaud's. My second thought was to ring the bell, but remembered there was no bell to ring. My third was, that there was nothing but the enamel paint, which had dissolved in boiling water. . . .'

even, so to speak, more so. His was an odd career. He was a Yorkshire-man who spent some years in Australia but was – and still is – associated in the public mind with London's poorer classes, with its guttersnipes and costers and charwomen and flower-girls and down-at-heel actors. (The East End types came into their own in Phil May's great decade, the Nineties, and can be found in its fiction and enjoying the limelight in its music halls.) His drawing, created with such superb economy, could translate a line of letterpress into vivid and sympathetic life. He had a very real sympathy with the people he drew, and behind his witty close observation there is affection, like all that has most Englishness in English humour.

The Victorian illustrator who has pleased me most, for all of seventy years, is John Tenniel. He had a long and happy life, perfectly arranged for him, beginning in 1820 and ending in 1914, just before Europe blew up and turned itself into the graveyard of youth. For his years of rather ponderous cartooning for *Punch* I care nothing, but in his illustrations for *Alice in Wonderland* and *Through the Looking-glass* (his drawings, like the text, becoming richer and stranger) he discovered a golden seam of Englishness. Later illustrators of *Alice*, together with stage producers and designers, have never begun to match him. Taking a holiday from the solemn and menacing world of politics and power struggles, he found himself at ease and inspired in this other and better nonsense world,

'Tweedle dee and Tweedle dum', illustration engraved by Dalziel after John Tenniel to *Through the looking-glass and what Alice Found there*, by Lewis Carroll, 1872

{194}

fascinating generation after generation of young readers. He was a happy man – and deserved to be.

At the risk of being accused of some appalling omission, I suggest we can find no comic artist of the highest class in the Edwardian and later years. (I am still excluding all living men.) But there have been some splendid funny men, all original. If there was good fun in E. T. Reed's *Prehistoric Peeps*, there was even better fun in the inimitable sketches of J. A. Shepherd, who could take his sketchbook round the Zoo and somehow contrive to satirize the whole human race without ever drawing one of its members. Heath Robinson drew a solemn-nonsense world of his

'Fish Tennis – a thrilling new Water Game', by W. Heath Robinson

(left) Illustration by Will Owen to *Light Freights*, by W. W. Jacobs

(right) 'Deeds that ought to Win the V.C. – the Sub-Lieutenant takes the Admiral's Queen', 1918, by H. M. Bateman

own, peopled with ancient baffled academics. H. M. Bateman took familiar predicaments into a furiously energized dreamland. Then I used to have a special fondness for the quiet little absurdities of George Morrow, whose every line was somehow droll. Max Beerbohm, of course, was never competing in this gallery, but his wit as a literary satirist gathered strength from his careful draughtsmanship. If I single out Will Owen from the illustrators it is because I always associate him with an old favourite of mine, a small-scale but genuine artist and equally genuine humorist, W. W. Jacobs, who was able to create a special little world of his own, filled with sleepy seaports, forgotten canals, remote villages, all manner of sailors hurrying ashore, innocent or cunning rustics. A giant contemporary of Jacobs who could have created a gigantic humorous world of his own was of course H. G. Wells, who gave us more than a glimpse of what he might have done in *Kipps*, parts of *Tono-Bungay*, and *Mr Polly*. But his mind was on other things, and he came to despise fiction. Nevertheless, in spite of his science and his angry attacks on the world's irrationality, there was from first to last a glowing lump of Englishness in the wonderfully gifted H.G.

A casual reference to the music hall in the Nineties is not enough. Though enjoyed by all classes, the music hall or Variety owed most – and certainly the greater part of its humour – to the working class, especially the working class of the industrial North and London, which contributed so many of its regular patrons and also most of its most successful performers, its comedians and comediennes. Its hilarious sketches, often in dumb-show, were not without a cheerful suggestion of surrealism, and their tours in the United States, together with the broad comedy of American vaudeville, were chiefly responsible for the development of slapstick in early silent films. Among the arrivals in

{196}

Los Angeles were Charles Chaplin and Stan Laurel, both fine comedians, with Chaplin finally turning himself into a masterly humorist with a world-wide audience. Variety in England reached its peak during the Nineties and its gradual decline probably began about 1911, in London, but later in the provinces. When its successor, Revue, aimed at laughter, it used wit (of a kind) rather than broad humour. Though illusionists and jugglers and comediennes, dashing on as soldiers, sailors, dandies out for the night, could be very popular and 'top the bill', I don't think I am being biased if I say that it was the renowned comedians, such as Little Tich, George Robey, the nonsensical Wilkie Bard, the outraged and furious Harry Tate, who were the most popular 'turns' of all. (Two or three of the best character comedians, I am sorry to say, were Scots; and the greatest of all music-hall clowns, the incomparable Grock, came originally, I think, from, of all places, Switzerland.)

What marked the music hall – to give it a position here – was the amount of genuine affection in its humour. First there was the affection of the performers for the characters they created. Then there was also the genuine affection of the audiences for these favourite performers. In all this, from the rough-and-ready surrealism, the wildly daft, to the constant display of warm affection, I find a great deal of Englishness, which began to dwindle after the First World War, though traces of it remained in films, particularly those made by Chaplin, and in the serial comedy of radio and TV.

But what about writing? Well, in the later 1920s a very cool and

(left) Little Tich
(right) Harry Tate

extremely clever young man, Evelyn Waugh, with his *Decline and Fall* and *Vile Bodies*, offered readers a new and highly original kind of comedy in fiction, which some of us welcomed just because it was so effective and unlike anything we had had before. His was 'dead-pan' comic writing. Its secret was that all affection had been removed from it. Here was the drollery of another and more dubious age. It was certainly English enough, but it was a long way removed from Englishness in humour, which had been kept warm for so long. Now we had comedy, like so many of our Americanized drinks, 'on the rocks'.

Men almost everywhere – and, to a lesser extent, women too – have their hobbies, their particular pastimes, their lasting interests, which must be distinguished from effervescent *crazes*, a notable American weakness. But this hobbying or hobbyism cannot be our subject here. For us there has to be a form of it governed by Englishness. If pressed I would agree that a man living in or within sight of Avignon, Leningrad or Philadelphia might possibly be our kind of hobbyist, but that would only prove that unexpected little blobs of Englishness, blown by the winds of the spirit, have descended on alien lands. What is certain, to my mind, is that England is the natural home of the mounted hobbyists, of the roving cavalry of hobbyism, and is the accepted pasture and stable and gallop-ground of that fantastic creature, bred out of Englishness and Individuality, the *Hobby-Horse*. Laurence Sterne, a master of the subject in *Tristram Shandy*, knew all about this creature:

> A man and his Hobby-Horse, tho' I cannot say that they act and re-act exactly after the same manner in which the soul and the body do upon each other: Yet doubtless there is a communication between them of some kind; and in my opinion rather is, that there is something in it more of the manner of electrified bodies; and that, by means of the heated parts of the rider, which come immediately into contact with the back of the Hobby-Horse, – by long journeys and much friction, it so happens, that the body of the rider is at length filled as full of Hobby-Horsical matter as it can hold; – so that if you are able to give but a clear description of the nature of the one, you may form a pretty exact notion of the genius and character of the other. . . .

Ignoring the *double entendre* that Sterne could never resist, I will try to explain his Hobby-Horse and those who ride it in terms of Englishness.

A man who merely has a hobby – perhaps placidly collecting anything from rare coins to matchboxes, doing a little woodwork or metalwork, taking a pride in his apple trees or roses – can lead a rational existence, well within the bounds of common sense. But Englishness, as we have discovered, does not favour rationality and can at any time shrug away common sense. It has its being in a hazy open-ended world that has no exact boundaries and can widen out, like a path going through a fairy-tale forest, into strange realms beyond any known laws. So it can create an atmosphere in which a man mounted on a Hobby-Horse can feel happy and free, waving goodbye to rationality and common sense. So strong is this atmosphere that men who have no Hobby-Horse don't condemn – though they may wonder at – the other men who are galloping away. 'Live and let live' is the motto of Englishness. (Notice that those narrow sections of the English who have been trained or have individually decided to reject and despise Englishness have long been notorious for their intolerance, social bigotry, contemptible prejudices, thin and sour arrogance. No Hobby-Horse for them – Good God – never!) And so far as Englishness can be said to have an army, then the Hobby-Horse men are its light cavalry, far out of sight, scouting or raiding. The war was often against ignorance. Civilization owes an immense debt to the generations of eccentric English gentlemen, with modest private means, who vanished on their Hobby-Horses to the ends of the earth,

Men arriving with their exhibits at the Southern Railwaymen's Fruit and Vegetable Show, August 1935

looking for rare flowers or birds or even rocks, and returning to add to this world's knowledge of itself.

I don't know what happens elsewhere, but certainly in England there can be multiple or group Hobby-Horses, carrying quite a crowd of men together to some solemn daftness. Thus – to take the first example I remember – I have been told that in Northumberland there are miners who spend their hours above ground cultivating gigantic leeks. These monsters are of a size and consistency that rule them out as possible vegetables for the table. Their growers soar high above any material level, probably to the disgust of their wives and feminine practicality. The mighty leeks are coaxed into existence as highly competitive trophies, and, I am told, are finally displayed, if worthy of the honour, in various miners' taverns, where their size and mysterious charms are compared and discussed over innumerable pints of beer. Many years ago, I employed a gardener who had won a prize at the local show for the biggest onion. Our whole garden seemed to me to be sacrificed, like an unfortunate body with a tumour, to produce bigger and bigger onions, unmanageable giants far from welcome in the kitchen. But then that gardener was not really existing on the same plane or in the same dimension; he was only pretending to be, while galloping, invisible to us, on his Hobby-Horse.

At the opposite extreme in Hobbyism to these ponderous vegetables, weighing too much, are ideas, weighing nothing. We are apt to forget that odd and wilful men can take to ideas as other men take to drink. If – going back to Sterne – Uncle Toby's Hobby-Horse always took him to fortifications, Mr Shandy's trotted unceasingly among peculiar ideas and astonishing opinions. And we must remember that Mr Shandy was a retired merchant, who had taken leave at last of exact calculations, his counting-house and his ledgers. It is my experience, long and thick because so many strangers have written to me during the past forty years or so, that it is the men who have retired from responsibly careful work – the chemists, the engineers, the surveyors – who go charging about on the Hobby-Horses of ideas, incredible theories, crazy opinions. It is they who send you, out of the wild blue of Hobbyism, new religions set out on two quarto sheets, at the same time challenging you to find a flaw in them. It is they who announce that all human history, past and future, has been marked out on the Great Pyramid; that spaceships from distant parts of the galaxy landed here in some remote age; that men and women once belonged to quite different species; that our moon is a satellite captured comparatively recently by the earth, which once had another moon; that all large-scale human affairs are directed by superhuman beings, no longer living in Tibet but scattered about, perhaps masquerading as a *restaurateur* in Marseilles, a jeweller in Hong

The London, Tilbury and Southend Railway Centenary, 1956. Ernest Marshall of Tilbury, one of the last drivers of the *Thundersley*, pointing out items of interest

Kong. But enough is enough: the Hobby-Horse ideas can be piled up like crazy pagodas. Moreover, most of these Hobbyists are not idly trifling with daft notions; they are driven by a furious energy, living in a snowstorm of pamphlets. I agree that they are not necessarily English, but I would say that England leads the amateur field, the professionals, not always innocent Hobbyists, usually heading for Los Angeles.

I don't know how it is elsewhere; no doubt the Hobby-Horse can gallop in many latitudes; but certainly where Englishness reigns, just as flowers attract the bees, the railways fascinate the Hobbyists. While more and more ordinary travellers and goods take to the roads, while steam engines have given way to diesel and electric trains, there is hardly a feature of past railway travel that has not its own crowd of dotty enthusiasts, Hobbyists to the last man and boy. Old timetables are pored over as if they were ancient scriptures. Maps and plans of disused lines are collected, retraced, deeply discussed. At least one group of happy crackpots has actually *bought* a fair length of disused line, together with an old steam engine and a few carriages; and they spend their weekends, bursting with joy and song, riding up and down their magic line, puff-puffing away with every care and sorrow forgotten.

We have seen for ourselves, on BBC Television, the middle-aged couple who now devote all their days to their miniature railway system. But the term *miniature* is deceptive. Their trains are not mere toys; they run, keeping good time, for at least a mile or so; and the system has stations, signals, telephone communication, and, for all I know, tiny tickets for invisible manikin passengers. Every morning, this man and his wife (a spellbound woman, for once) put on uniforms to run their railway, where they may be heard gravely declaring, 'The 11.10 is nearly two minutes late.' If they were in charge of the old *Flying Scotsman*, with the Royal Family and the Cabinet among the passengers, they could not smile less nor suggest more deep concern. There is not a more solemnly conscientious couple in England; but it is easy to see they are happy indeed, living in a kind of railway fairyland.

Among other riders of the Hobby-Horse was a man who on his retirement took to painting. This is common enough – and very sensible – but with this particular Hobbyist it was art with a difference. His subjects were rigidly confined to the old-fashioned road-engines, the ponderous steam-rollers no longer to be seen – except of course in his loving portraits of them, all types, mostly drawn and coloured from memory. I never learned what happened to his pictures, but I am quite willing to believe there are groups of road-engine enthusiasts ready to buy them, some favouring the taller funnels, others the shorter. And now I have suddenly remembered, after forty years, that moon-struck happy Cotswold squire I visited when I was writing *English Journey*, surely the king Hobbyist of all my acquaintances. A bachelor – he would have driven a wife out of her mind – he lived and had his workshop in an outhouse, filling his manor, rather beautiful if crazy inside and out, with collections, crowding one dim panelled room after another, of spinning wheels, sedan chairs, model wagons, ancient musical instruments, Chinese lacquer, old costumes – crinolines, uniforms, bonnets, beaver hats, cockades, enough to dress several opera companies. This is what I wrote:

Neither in one house nor the other (the outhouse) did I catch the smallest glimpse of a modern book or a newspaper or anything else that belongs to our age. The twentieth century was nowhere in evidence and the nineteenth had only just dawned there. But the owner no longer spent his time collecting these relics of the past; his hobby now was the construction of a whole miniature old-fashioned seaport; boys' play on a smashing adult scale, defying all commonsense but glorious in its absorption in the exquisitely useless. The miniature seaport . . . has a proper harbour in one of the ponds in the garden. It has its quay, its fleet of ships, its lighthouse, its railway system, with station, sidings and all, its inn, main street and side streets, thatched cottages, and actual living woods, made up of dwarf trees in the garden. The owner, who has had some architectural training, has designed, built and painted the whole village himself. It is portable, except for the harbour works, and is brought out and erected during the summer and then

The magic and mystery of an English garden in spring is marvellously evoked in this watercolour drawing by Samuel Palmer, 'In a Shoreham Garden', 1829.

taken into the house in winter. Its creator has now decided that it should have a castle, and he showed us an excellent preliminary drawing of this imposing building, which will be several feet long and will easily dominate the place. I hope there will be no trouble in the village with the two-inch lord of this castle, for by this time the place may have settled down to an easy democratic existence and it may resent this sudden descent into the feudal. . . .

I can remember even now how, towering over this village and seaport and its ships, I felt like another Gulliver in Lilliput; and how, scaling myself down to land properly at a seaport two feet high, I could imagine myself in a harbour where the goldfish – and they were real, and big fat fellows up to nine inches long, some of them – would then seem to come glittering in like whales of red gold. What a Hobbyist that Cotswold squire was! Taxation and anxiety and pills may prevent our ever seeing his like again.

In August 1771, Horace Walpole, then in Paris, wrote to his friend John Chute:

Methinks, I should be as glad of a little grass, as a seaman after a long voyage. Yet English gardening gains ground here prodigiously – not much at a time, indeed – I have literally seen one, that is exactly like a tailor's paper of patterns. There is a Monsieur Boutin, who has tacked a piece of what he calls an English garden to a set of stone terraces, with steps of turf. There are three or four very high hills, almost as high as, and exactly in the shape of, a tansy pudding. You squeeze between these and a river, that is conducted at obtuse angles in a stone channel, and supplied by a pump; and when walnuts come in I suppose it will be navigable. In a corner enclosed by a chalk wall are the samples I mentioned; there is a stripe of grass, another of corn, and a third *en friche*, exactly in the order of beds in a nursery. . . .

Horace Walpole – who rode his own Gothick Hobby-Horse at Strawberry Hill – could afford to be ironical in his account of such puny French efforts. Though no wealthy landowner himself, among his titled friends there must have been several, then and later, who spent fortunes on enormous and carefully landscaped gardens, with experts like 'Capability' Brown and Humphry Repton planning and directing. The landscaping fashion survived the eighteenth century, for in his *Headlong Hall* (1816) Peacock has his Mr Milestone, the expert landscaper, explaining how he has planned an effect of *surprise* in one part of the grounds; only to be asked, by one of Peacock's amused young women, how he would describe the effect to anybody who had gone round a second time.

Six years later than *Headlong Hall* came Loudon's successful *Encyclopaedia of Gardening*, which I must confess I never heard of until I read the Hadfields' *Gardens of Delight*, a fine treasure-house to plunder. The *Encyclopaedia* offered some severe instruction to the young gardener,

The elaborate topiary shown in this detail of Stanley Spencer's painting of a cottage at Burghclere shows the English farm-worker doing his utmost to emulate the conceits of the great landscape gardeners

who might in those days be only one out of twenty, thirty or forty. Here are some specimens of it:

> *Decorum* is the refinement of propriety. It is in order to procure stable-dung for hot-beds, it is proper to do this at all times when it is wanted, but it is decorous to have the work performed early in the morning, that the putrescent vapours and dropping litter may not prove offensive to the master of the garden, should he, or any of his family or friends, visit that scene. . . .

We are lucky today to find a gardener at all, even if he *indecorously* slaps down manure under our very noses. But again:

> *Finally, attend to personal habits and cleanliness.* Never perform any operation without gloves on your hands that you can do with gloves. . . . No gardener need have hands like bears' paws. . . . Let your dress be clean, neat, simple and harmonious in form and colour. . . .

We know that Beau Brummell in his best years lived up to that precept, but it is asking a lot of a working gardener. And there are greater demands to come:

> Elevate, meliorate, and otherwise improve, any raw, crude, harsh, or inharmonious features in your physiognomy, by looking often at the faces of agreeable people, by occupying your mind with agreeable and useful ideas, and by continually instructing yourself by reading. This will also give you features if you have none. Remember that you are paid and maintained by and for the use of and pleasure of your employer, who may no more wish to see a dirty, ragged, uncouth-looking, grinning or conceited biped in his garden, than a starved, haggard, untutored horse in his stable.

This is not sensible advice: two quite different standards are represented in it. A gardener – or any other man – might never be dirty and ragged and yet be unable to improve his own features by staring at other people's, by thinking hard but cheerfully, by reading and reading, always for instruction. After all, he is not asking for a gardening job in Plato's Republic.

It is easy to think of English gardens at two extremes, those associated with the great country mansions and the cottage gardens that have often bloomed prettily for centuries, though now perhaps under sentence of death from motor-road planners. In the great gardens, obviously the professional masculine element prevails, but I cannot help believing that many of the cottage gardens are maintained by the men, even though, back in the sixteenth century, Tusser could write:

> In Marche and in Aprill, from morning to night:
> in sowing and setting, good housewives delight;
> To have in a garden, or other like plot:
> to trim up their house, and to furnish their pot.

However, during the nineteenth century and increasingly during this age of ours, another sort of garden and another kind of gardener came into existence. Both were products of the middle class, neither rich enough to employ a highly professional staff nor yet too poor (except after the Second World War) to afford a man and a boy. Such people either contrived to keep a smallish country house going while the city, where the husband had his office, was still their headquarters, or they bought a house with a promising garden for their retirement. And this is when and where the Englishwoman, hardly mentioned so far in this section, mounted and rode her own Hobby-Horse. I am now referring to something beyond the natural feminine desire to be among and to tend living things, after years of streets, office buildings, town halls. I have in mind – and God knows I have met it often enough – a late but impassioned love affair now with a garden, a true Hobbyist's happy lunacy. Her favourite reading will be the blazing catalogues of the seed merchants and perhaps a well-thumbed edition of *Pot-Pourri from a Surrey Garden*. Gone now for ever will be any hesitation about boring and glazing the eyes of visitors, who must share this horticultural madness or stay away. There have been so many jokes about these spellbound ladies, often cheerfully surviving widowhood for twenty years and creeping out with a trowel in their late eighties, that it is not worth quoting one. Certainly at least in England, the gardens did it when nothing else could do it: they compelled Woman to gallop away on her own Hobby-Horse and never dismount until her last fatal illness. And even then, when all is supposed to be over, she may be haunted by dreams, teasing but yet delightful, of bigger and still brighter flower-beds, of rose gardens out of the *Arabian Nights*, of sweet peas in trembling swarms, delphiniums bluer than the heavens. So much for the last – and perhaps the best – of all the hobbies, half-crazy, half-felicitous, born under Englishness.

'Miss Jekyll's gardening boots', 1920, by Sir William Nicholson.
'No carpenter likes a new plane; no house-painter likes a new brush. It is the same with tools as with clothes, the familiar ease can only come of use and better acquaintance. I suppose no horse likes a new collar; I am quite sure I do not like new boots!' From Gertrude Jekyll's *Home and Garden*

A PORTRAIT GALLERY

✿

I T is of course a tiny portrait gallery, with no more than seven framed heads in it, for there really is no room for others. After much reflection I chose the following: Raleigh, Pepys, Dr Johnson, Charles Lamb, Michael Faraday, R. F. Burton and C. B. Fry. All of them wrote, some copiously, but not one is here primarily as an author. They were all English, of course, and they have been selected to represent and illustrate – obviously in very different ways – certain varieties of Englishness, which, while maintaining its central and essential character, can express itself in surprisingly varying forms. Not one of them, not even Raleigh, could have been awarded a place in Chapter 3, among my 'Lords and Masters', for they never occupied any really high office, never exercised great power; yet with the possible exception of Burton – and I have my own reasons for putting him into this gallery, as I hope to show – in one way or another these men caught and held the imagination or the affection (or both) of a large number of their fellow countrymen. Indeed, some of them are deeply remembered by people who have forgotten all but a few of the lords and masters, the men of power. Even so, I make no claim that my choices are inevitable, and I hope some readers will amuse themselves furnishing their own little portrait galleries, perhaps for Scotland, Wales, Ireland, America, as well as for England. Meanwhile, the door here is open.

It seemed to me we ought to begin with a splendid figure of a man, to represent the Elizabethans. James Thomson (a Scot himself), turning to them in *The Seasons*, cried:

> But who can speak
> The numerous worthies of the maiden reign?
> In Raleigh mark their every glory mix'd

Which Macaulay enlarged for us: 'Raleigh, the soldier, the sailor, the scholar, the courtier, the orator, the poet, the historian, the philosopher.

. . .' Though greatly helping to bring the New World into existence – and he has been called 'The Father of the United States' – he can be looked at from the other end, so to speak, and seen as the last magnificent specimen of Renaissance Man. In spite of all the books devoted to him – and no Elizabethan except Shakespeare and the Queen herself can have had more – he exists as a figure in the English mind that is both clouded and enhanced by legend, almost mythology. Biographers and historians have told us a great deal about him, yet he remains ambiguous to them and still looms mysteriously to us. There seems a lot of him left over when so many of the facts are known.

His legend resists the records. Did he, as a poor young man, first gain favour with Elizabeth by throwing down his only fine cloak over that patch of mud? Can we credit him with opening North America to the English, taking the potato to Ireland, bringing tobacco and pipes to us here? (We know that he smoked himself and presented to his friends various pipes with silver bowls – well meant, but not a good choice of material.) Was he simply in favour of religious toleration and free discussion, or was he in truth at one time, as rumour declared, a downright dark atheist, mocking God with Christopher Marlowe? No matter; but he moves through our minds in an atmosphere, both bright and then murky, of the legendary, almost like some mythological being.

The various portraits of him – though I cannot pretend to have examined them all – do not tell us very much, and indeed seem to contradict contemporary reports of his bold proud carriage, of his beard 'turned up' or perhaps bristling, of his face deeply tanned after hard service both on land and at sea. We are told more than once that he took to London with him a broad Devon accent that he made no attempt to disguise all the rest of his life. Is this important? I think it is, as one clue to his character, because a careful and smooth-tongued careerist would have rid himself of that Devon accent soon after succeeding at court. Another clue is that he was the friend, not simply the grand patron, of poets, bringing Spenser to the Queen and attending, perhaps often arranging, those evenings of poetry, wit and carousing at the Mermaid Tavern. None of this suggests the pride and arrogance, greed and ferocity, charged against him by his enemies.

No doubt he was a hard man when in hard company. And if, while he was still young, there was to be swaggering, he would swagger with the best of them. After all, he was a provincial outsider, well connected in his own county but not closely related to any of the great families. A seasoned campaigner but still poor, he had to attract the Queen's attention, making the best use he could of a handsome appearance and a sharp wit. I feel that Queen Elizabeth, once she had smiled on him, treated him badly. She should have given him less or given him more.

Had she given him less, not showering on him estates, licences, unearned wealth, he would have aroused less envy and suspicion and have had fewer enemies. Had she given him more, a grander title and then high command, which he was capable of filling as poor Essex never was, his career would have been very different. But she tried to turn a man, Raleigh, into a toy, while weakly agreeing to turn a toy, Essex, into a man. Her fury at Raleigh's 'seduction' of Elizabeth Throgmorton, condemning her to the Tower with him, was stupid and contemptible, for the girl was in love with him and stayed in love with him throughout their married life. (A grisly piece of evidence here, for after Raleigh's execution she had his head embalmed and kept it close to her, in a red velvet bag, until her death – at eighty-two.)

Unlike so many Elizabethan grandees, Raleigh made a good husband – another clue to his real character, very different from his dubious

{210}

public reputation. (But the way his star continually rose and fell, to shine steadily after his death, shows us how fickle public opinion can be.) Certainly he was ambitious, perhaps over-ambitious, and acted with ferocity on occasion, but most detailed accounts of his behaviour to people in his care show him to have been reasonable and, for those grim times (not to be seen through a haze of poetry), compassionate. He was the opposite of his rival, Essex, who, until his miserable end, had the luck but no judgment. Raleigh had judgment but no luck. A fighting seaman, he was kept out of the fleet challenging the Armada, to go scurrying round the country. He saved the day at Cadiz by insisting upon a seafight, but it was Essex who returned in glory. He ran out of luck in attempting to colonize his 'Virginia', also in the piratical Azores venture with Essex, who denounced an independent action Raleigh had been compelled to take and then turned mere jealousy into steady hatred. Everything, in fact, began to go wrong. But it went much worse as soon as James came to the throne, for Essex and his friends had sent word to Edinburgh over and over again that Raleigh was deeply hostile to the Stuart succession; and even Cecil, in the Queen's last weeks, told the same tale. Moreover, James's policy was to conciliate Spain, where Raleigh was feared and detested.

In 1603 Raleigh was tried on trumped-up charges, with Attorney-General Coke yelling that he was a coward (of all things) and 'the most vile and execrable traitor that ever lived'. He was condemned to death, but, probably because public feeling was running in his favour, a last-minute reprieve was granted, and he was committed to life imprisonment in the Tower. This was not as bad as it might sound, for he had his own rooms and his wife and family were with him for a time. Even so, he could not move from the Tower; and he had been very much a man of action – and an impatient man of action at that. But instead of wearing himself out, pining for freedom and fresher air, he fully opened another side of his rich nature and turned full-time poet, prose historian, student of science, literature and politics. To my mind it is not what he accomplished then – though it includes some famous eloquent passages and a *History of the World* that went through many editions – but the fact that he did it at all that proves his greatness. (He is the most impressive example I know of what Maslow, the American psychologist, called 'self-actualization'.)

Having among other things an Elizabethan romantic imagination, which probably explains his reputation for embroidering fact, he was still haunted by the idea of Eldorado, the city of gold somewhere in the jungle near the upper reaches of the Orinoco; and in 1616 he was allowed to set out, with a dangerously small expedition, and discover it. After many early setbacks, everything went disastrously wrong. Raleigh

{211}

himself was down with fever and had to remain behind while five of his smallest ships, with depleted crews, sailed up the river; his son was killed in a skirmish with the Spaniards (which Raleigh had promised to avoid); the captain who returned with the dreadful news committed suicide; and when Raleigh finally crept home he had to face the accusations of the sly and deadly Francis Bacon and was duly sentenced to be executed. In 1618 he faced the axe as magnificently as he had always lived. Told when he put his head on the block that it should be facing the east, he replied, 'What matter how the head lie so the heart be right', and none of his enemies, from the slobbering cowardly King James downwards, ever said anything braver and better. And by this time his star had risen again, to blaze steadily for generation after generation of the English. And even an eighteenth-century poet from Scotland could declare, 'In Raleigh mark their every glory mix'd.' He was the last of the many-sided splendid Renaissance Men, who yet planned, toiled and fought to open a New World. And if he is not worth a place in my little gallery, then who is?

However, we must have men of various sorts, though they must be English, have some claim to Englishness, and not lack a certain legendary appeal. So in England we have only to hear 'And so to bed' or 'My wife, poor wretch!' to remember Samuel Pepys. And both here and in America comic journalists have paid their rents and part of their liquor bills by borrowing his mannerisms for their columns. I like to keep a few odd old-fashioned reference books and collections of quotations, and turning in one of them to the entry *Samuel Pepys* I found some astonishingly varied judgments. That cold and conceited man, Lockhart, calls Pepys 'a vain, silly, transparent coxcomb, without any solid talents or solid virtues'. But Lockhart's wise father-in-law, Walter Scott, could write:

> The variety of Pepys' tastes and pursuits led him into almost every department of life. He was a man of business, a man of information, if not of learning; a man of taste; a man of whim; and, to a certain degree, a man of pleasure. He was a statesman, a bel-esprit, a virtuoso, and a connoisseur. . . .

The old *Quarterly Review*, which so often combined abuse and humbug, called him 'A man of an essentially vulgar and coarse stamp'. Yet in a serious reference work, perhaps rather earlier, we read:

> It may be affirmed of this gentleman that he was, without exception, the greatest and most useful minister that ever filled the same situations in England: the Acts and Registers of the Admiralty proving this fact beyond contradiction. . . . He was a person of universal worth, and in great estimation among the literati, for his unbounded reading, his sound judgment . . . and all polite accomplishments of a gentleman, particularly those of music, languages, conversation, and address.

Sir Walter Raleigh and his Son, 1602, by Nicholas Hilliard

1602
Sr Walter Ralegh Knight Lord Warden of
the Stannries of the
& of the Isle of Jarsey & her M. Lieute
nant generall of the Counties of Devonshyre & Cornwall

No doubt that is overstating his case, but he was in fact a valuable civil servant, a very able administrator and sensible reformer, and was President of the Royal Society for two years. He was finally dismissed as Secretary of the Admiralty when the Revolution turned out James II, who as Duke of York had long been Pepys's chief patron. On his retirement Pepys was able to enjoy a fairly wide reputation as a critic of music and a collector of pictures, books and manuscripts. So where do we find here 'the vulgar and coarse stamp' or the 'vain, silly, transparent coxcomb'?

Yet, though Lockhart and the *Quarterly Review* were wrong most of us cannot help thinking of Pepys as a comic little man. We remember his *Diary* and not his career and the serious interests of his later life. He began the *Diary* in 1660, still in his twenties, and ended it in the middle of 1669, when the shorthand he used, which afterwards proved to be so difficult to decipher, severely tested his eyesight. (These years, 1660–9, not only give us the initial period of the Restoration but also the Plague and the Great Fire, which Pepys describes out of his own experience.) But why did a busy and ambitious man, who often rose at dawn to start work, go to all this trouble? Many people have kept diaries to show posterity how good, how wicked, how important they were. But I am sure Pepys hadn't posterity in mind. His *Diary* didn't exist to prove anything. I see his diary-keeping as a part of his eagerly experiencing style of life, his desire to try and to taste everything. He had been brought up rather strictly in a puritan England, and now here he was, with a pretty French wife, still only twenty, in the rip-roaring London of the Restoration and Charles II, a city of music (which he genuinely loved), theatres with wickedly fascinating *actresses* –

> Comes Mrs Knipp to see my wife, and I spent all the night talking with the baggage, and teaching her my song of 'Beauty Retire', which she sings and makes go most rarely, and a very fine song it seems to be. She also entertained me with repeating many of her own and others' parts of the play-house, which she do most excellently; and she tells me the whole practices of the playhouse and players, and is in every respect most excellent company. . . .

It was a city filled with talk of mistresses, the King's included, with crowded taverns and assignations and late-night suppers and glimpses of white breasts and enchanting legs, but also with darkness and violence and death never far away. Much has been made of Pepys's drinking bouts and wandering lusts and infidelities, but by Restoration standards he was a well-behaved man. The few setbacks in his career were concerned with politics and religion and had nothing to do with loose living.

The point is, with his *Diary* he took the lid off himself, and told all. If we think him a comic little man – even though his quaint seventeenth-

Samuel Pepys, 1666, by John Hayls

{215}

century manner encourages us – it is chiefly because we meet him with the lid off, whereas we know most men with their lids screwed on hard. If we knew as much about many of the youngish men now working in the Treasury and the Foreign Office they would seem comic, pathetic or disgusting – preferably comic. The Lockhart or *Quarterly Review* contemptuous dismissal of Pepys is simply a display of hypocrisy and humbug. No telling all, no lids off, for them! Can we imagine Lockhart or some other solemn editor of the *Quarterly* or, for that matter, some civil servant or junior minister of our time, telling us what follows –

> . . . At night my wife and I did fall out about the dog's being put down into the cellar, which I had a mind to have done because of his fouling the house, and I would have my will; and so we went to bed and lay all night in a quarrell. . . .

> . . . And so home to see Sir J. Minnes, and after staying talking with him awhile I took leave and went to hear Mrs Turner's daughter play on the harpsicon. But, Lord! it was enough to make any man sick to hear her; yet I was forced to commend her highly. . . .

> . . . To the Theatre, where I saw again, 'The Lost Lady', which do now please me better than before; and here I sitting behind in a dark place, a lady spit backward upon me by mistake, not seeing me; but after seeing her to be a very pretty lady, I was not troubled at it at all. . . .

And now, just to see what we can learn from him, a last but longer passage, chosen almost at random, this old edition of Pepys's *Diary* having eight hundred closely printed pages that worry my sight as the shorthand began to worry his. It is dated 15 June 1664:

> At home, to look after things for dinner. And anon at noon comes Mr Creed by chance, and by and by the three young ladies [the daughters of his patron, Lord Sandwich]; and very merry we were with our pasty, very well baked; and a good dish of roasted chickens; pease, lobsters, strawberries. And after dinner to cards; and about five o'clock, by water down to Greenwich; and up to the top of the hill, and there played upon the ground at cards. And then so to the Cherry Garden, and then by water singing finely to the Bridge, and there landed; and so took boat again and to Somerset House. And by this time, the tide being against us, it was past ten of the clock; and such a troublesome passage, in regard of my Lady Paulina's fearfulness, that in all my life I never did see any poor wretch in that condition. Being come hither, there waited for them their coach; but it being so late, I doubted what to do to get them home. After half an hour's stay in the street, I sent my wife home by coach with Mr Creed's boy; and myself and Creed in the coach home with them. But, Lord! the fear that my Lady Paulina was in every step of the way: and indeed at this time of the night it was no safe thing to go that road; so that I was even afraid myself, though I appeared otherwise. We come safe,

however, to their house; where we knocked them up, my Lady and all the family being in bed. So put them into doors; and leaving them with the maids, bade them good night.

First, we have the merry dinner (with lobsters casually mentioned with vegetables and fruit); then the little idyll of Greenwich Hill and Cherry Garden; then the earlier water trip, singing away; then the later rougher trip, alarming poor Paulina; then the coach, the road, the night, perhaps hiding drunken marauders, footpads, highwaymen: a strange lost London recovered here for us. No historian, not even Macaulay with his prodigious memory, can do as much for us. We owe more than smiles to this busy, brave (he stayed and worked in London throughout the Plague), cheerfully candid little Pepys, who probably looks better with the lid off than most of us would do. He well deserves to remain a national figure, his legend still bright.

Our eighteenth-century man must be Samuel Johnson, partly because of the sheer size and weight of him but also because Boswell's *Life* has been so great a favourite with English readers. However, we go badly wrong if we think of him as a representative figure of his age. He stands four-square against his age, never accepting its rationality. He is the very opposite of an eighteenth-century intellectual. (Horace Walpole loathed him: . . . 'an odious and mean character' – 'By principle a Jacobite, arrogant, self-sufficient, and overbearing by nature, ungrateful through pride and of genuine bigotry' – together with much more of the same.) I see Dr Johnson as a vast lump of character hewn out of Englishness, which I am using strictly here in the meaning it has throughout this book. There could be no question with him of barring out the unconscious: he lived in its shadow.

In his private life, Johnson represents the darker side of Englishness. Physically an unusually courageous man, capable of separating savage dogs or defying three or four ruffians, he was spiritually fearful of death and the dreadful judgment that would follow it. His constant prayers echo those fears: 'Grant that, by the assistance of the Holy Spirit, I may improve the time which thou shalt grant me, to my eternal salvation' – and again, 'Enable me to proceed in this labour, and in the whole task of my present state; that when I shall render up, at the last day, an account of the talent committed to me, I may receive pardon, for the sake of Jesus Christ.' There may have been medical reasons why, to the very end of his life, he suffered from long spells of depression and indolence. After all, he had passed half his adult life facing poverty, drudgery and humiliation. But behind these fits were profoundly irrational fears that he might be doomed to a terrible eternal judgment, in spite of all his efforts, his attempt to live a decent life, his natural kindness and compassion. He was not merely looking for a suitably grave subject when he

began to write *The Vanity of Human Wishes*. He belonged, in an evil world, to a wretched struggling species.

Dr Samuel Johnson, by James Barry

We must remember that when Boswell began to report almost everything Dr Johnson said in his hearing, the worst, in the ordinary sense of living, was over. Dr Johnson had his pension, his enormous prestige and, what was very important, many good friends. (Boswell was a wonderful piece of luck for Johnson, but the idea, held by some critics, that the tireless, hero-worshipping little Scot really *created* Johnson will not do: the same character, though not so carefully drawn, appears in too many other contemporary records.) Though the unwieldy battered ship has arrived at last in harbour – and Boswell shows us the lighted supper table or the circle of friends round the fire – that ship has come out of the dark and will vanish in darkness again. In other words, while we are reading Boswell we must never forget that fearful, gloomy, deeply pessimistic background I have already sketched. I think Johnson never did.

Consider one of his famous remarks: 'If I had no duties, and no reference to futurity, I would spend my life in driving briskly in a post-chaise with a pretty woman' – but notice the *reference to futurity*. His political opinions, his High Tory bigotry ('I have always said, the first Whig was the devil'), were shaped in that dark background. To give him some sense of security, he needed a fixed social hierarchy, even though mixed somehow with his respect for it was a manly feeling of independence. (This is very English.) Radical desires for change, reform, improvement, were either wicked or so much cant because in a world as bad as this one, with human nature being what it is, we are fortunate to be where we are at present. When he told Boswell that he believed a wise Tory and a wise Whig would agree, he was assuming that a wise Whig would disturb nothing. When some unwise Whigs annoyed him, as Boswell suggested, he declared that 'Public affairs vex no man', that he had never slept less nor eaten less because of them. Not wishing to fall back on his deep-seated pessimism, to explain his political bigotry, he made light of government altogether, now asserting that one was as good as another in terms of the happiness of the individual, that if tyranny should exist it would soon be remedied; and making similar statements that were preposterous then and now seem monstrously ridiculous. But on these occasions, Dr Johnson was not being honest either with himself or his listeners: he knew better than that.

Where I feel he was being completely honest was in his praise of London, of a club, of a good tavern, of an evening of talk in excellent company. (Certainly he was inclined to show off, but this was often the fault of Boswell, who would hurry to London as if he had there a three-ring circus, with the same elephant in each ring.) Johnson meant it, too, when he urged us – yes, us as well – to try to form new friendships and even to find plenty of acquaintances. When he came lumbering out of his private darkness, his melancholy and fearfulness, for all his huffing and puffing and rough answers he loved company and conviviality because they shone all the brighter. Though most of us know it so well, I cannot resist quoting Boswell's account of how the grand old boy – he can be called that out of sheer affection – was disturbed at 3 a.m.:

> One night when Beauclerk and Langton had supped at a tavern in London, and sat till about three in the morning, it came into their heads to go and knock up Johnson, and see if they could prevail on him to join them in a ramble. They rapped violently at the door of his chambers in the Temple, till at last he appeared in his shirt, with his little black wig on the top of his head, instead of a nightcap, and a poker in his hand, imagining, probably, that some ruffians were coming to attack him. When he discovered who they were, and was told their errand, he smiled, and with great good-humour agreed to their proposal: 'What, is it you, you dogs! I'll have a frisk with you.'

And soon he was dressed, and off they went. (It is hard to imagine later authorities on Literature, let us say Matthew Arnold or T. S. Eliot, frisking in this style.) Johnson enjoyed the right sort of company so much that, with Boswell at hand, he would talk to tease, to startle, as another man might do card tricks. Into the accepted beliefs, the opinions held in common by other people present, he would toss a grenade. For the time being he would be perverse on principle, with the result that many of his best-known sayings will not stand examination. Let us take a few at random.

There are few ways in which a man can be more innocently employed than in getting money. Not true then; even more wildly wrong now. *There is more knowledge of the heart in one letter of Richardson's, than in all 'Tom Jones'.* Nonsense; and said because he had received some help from Richardson. *Marriages would in general be as happy, and often more so, if they were all made by the Lord Chancellor.* But even an eighteenth-century Lord Chancellor would not have decided that young Samuel Johnson should marry a widow twenty years older than himself – and Johnson truly loved his odd wife. *No man but a blockhead ever wrote, except for money.* Obviously untrue, and indeed if a man, then or now, thinks first about money, then he is a fool to write at all when he might be making shoes or sausages. *We would all be idle if we could.* Possibly true of himself and most labourers, but we have seen how even the so-called 'idle rich' invented fashionable commitments to keep themselves busy. *Every man thinks meanly of himself for not having been a soldier, or not having been at sea.* Generously spoken by a man who had known no service on land or sea, and I cannot test its truth with my own feelings, having been a soldier (of a sort, but in a hard war), but I have never found any evidence, in a long life, that favoured this statement. However, I would make a distinction between sayings like these and those in which the sad dough of prejudice is leavened by wit, as for example, *The Irish are a fair people; – they never speak well of one another*, or, of the Scotch (and a shocking slander), *Their learning is like bread in a besieged town; every man gets a little, but no man gets a full meal.*

What emerges from Boswell's *Life* is a tremendous character, English-ness on a grand scale, displayed in the round, menacing in a few aspects and lovable in most others, wise at one moment and absurd at the next. But no, I ought to modify that 'displayed in the round', if only because I was about to add that it seemed to me a pity that for every hundred persons who have read Boswell – and, of course, have enjoyed him too – probably only one has read Johnson's *Lives of the Poets*. Here, instead of astonishing or dismaying his company, he can be found working steadily and sensibly, not a great critic but a very good one, and one who could use as the basis of his biographical notes his own searching experience. True, in some matters his heart was better than his head. He could place pennies on the closed eyes of wretched boys sleeping in the streets so that they could pay for a breakfast. But when he declared, *Most schemes of political improvement are very laughable things*, it ought to have occurred to him that some possible scheme might be devised to take those boys out of the streets and put them into a warm room and a bed. There is no personal hostility here; I am merely claiming the right as one free Englishman – even though two centuries separate us – to talk politics back at an Englishman who talks politics at me. And indeed I have a special affection for Dr Johnson here and now if only because he illustrates so well my idea of Englishness, defying cold rationality in the very age famous or notorious for it, enjoying the tavern fire and the talk because he was always aware that somewhere beyond this little lighted place was darkness, death, mystery. So now in he goes, together with the best carved and gilded frame the gallery can afford. And if a few foreigners drift in later, to stare, to wonder, to mutter and titter – well, let 'em! Samuel Johnson wouldn't have cared, and neither do I.

Charles Lamb is next, to represent that age crammed with character, the Regency. And how did Carlyle describe him?

> He was the leanest of mankind; tiny black breeches buttoned to the knee-cap and no further, surmounting spindle-legs also in black, face and head fineish black, bony, lean, and of a Jew type rather; in the eyes a kind of smoky brightness, or confused sharpness; spoke with a stutter; in walking tottered and shuffled, emblem of imbecility, bodily and spiritual (something of real insanity, I have understood), and yet something, too, of human, ingenuous, pathetic, sportfully much enduring. Poor Lamb! he was infinitely astonished at my wife, and her quiet encounter of his too ghastly London wit by a cheerful native ditto. Adieu! poor Lamb!

And Adieu! poor Carlyle, doomed to squash most of that cheerful native wit out of his wife. 'Emblem of imbecility, bodily and spiritually' – what arrogance, what stupidity, what ignorance! (But then Lamb wrote, 'I have been trying all my life to like Scotchmen, and am obliged to desist from the experiment in despair.') Strange as it may at first appear, I declare that of these two famous men, Lamb had the stronger character and could be depended upon when Carlyle could not. True, Lamb occasionally drank too much gin, stammered out absurd puns to wreck solemn talk, mocked self-important fellow guests. (The woman who sat next to him at dinner went on and on praising some man she admired, ending at last with, 'And well I know him – bless him!' To which Lamb replied, speaking for us all, 'Well, I don't – but damn him at a hazard!') But the truth is, there was in his time – and has been ever since – too much 'Poor Lamb' and 'Gentle Lamb' and too many helpings of syrup.

A few facts would help us here. He grew to manhood, in a poor household, to accept the responsibility of earning a steady living as a clerk and looking after his elder sister, Mary, who in a fit of insanity had killed their mother. For the rest of his life he had to watch Mary carefully, for she had been released from the asylum into his care, and when the warning signs returned he had to take her back to the asylum. Though her mental health improved later, it was this that decided how and where they lived. 'This', as his friend Barry Cornwall said, 'was substantially his life. His actions, thoughts, and sufferings were all concentrated on this end. It was what he had to do; it was within his reach; and he did it.' He worked at his desk, in the East India Company's office, conscientiously and manfully, for thirty-three years until at last he was given his freedom and a pension, without complaining, giving only an occasional glimpse of the dark bewilderment, struggle and suffering below the surface. His humour, the truest and profoundest of his time, rises like a flower out of this hidden soil.

But that is not all. This 'Poor Lamb', this 'emblem of imbecility', not only carried his own load but was always eager to help a friend or even any new young acquaintance. No other author of his time was so quick in sympathy, so full of helpfulness, or, behind his jokes and nonsense, so sound and brave in his judgments. He *played* the clown, just as Carlyle, uncertain, neurotic, played the incorruptible strong man. This incomparable Lamb mixture, to be enjoyed in any pipe, is to be found, of course, in his letters, which are fine literature at ease and in slippers. His *Elia* essays, in spite of their autobiographical material and playful asides to friends, are definite creations, *Elia* not being simply a pseudonym for Charles but an extension of one side of his personality, presented with enormous skill. Because we meet them too early, at school, when we are not yet ready for such prose sonatas and fantasias and prefer brisk and blunt statements, we tend later to underrate or ignore these essays. Equally important, however, is his criticism. This was an age of some of the best and the worst critics English Literature had known. After sitting up late, with his pipe and glass, over his precious folios of Elizabethan or Jacobean dramatists or the new works his friends sent him, then making a few notes or writing a letter or two, Lamb transformed himself into a superb informal critic. Without Coleridge's range or Hazlitt's force, he was their equal – in some respects, notably in his sureness of touch and originality, perhaps their superior. He explored the old dramatists for gold – and found it, just enjoying himself in the night, forgetting his waking life, which, he once wrote, 'has much of the confusion, the trouble, and obscure perplexity of an ill dream'. Add to this his criticism and essays, the Ali Baba's cave of his letters, which have been republished over and over again, what he left us – along with the unique memorial of him as a person – is far more solid and generous than we might at first imagine.

Charles Lamb, 1804, painted by a fellow essayist, William Hazlitt

To choose one letter, just as a taste of his quality, has been as teasing as he often was, but, rejecting so many early letters, bubbling with nonsense, I have decided on a late one. His final move, for the sake of Mary's health, was well out of the City to Enfield, not a happy move for him as it took him away from his friends and the London he loved. He is describing what he feels about living in Enfield, in a long letter to his solemn friend, Wordsworth, who might be said to be in the simple-country-life business so that Lamb was always tempted to mock it:

... In dreams I am in Fleet Market, but I wake and cry to sleep again. I die hard, a stubborn Eloisa in this detestable Paraclete. What have I gained by health? Intolerable dullness. What by early hours and moderate meals? A total blank. O! never let the lying poets be believed, who 'tice men from the cheerful haunts of streets, or think they mean it not of a country village. In the ruins of Palmyra I would gird myself up to solitude, or muse to the snoring of the Seven Sleepers; but to have a little teazing image of a town about one; country folks that do not look like country folks; shops two yards square, half a dozen apples and two penn'orth of overlooked gingerbread for the lofty fruiterers of Oxford-street; and, for the immortal book and print stalls, a circulating library that stands still, where the show-picture is a last year's Valentine.... The very blackguards here are degenerate; the topping gentry stock-brokers; the passengers too many to insure your quiet, or let you go about whistling or gaping, too few to be the fine indifferent pageants of Fleet-street.... O! let no native Londoner imagine that health, and rest, and innocent occupation, interchange of converse sweet, and recreative study, can make the country any thing better than altogether odious and detestable. A garden was the primitive prison, till man, with Promethean felicity and boldness, luckily sinned himself out of it. Thence followed Babylon, Nineveh, Venice, London, haberdashers, goldsmiths, taverns, playhouses, satires, epigrams, puns, – these all came in on the town part, and the thither side of innocence. Man found out inventions. ...

Merely a letter to an old friend, yet a little work of art, in which humour bubbles and sparkles to hide regret, a darkening sadness.

Landor, hardly a sentimental enthusiast, after the death of Charles Lamb cried, 'Few are the spirits of the glorified / I'd spring to earlier at the gate of Heaven.' But Landor would not have found Lamb there – we know about Elia's doubts of Heaven. I think Lamb would have deliberately chosen at least a long spell in Limbo, still stammering outrageous puns, joking with a melancholy face, instantly if shyly offering help and consolation – a saint in voluntary exile, with the reek of gin and tobacco still about him, his halo, invisible to him, genuine enough but a trifle shabby. And if I could choose only one of my gallery men to spend an evening with, he would be my first choice.

About sixty-five years ago, while still at school, much against my will

Michael Faraday, 1842, by
Thomas Phillips

I would be compelled to go down to the physics lab at tediously regular times. Attempts would be made in that basement of dehumanized abstractions to instruct me, among others of course, in electricity and magnetism. A genuinely brilliant scholar in all subjects that showed me human beings playing a leading part, I made nothing of electricity and magnetism. And though I have just been trying to read round them, in a feeble sort of way, I still make little or nothing of them, though enjoying the benefits that researches, experiments, developments, have brought me. But it is not out of shame, to do penance, that I have decided to bring into my gallery, as its fifth national figure, no other than Michael Faraday. Nor is it, strictly speaking, because of the breadth and depth of his discoveries, because he is one of the great inspirers and founders of modern science, because he is the English father of electrical engineering, a man to remember and thank every thousandth time we switch on a light. He would still be a remarkable man even if every patient experiment had failed.

To begin with, as all evidence testifies, he was a tremendously lovable man. So Tyndall could say, 'You might not credit me were I to tell you how lightly I value the honour of being Faraday's successor compared with the honour of having been Faraday's friend. His friendship was energy and inspiration. . . . Surely no memory could be more beautiful. He was equally rich in mind and heart. . . .' Nowadays most of us laymen cannot help giving scientists dubious and sideways looks; we wonder gloomily what they will be up to next; some of their hubristic pronouncements chill the spine; and out of our puny resentment we imagine them driving themselves mad and then put them into science fiction and horror films. I am not saying that this is entirely justified, and indeed I would say that most great scientists, as distinct from so many of their narrow and conceited camp-followers, have had – or still have – lovable qualities that almost always include a certain innocence. Even so, Faraday, equally rich in mind and heart, seems to have been exceptional, a paragon. This brings me to my final point, to justify his place in the gallery. I see his character and career as a triumph of Englishness.

For more than one good reason, it is worth taking a look at how Faraday began. Born in 1791 in Surrey, the son of a blacksmith, he was first, at twelve, an errand-boy at a bookbinder's and stationer's, and then an apprentice. In his teens he was already reading hard and attending any lectures he could find on 'natural philosophy'. In 1812 a customer of the shop, impressed by this thoughtful youth, gave him tickets for four lectures to be delivered by Humphry Davy (he received his title later that year) at the Royal Institution. Faraday attended the lectures, made careful notes, wrote them up fully afterwards, then bound what he had written into a quarto volume. He sent this to Davy, together with a letter asking how he could get out of trade, which seemed to him selfish and vicious, and give his life to science. After an interview at the Royal Institution, Davy offered him a job as general assistant at twenty-five shillings a week, not bad 'take-home' pay for a young unmarried man in those days.

In the autumn of 1813 Sir Humphry and his wife (a silly woman who made difficulties) took Faraday abroad, on a protracted scientific tour of France, Switzerland, Italy and the Tyrol, and they were away nearly two years. I would agree that Davy was an odd type of scientist and professor: he was a close friend of Coleridge and Southey when they were all young together at Bristol, and he himself was constantly writing verse. But I cannot help contrasting what happened then, when there was a certain looseness and flexibility about academic society, with what would happen now. To engage an assistant these days, Davy, after reporting to a committee, would have to advertise, demanding detailed applications in triplicate that would have to name various referees, then there would be a short list compiled in conjunction with the committee, then those on that list would be interviewed before the final decision could be made, while any ingenuous youth working at a bookbinder's would have had his application dismissed during the first shuffle. (Remember, too, Darwin's rather casual appointment to the *Beagle*.) And then that long and leisurely foreign tour – in a Europe, too, that still had war rolling around it – would be impossible in our time. But then in 1807 Davy had been awarded a prize of three thousand francs by the Institute in Paris when France and Britain were officially at war! So much for progress! However, in 1812 an eminent scientist like Davy could be credited with a certain amount of intuition. (Englishness again?) When he was being praised much later for his important discoveries, we are told he replied, 'My best discovery was Michael Faraday.'

All accounts agree that Faraday was an uncommonly appealing man. He was shortish but well built and energetic. His head was unusual, so long from back to front that he had to have his hats specially made for him; but there was nothing austere and formidable about his looks, as may be seen from his portrait: he had an attractive mobile face. He appears to have been entirely without false pride, egoism, greed for fame and applause. If he disagreed, he could do it calmly, without the aggression and rancour not unknown among scientists. He was a superb lecturer, we are told, both to adult and juvenile audiences. In private he could be lively company, had a hearty laugh, enjoyed good simple meals and a glass of wine, and was fond of the theatre. There would be nothing surprising in this if it were not for the fact that all his life Faraday was deeply religious, and the further fact that he was a fervent member of what he himself called 'a very small and despised sect of Christians,

known – if known at all – as Sandemanians'. Small sects were generally puritanical, considering merry evenings, wine and playgoing as signposts to damnation. The Sandemanians – and Faraday in time became one of their 'elders' – were unshakeably devout, believing beyond question they had a direct personal relationship with God – but were not just another collection of evangelical bigots. Their founder, a Scot called Glas, was an excellent scholar and no screamer for 'conversion', who moved away from presbyterianism, rejecting any state of interference with religion, and came much closer to the Quakers, though differing from them in various practices. Robert Sandeman, a disciple of Glas and his son-in-law, was another Scot, an energetic writer and preacher, who in 1760 was able to establish the sect in London. Four years later he sailed to New England and was successful in creating groups of 'Sandemanians' in various places. But the political tide ran hard against him, because he preached the duty of the colonies to remain loyal to the United Kingdom, and he was even brought to trial in Connecticut a year before his death in 1771. However, in the Sandemanian congregation he left behind in London were most of the older relatives of Michael

Faraday, who to the end of his life was faithful to the principles and practices of John Glas, clearly set forth in 1733 in his first meeting house in Perth.

In 1821 Faraday, thirty years of age, married Sarah Barnard, who was twenty-one. He was deeply in love, and though Sarah may or may not have enjoyed visits to the laboratory, to discover what was happening between a magnetic needle and an electric current, the marriage in fact was a very happy one. But only a month after the ceremony, Faraday, following a Sandemanian custom, made his public confession of sin and profession of faith before the congregation. When the rather bewildered Sarah asked him why he hadn't told her what he was going to do, for once he was curt, replying, 'That is between me and my God.' We may think him mistaken (as I do) in believing that such a direct personal relationship existed between a human being and the unimaginable Creator of the universe, but this was the core and heart of his faith, from which he never wavered.

I make this point again here because we must now face the fact that in 1841 Faraday suffered a breakdown that lasted over three years. It was certainly not physical; he probably spent more time and energy, exploring the lower slopes of the Alps, than most men his age, over fifty now, would want to do. But he was unable to continue his scientific work, even to undertake any serious reading, and there were times, at hotel dinner tables, when even conversation was difficult or impossible. It would be all too easy to attribute this breakdown to a deep-seated conflict – on familiar nineteenth-century lines – between his science and his religion. But this, I believe, would be wrong. When he returned to work, beginning with what he called 'the magnetization of light, and the illumination of the lines of electric forces', the peaceful relation between his science and his religion was exactly as it had been before. I believe that what brought him down – and it happened to other scientists of the creative first rank – was the long-continued high pressure of his work, which demanded that two very different sides of his mind should collaborate. As the wonderland of electricity and magnetism opened out, there was all the excitement of the imaginative and intuitive flashes of inspiration. At the same time, these had to be checked by careful and patient experiment, often with improvised and rather rudimentary apparatus. Like all scientists on this highest level, he might be compared to a man who found himself at last in Eldorado but had to stop every few minutes to examine very carefully his compass and pedometer. And Faraday was no cold fish; his was an open, warm, generous nature; he would be particularly vulnerable; and a world nourished by his omelettes could forgive him if at last he spent a few years staring at broken eggshells.

Later, in 1854, in a lecture on education, published afterwards to conclude his *Researches in Chemistry and Physics*, he made his position as clear as he could:

> . . . I must make one distinction which, however it may appear to others, is to me of the utmost importance. High as man is placed above the creatures around him, there is a higher and far more exalted position within his view; and the ways are infinite in which he occupies his thoughts about the fears, or hopes, or expectations of a future life. I believe that the truth of that future cannot be brought to his knowledge by any exertion of his mental powers, however exalted they may be; that it is made known to him by other teaching than his own, and is received through simple belief of the testimony given. . . . It would be improper here to enter upon this subject further than to claim an absolute distinction between religious and ordinary belief. I shall be reproached with the weakness of refusing to apply those mental operations which I think good in respect of high things to the very highest. I am content to bear the reproach. . .

It was probably the only reproach he had to bear. In his sixties he realized, probably before anybody else did, that his memory and ability to concentrate were failing him, and quietly, without any fuss or complaint, relinquished work for which he felt himself unfit and gently refused any positions of authority. Moreover, we are told that when he could no longer turn to science at all, 'he remained content and happy in the exercise of those kindly feelings and warm affections which he had cultivated no less carefully than his scientific powers' – though I would have thought that those feelings and affections hardly needed careful cultivation but came naturally to him. I feel we do not need to be Sandemanians to accept as truth everything found in the Bible, to believe in that direct relationship with God or even the whole Judaeo-Christian tradition itself, to understand that this remarkable and extremely lovable man was nourished by being rooted both in the visible world of phenomena in space and time and the invisible world of the spirit, outside space and time. He accepted both his science and his religion, and refused to allow them to tear him to pieces. He gave both sides of his nature full play. As well as an innate nobility of character, there was a lot of Englishness in Michael Faraday.

I announced at the beginning of this chapter that Richard Burton would be my sixth choice, and many readers may still be wondering why I preferred him to some of their own Victorian favourites. I agree – and said as much when I was opening this gallery – that unlike the other six he enjoys no great warmth of public affection. Possibly if we had met him, at a dinner party or in a club, we might have felt impressed, but would not have taken to the chap. In that well-known Leighton portrait he looks a magnificent figure of a man, but I cannot help feeling that

nobody has to look as fierce as that: he is overdoing it. But as soon as I forget his appearance and all that showing-off, not only do I appreciate his essential character, his courage and ability, but also (though this would have annoyed him) I feel extremely sorry for him. I have my reasons and these will appear shortly. Meanwhile I can offer one reason – though it is not the only one – for his appearance here. He represents on a high imposing level a type of Englishman discovered all over the place in the nineteenth century – the restless, exploring, intensely curious, knowledge-seeking, language-speaking kind of Englishman, the men who were fascinated by the blank spaces on the map or the shaky little entries in the encyclopedias. And of all these Burton is the awe-inspiring monarch. On his occasional appearances in London society, tearing and trampling on its veils of Victorian timidity, conformity, complacent humbug, he might have been at the head of a terrible invading army. Yet for all his audacity, his extraordinary adventures and accomplishments, the feverish activity of his mind, he was in the end, I feel, at the mercy of that society, which flattened him, beat him down, humiliated him – a tiger with his teeth drawn, his claws cut.

One question about Burton must be answered immediately. Should he be given a place at all among the English? His father, a lieutenant-colonel in the regular army, was born in Ireland, and was always regarded as a typical Irishman. But his paternal grandfather only settled in Ireland on being appointed a rector there, and was a member of a Westmorland family. Burton's mother belonged to a Hertfordshire family, though in part it was descended from the MacGregors. We are told, 'There were even those, including some of the Romany themselves, who saw gypsy written in his peculiar eyes and in his character, wild and resentful, essentially vagabond, intolerant of convention and restraint.' But some of this can be explained by his childhood and early youth, which he spent wandering round France and Italy with his parents (his father had retired from the army), receiving no regular education, well away from the discipline and tedium of schools. This is the way for a clever child to pick up languages, hearing them all round him and not being drilled in them. And I suggest that Burton's character, his abilities and audacities and prejudices, both his strength and his weakness, were all rooted in this unusual childhood.

In spite of his obvious brilliance, he lasted only five terms in Oxford. Service with the East India Company's army was better, even though its routine drove him half-crazy with boredom, irritation and impatience. But India itself, with its huge variety of customs and tongues, delighted him, and, still in his early twenties, he grabbed any appointment, like that of an assistant in the survey of Sind, that let him loose among the people. His character and future career might be said to be fixed. He had an astonishing talent for acquiring languages, dialects and all, and was credited finally with a mastery of no fewer than thirty-five of them. Secondly, not only did he reject academic and military routine, but he also rejected, once and for all, the customs, prejudices and values of a Victorian Christian gentleman, recklessly admitting his sympathy with Eastern modes of living, and this at a time when all 'natives' were regarded as mere riff-raff. Thirdly, depending upon audacious enterprise, courage and a capacity for endurance, he decided upon a career that seemed to promise great rewards but always left him short of money; a career that brought him fame but no secure place in the society of his time.

Lord Stanley said that before Burton had reached middle age he had crowded into his life 'more of study, more of hardship, and more of successful enterprise and adventure than would have sufficed to fill up the existence of half a dozen ordinary men'. Certainly Burton was no ordinary man. After India and his famous journey to Mecca hazardously posing as a genuine pilgrim, he vanished into unknown East Africa, and before gout and age made expeditions impossible, he had roved from Iceland to Paraguay, the Gold Coast to Salt Lake City, his explorations covering so wide a range that they seemed to belong to a legendary character. And on most of these journeys he was taking note of every-

thing for future lectures, articles, books. Those books would fill a very long shelf, though only anthropologists would want to disturb it. Burton was not a natural writer, was heavy-handed, and generally told his readers more than they wanted to know. Even his most successful work, his *Personal Narrative of a Pilgrimage to El-Medinah and Meccah*, would please more general readers if it were carefully abridged. But he worked hard and well at translation, especially with his favourite poet Camoëns and of course with his *Arabian Nights*. Yet in 1861, the year of his marriage, in need of a regular income he entered the consular service, where he remained for the rest of his life – rather like a Grand National winner transferred to a girls' pony club. And even within that service he had no luck. After years in West Africa and South America, he was appointed to Damascus, the very place for him, where his knowledge and understanding of the Middle East could be of great value. But in under two years he had run into trouble, and was then moved to Trieste, his official post – though he spent a lot of time away from it – from 1872 until his death in 1890. Was this all, together with a few gold medals and a very belated knighthood, his country could do for a man with such an astonishing record?

Burton was a formidable personage, a notable character, in an age of over-life-size figures; and he had a large helping of the qualities that make a great man. But he never enjoyed the good fortune that so many great men have known. Indeed, we could say he was born at the wrong time. Three hundred years earlier he could easily have been one of the tremendous Elizabethans, adventuring by the side of Raleigh. Again, if he had been born in 1921 instead of 1821, by this time he would have been one of our most admired and highly rewarded anthropologists, with an indulgent professorship in America and a pot of money from a book-of-the-month-club choice and the paperback rights of his more erotic works. And what about Burton's marriage? Out of many examples of gushing references to it, I take what Stanley Lane-Poole wrote in his 1913 Introduction to the *Pilgrimage*:

> . . . Of all the exploits of his varied career there was none which so honoured him as his power to win that rare and exquisite devotion with which she worshipped and served him through nearly thirty years of trial, hard work, poverty, exile, deadly climates, official difficulties, and latterly frequent illness. . . . No man could dare to call himself worthy of such devotion. Unlucky in many things, 'Ruffian Dick' was supremely fortunate in his marriage.

But it appears to me he was unlucky in this as well. Isabel Burton was a devout Roman Catholic, a novelette-heroine-romantic (we are told she fainted at the first sight of Burton), and entirely humourless – a dubious combination quite wrong for a man like Burton. Undoubtedly she worked hard and endured much for his sake. But what he needed was not an ultra-romantic heroine, a devotee, a worshipper; he would have fared better with a loving but fairly clear-sighted mate, ready to modify his moods with feminine common sense and humour. Out of a fundamental loyalty to her man, such a wife would have been incapable of destroying, as Isabel did, the work so close to her husband in his last years, just because it offended her sense of propriety. What Isabel Burton did – greatly to our loss – came out of egoism rather than genuine devotion. Again, she is praised for her desperate efforts in London to further his career, and I suspect she did him more harm than good, too much wifely pressure being resented, especially in official circles.

Indeed, Lane-Poole's 'thirty years of trial, hard work, poverty, exile, deadly climates, official difficulties' were not inevitable. Was there nothing left to Burton but the consular service? And if he had to turn consul, did he have to spend four years at Fernando Po on the Gold Coast, then another four years at Santos in Brazil? Clearly this remarkable man was no favourite in some influential circles. In my first chapter I indicated one long-lasting feature of English public life. This was the constant appearance in it of apparently important men, ennobled, decorated and beribboned, who had really never done anything in particular, 'sound' fellows who had always been about and given no trouble. At the other extreme, there have always been the 'unsound' types, brilliant fellows no doubt but not to be depended upon to toe the line, not rock the boat, play the game, and these have almost always been brushed off by the Establishment – *except in wartime*. (And of course I have in mind the world wars of our century, not idiotic campaigns in the Crimea, where

C. B. Fry

Burton was seconded to the Bashi-Bazouks stationed at the Dardanelles and never saw any active service.) Richard Burton, so astonishingly gifted, seems to me a striking example of this unfortunate type; which is another reason why he is here in the gallery, and why (though he would have hated it) I feel sorry for him.

In picking C. B. Fry as my seventh and last man I am not giving myself any advantage. Unlike the other six, Fry was a man of our time (1872–1956) – yet I have to confess that I never met him, never even set eyes on him. The fact that as a small boy I used to read *The Captain*, which he helped to edit, hardly takes me any closer to him. But even without any direct personal knowledge, I don't believe I could have made a better choice. I have a special fondness for versatile men, natural all-rounders, arriving belatedly among us from the Renaissance; men who even in their own time loomed as legendary figures. I opened this gallery with one of them, Raleigh, and I close it with another, Charles Burgess Fry. Among his companions and rivals when he was at Wadham, Oxford, were F. E. Smith (Lord Birkenhead) and John Simon, who were to march forward to become renowned or notorious politicians, to enjoy great power, both political and legal, to receive public honours quite beyond Fry's reach; yet I see him as a better man than either of them. And I am not simply thinking now about his extraordinary record in games and athletics, though we had better take a look at it.

When he left Oxford he had been Captain of the University Cricket Club, Captain of its Football Club, President of its Athletic Club. He had broken the world record for the long jump – and, we are told, putting aside the cigar he was smoking to do it. If this is not strictly true, then it ought to be, being a dramatic example of his style. He never seems to have been discovered preparing himself for the next game or athletic event, solemnly training anywhere. He went on to captain England at cricket (actually recalled at the age of fifty), to score over 30,000 runs, to be the only English batsman to make six successive centuries. He played association football for the legendary Corinthians and for England. Going over to the Rugby game, he played for Blackheath and the Barbarians, and it was only because he was injured that he missed a place in the England team. When, much later, he was asked by Trevor Wignall, the sports writer, if he had enjoyed his sport, Fry leaned forward and declared emphatically, 'Every second of it.' He took his games seriously, throwing the whole of his formidable self into them, but not solemnly and ritually, nor with the rather sour, grinding application of so many of our professionals. He was enjoying himself, not earning a hard living. He was one of the last of his kind – and certainly the finest

The game that Fry invented: Diabolo at Bournemouth, 1907

specimen of it – the amateurs, the smiling gentlemen of games, intensely devoted to the skill and the struggle but always with a certain gaiety, romantic at heart but classical in style. Throughout his long career in cricket, he had a certain disdain, I suspect, for the mob of spectators, jeering one moment, applauding the next. I cannot imagine him saying, like many TV commentators today, that the crowd was getting value for money: he was not concerned with the commercial aspect of the game.

Even so, though naturally attracted to a grand style of living, he was from the first a man who could not depend upon a private income. When he went up to Oxford, he tells us, he had no allowance from home, about £3 in his pocket, and an £80 scholarship that would vanish in college fees. And when he departed in glory – for in addition to his athletic fame he had been a Senior Scholar at Wadham and had taken a first in 'Mods' – he had a living to earn. After a spell as assistant master at Charterhouse, he took to journalism, first becoming Athletics Editor of *The Captain* and then founder-editor of *C.B. Fry's Magazine*. Here I must add, to my regret, that I never remember reading this magazine, though from his account of his editorship in his lively autobiography, *Life Worth Living*, it must have been well worth reading. (Among other things he was partly responsible for the 'Diabolo' craze, which I distinctly remember. Even the very name, he tells us, was his invention.) Finally, with the arrival of the Australians in 1934, he was asked if he would like to attempt a new, sharper and more personal style of cricket reporting and commentary, and was given a trial run at the Australians' opening match at Worcester. We go now to his own account of what happened there:

> I arrived at Worcester about an hour before the match, and having found a bedroom in a small hotel, thought well to write out about a column in advance, sitting on the bed. This took me half an hour. I stuffed the sheets into my pocket and crossed the Severn and the Rubicon. Just before noon a young man from the *Evening Standard*, sent down to help me, bearded me with, 'Will you be able, sir, to let us have half a column in an hour's time?'
> 'Oh yes,' I replied, 'and here is something meanwhile.'
> Before the hour was out, and before I had sent in anything about the actual play, I got a telegram from headquarters as follows: 'Splendid stop great success stop this is the stuff to give the troops stop Editor.'

This success, which continued, gave Fry the chance of playing the sporting journalist in the grand manner, amusingly described by Denzil Batchelor, his friend-cum-secretary during these years:

> It is half-past ten; time for the caravan to start from Brown's Hotel, London. The Bentley is at the door; Mr Brooks, the chauffeur, is wise-cracking out of the side of his gutta-percha mouth. Aboard are writing pads and binoculars

and travelling rugs, a copy of Herodotus, a box of Henry Clay cigars and reserve hampers of hock and chicken sandwiches in case there has been a strike of caterers in North-west London. A monocle glitters. A silver crest passes, high and haughty above the cities of the plain, C. B. Fry is off to Lord's. . . .

But this is an account of C. B. Fry having fun as well as games. It must not be allowed to be misleading. Not only did Fry stand as a Liberal candidate in three general elections, he gave more than half a lifetime to the training-ship *Mercury*, which soon became more than a ship, for its 'shore establishment' had all manner of buildings, ranging from a church to a theatre. Fry – enthusiastically assisted by his wife – accepted the responsibility of raising funds for the *Mercury* and then running it because there was an urgent need for a training-ship of this kind. Troublesome lads, juvenile delinquents, could be trained for service at sea, if only to keep them out of mischief, but there was nothing for a well-behaved boy, probably belonging to a working-class family, who might want to go to sea. In *Life Worth Living*, Fry writes:

> If you take on an adventure like running a training-ship you must expect to stand some of the racket. The *Mercury* finance would certainly have failed had the full complement of staff been paid. The fact that my wife and I between us have, ever since 1908, performed the functions of Captain Superintendent, Second-in-Command, Organizing Secretary, and for a good part of the time Head Schoolmaster, has in that period saved about £40,000 of cost. As we have also found about £24,000 towards the cost of running the establishment, it will be seen that a ship like the *Mercury* cannot be run, or anything like it, from the State grants or the usual available sources. As there are, I believe, a number of people who fancy that my wife and I have been advantaged by taking up this work and carrying it on for the past thirty years, I take this occasion to exhibit that this is not so. In fact, we have paid heavily for such satisfaction as we may derive from having helped to carry on one of the best training establishments of its kind in the world.

He goes on to point out that the number of *Mercury* boys who had risen to commissioned rank in the Royal Navy, entering by the lower deck, was remarkable; and so was the number who had risen to be masters and first and second officers in the Merchant Service:

> This is due to the boys under training in the *Mercury* being given responsible work every day of their lives, and being effectively introduced to the idea that it matters very much indeed how they do it.
>
> Lord Birkenhead asked me once how we got such results. I told him that a boy in the *Mercury* discovered in his first fortnight that it is worth while to make a fine art of cleaning a bucket. He said it was a pity he and I had not been brought up like that.

Fry's autobiography, published in 1939, is still very good reading. It is a full life presented by a full mind. (I except two chapters: one on his visit, by invitation, to Nazi Germany, the other describing his month's stay with Aubrey Smith in Hollywood; for both are naïve, Fry being for once – or indeed twice – out of his element.) Sir Neville Cardus, who wrote an even better autobiography, is both humorous and affectionately appreciative on Fry. After describing how Fry, in an hotel lounge in 1934, walked round making batsman's motions, trying to account for a bad stroke that cost him his wicket in *a game played thirty years before*, Cardus goes on:

> I have been told that if Fry had not 'squandered' his talents on games and pursuits diverse and sometimes mutually exclusive, he might have distinguished himself in (1) politics, (2) the theatre, (3) law, (4) literature. For my part I think there are politicians and actors and K.C.s and authors enough; there has been only one C. B. Fry. I have heard only one man talk more to the dozen than Fry on all subjects and that was J. L. Garvin. Fry was a master of ellipsis and the rhetorical question. We voyaged to Australia together in 1936–1937; and every morning Fry held court amongst the deck-chairs on the *Orion* as she ploughed patiently through the seas. He dressed differently every day; sometimes with topee and short leather trousers, as though about to trace the source of the Amazon; or in a scaled green sort of costume which made him look like a deep-sea monster; or in a bath towel worn like a toga. One day, to tease him, I said: 'Good morning, Charles. No hemlock yet? Give us your ideas about the Iambic.' In full spate came forth a swift survey of the origin and development of the Iambic, with quotations from all periods and writers. . . .

Are there any such men left – and, if so, why are we always going to the wrong places to meet the wrong people?

So, with this tremendous all-rounder, Charles Burgess Fry, we come to the Exit of my little National Portrait Gallery. Its characters are all quite different, yet I find it impossible to imagine them 'Frenchmen and Dutchmen / And Spaniards and such men.' They all seem to me to be English in bone and marrow, men refusing to accept the limitations of strict rationality, ready to ignore any timid conventional pattern of thought and behaviour, but not in any more profound sense unreasonable. In their several ways they were aware of instinct and intuition, of the mysterious promptings of the unconscious, and indeed of all that belongs to Englishness. Shall we – or our children's children – see their like again? Is our age, so very different from anything these men knew, with its mass media, Admass and computers, already moving towards a portrait gallery of the faceless – or perhaps no gallery at all? Any attempt to answer these questions demands another – and last – chapter.

THE FUTURE OF THE ENGLISH

To write about the English in standard and cosmopolitan political terms, the usual Left-Centre-Right stuff, is almost always wasting time and trouble. The English are different. The English are even more different than they *think* they are, though not more different than they *feel* they are. And what they feel – Englishness again – is more important than what they think. It is instinctive feeling and not rational thought that shapes and colours actual events in England.

For example, although the English seem to be so sharply divided, always indulging in plenty of loud political abuse, there are nothing like so many Communists or neo- or potential Fascists in England as there are in most other countries. Again, although the English seem to have more than their share of rallies, protest marches, confrontations with authority, what could begin to look like a murderous encounter in France or America, or might be a bloody street battle in Japan, would in England end at the worst in a few scuffles and arrests. This is because there are fewer fanatical believers among the English, and at the same time, below the noisy arguments, the abuse and the quarrels, there is a reservoir of instinctive fellow-feeling, not yet exhausted though it may not be filling up. Not everybody can draw on that reservoir. No doubt there are in England some snarling shop stewards who demand freedom for the workers when what they really want is to bring the whole system crashing down, together with every guarantee of liberty. No doubt there are wealthy employers who smile at the TV cameras and declare that all they desire is the friendliest relation with their work force, when at heart they would like to take a whip to the whole idle troublesome mob of them. But there are not many of these men, either on the board or the shop floor, and they are certainly not typical English. Some cancer in their character has eaten away their Englishness.

The real English, who are 'different', who have inherited Englishness and have not yet thrown away their inheritance, cannot feel at home in the contemporary world, representing the accelerated development of our whole age. It demands bigness, and they are suspicious of bigness. (And there is now not only Industrial bigness; there is also Scientific bigness, needing more and more to discover less and less.) Clearly everything cannot be done by smallish and reasonably human enterprises. No cosy shipyard can undertake to build a 150,000-ton ship, though we may not be in our right minds if we want such a ship. But it is safe to say that while Englishness may reluctantly accept bigness, its monsters are never heartily welcomed. They look all right in America, itself so large, but seem altogether out of scale in England. Along with the demand for bigness goes a demand for severe efficiency, often quite rational but not reasonable, therefore alien to Englishness. A further necessary demand, to feed the monster with higher and higher figures and larger and larger profits, is for enormous advertising campaigns and brigades of razor-keen salesmen. Finally, from the monster and all its spokesmen comes a message, endlessly repeated. It runs more or less as follows: 'You ought to be happy. But you are not happy. You can be happy, though, if you buy what we are making for you.' And a postscript might be added from Iago: 'Put money in thy purse.'

I like to call this 'Admass', and will do so from now on. I will also announce what the future of the English hangs upon, while at the same time, unlike almost everybody else, keeping well clear of economics. It hangs upon the final result of a battle that has been going on for some years now and that explains why the English seem so odd, eccentric, unsatisfactory, not only abroad but to many persons at home. It is a battle that is being fought in the minds of the English. It is between Admass, which has already conquered most of the Western world, and Englishness, ailing and impoverished, in no position to receive vast subsidies of dollars, francs, Deutschmarks and the rest, for public relations and advertising campaigns. The triumphs of Admass can be plainly seen. It operates in the outer visible world, where it offers more and more things – for more and more money of course – and creates the so-called 'Good Life'. Against this, at least superficially, Englishness seems a poor shadowy show – a faint pencil sketch beside a poster in full colour – belonging as it really does to the invisible inner world, merely offering states of mind in place of that rich variety of things. But then while things are important, states of mind are even more important.

It is easy to understand why there should be this conflict between Admass and Englishness. What is central to Admass is the production and consumption of goods. If there is enough of this – though of course there never is, because dissatisfaction is built into Admass – there will be sufficient money to pay for its 'Good Life'. But it is worth noting along

The Englishwoman's recreation, 1973: Bingo at Peckham

the way that while America has been for many years the chief advocate of Admass, America has shown us too many desperately worried executives dropping into early graves, too many exhausted salesmen taking refuge in bars and breaking up their homes, too many workmen suffering from monotony or time-and-motion studies and wondering how the hell they got into these traps. And America, to its credit, can also show us a lot of sensible men and women who have denounced all this and have walked out of it. But this book is about the English, not the Americans. Now Englishness, with its relation to the unconscious, its dependence upon instinct and intuition, cannot break its links with the past: it has deep long roots. Being itself a state of mind, it cannot ignore other states of mind and cannot help feeling that Admass, with its ruthless competitiveness, its idea of man simply as a producer and consumer, its dependence upon dissatisfaction, greed and envy, must be responsible for bad and not good states of mind. Furthermore, while Englishness is not hostile to change, it is deeply suspicious of change for change's sake, rejecting the idea that we are now committed to some inevitable mechanical progress. Here we might take a concrete example. Englishness would support an immediate demand, at the expense of many other things, for more and better housing. Without adequate shelter and a decent place to call their own, people feel wretched. But people in England, not a big country, do not have to have more and more and larger and larger cars, with longer and wider motorways, wrecking the countryside, to take the cars. If they think they do, this is Admass at work. People have wanted houses for centuries, and cars of their own only for a very short time. To put cars and motorways before houses seems to Englishness a communal imbecility.

The battle that will decide the future of the English is going on all round us. At this time of writing, we in England are in the middle of it.

I must add that while Englishness can still fight on, Admass could be winning. There are various reasons why this may be happening. To begin with, not all the English hold fast to Englishness. Some important and influential men carefully train themselves out of it – politicians, academics, bureaucrats, ambitious financiers and industrialists, can be found among these men – and a horde of others, shallow and foolish, wander away from it, shrugging off their inheritance. Englishness is not as strong as it was even thirty years ago. It needs to be nourished by a sense of the dignity and possible destiny of mankind. It must have some moral capital to draw upon, and soon it may be asking for an overdraft. The *Zeitgeist* seems to be working for Admass. So does most of what we read and what we hear. Even our inflation, which keeps everybody nudging everybody for more money, is often seen not as a warning, not as an enemy of the genuine good life, but as a proof that we need more and not less Admass.

Some battles have been won or lost because the commander of a large force, arriving late, decided almost at the last moment to change sides. I feel that a powerful section of English workers, together with their union bosses, is in the same situation as that commander just before he could make up his mind. These men believe that if there is a 'Good Life' going, then it's high time they had their share of it. But some remaining Englishness in them whispers that there may be a catch in it. Where's this 'Good Life' in sweating your guts out, just because the managers are on the productivity-per-man-hour caper? It's all a racket anyhow. If we don't work like the old man used to do, we're not turning out the honest stuff the old man was expected to turn out. It's the profit now, not the product. Half the time, we cheat the foremen, the foremen cheat the management, the management cheats the customers. Okay, we want shorter hours, more holidays, bigger pay packets – then the 'Good Life' of the adverts for us. Or are we kidding ourselves?

Now I am not pretending that something like this is being said in every branch of English industry, and certainly not where there is a genuine – if rather old-fashioned – pride in the work on hand. But something like it is being said, thought or felt, in the very places where there is the most money, the most boredom, the most trouble and 'industrial action', and indeed the most Admass. Behind the constant bickering, the sudden walk-outs and strikes, the 'bloody-mindedness', which bewilder so many foreign commentators, is the conflict between Admass, offering so much, and the Englishness that instinctively recoils from Admassian values and life-style. There are, of course, people on the management side who may be aware of this conflict in themselves, but it is probably nothing like so sharp, the Admass spoils being greater for them and their instinctive feeling not being so strong. (In Chapter 4, describing the common people, I argued that they clung harder to tradition than any other class.) In addition to this conflict, all the more worrying because it is hardly ever openly discussed, there is something else that must disturb many officials and members of the more powerful trade unions. This is the anomalous position of these huge organizations. What exactly are they? One day they describe themselves as existing simply to negotiate rates of pay, hours and conditions of work. Another day they talk and behave as if the country was moving towards syndicalism and they were in the van. A week later they will be back in their purely negotiating role. They make the rest of us feel that either they should be more important and if possible creative, or less important, just minding their own business. As it is they are like a hippopotamus blundering in and out of a pets' tea party. Moreover, sooner or later they will have to put an end to this conflict between Admass and what remains of their Englishness, coming down decisively on one side or the other, for *they cannot enjoy both together*. The future of the English may be shaped by this decision.

There are, of course, people belonging to all classes who do not want to be fascinated and then enslaved by Admass, and who if necessary are ready to make a few sacrifices, largely material, to achieve a satisfying state of mind. They probably believe, as I do, that the Admass 'Good Life' is a fraud on all counts. (Even the stuff it produces is mostly junk, meant to be replaced as soon as you can afford to keep on buying.) Such people can be found among workers in smallish, well-managed and honest enterprises, in which everybody still cares about the product and does not assume the customers are idiots. They can be found, too – though not in large numbers because the breed is dying out – among crusty High Tories who avoid the City and directors' fees. But they are strongest and, I fancy, on the increase in the professional classes, men and women who may or may not believe in my Englishness but have rejected Admass. They are usually articulate; they have many acquaintances, inside or outside their professions, ready to listen to them; and not a few of them have a chance to talk on TV and radio. If the battle can be won, it will probably be these men and women who will swing it.

But what about the young? Here we might remember that as soon as we consider even the fairly immediate future then our young will not be the young any more; some other young will have arrived. It is one difficulty the American counter-culture enthusiasts have to face – that while they are still praising the rebellious young, half those lads and girls may have already lost their youth and may be as busy conforming to Madison Avenue as they conformed earlier to Hippy California or the road to Katmandu. So far as the English young are concerned, I am dubious about the noisy types, whether they are shouting in the streets or joining the vast herds at pop festivals. Too many of them lack the individuality to stand up to Admass, which can provide them with another and even larger herd to join. I have far more faith in the quieter young, who never swaggered around in the youth racket, who may have come under the influence of one or two of those professional men and women, who have probably given some thought to what life may be like at forty or forty-five. They, too, might help to swing the battle.

What follows does not apply to old-age pensioners, to people still overworked and underpaid, to all the English who have some integrity, some individual judgment and real values. Far too many of the other English – though I don't say a majority – are sloppy people. They are easy to get along with, rarely unkind, but they are not dependable; they are inept, shiftless, slovenly, messy. This is not entirely their own fault. Unlike their fathers or grandfathers, they have not been disciplined by grim circumstances. They are no longer facing starvation if they don't work properly or go on strike, no longer told to clear out if they aren't properly respectful and start answering back, no longer find themselves the victims of too many hard facts. And this, in my opinion, is how things should be in a civilized society. But people who have been liberated from the harsh discipline of circumstance should then move on to acquire some measure of self-discipline. Without self-discipline a man cannot play an adequate part in a civilized society: he will be just slopping around, accepting no responsibility, skimping the work he is supposed to be doing, cheating not only 'the bosses', the capitalists, but even his neighbours. And unless he is an unusual type, he will not even find much satisfaction in this scrounging messy existence, which does nothing for a man's self-

The Englishman's sport, 1973: a betting shop at Elephant and Castle, London

respect. (I am keeping this on the male side, if only because a woman's problems are generally more personal, immediate, emotionally urgent, so that unless she is a hopeless case she has to face and deal with some of them.) And this is the situation that many of the English, decent at heart, find themselves in today. Bewildered, they grope and mess around because they have fallen between two stools, the old harsh discipline having vanished and the essential new self-discipline either not understood or thought to be out of reach.

Boredom is a menace, now and in the future. All heavily industrialized societies are in the boredom business. This is not simply because so much of the work they offer is boring. It is also because, after having shattered the slow rhythms, the traditional skills, the closely knit communities of rural societies, they crowd people together, excite them by large promises that cannot be kept, so drive them into boredom. Now the English – at least the contemporary English of my experience – can soon feel bored, which largely explains why they gamble and booze so much and enjoy any dramatic change in public life, any news that encourages excited talk: the urban English have always seemed to me a *dramatic* people. When boredom can't be banished, there is always danger ahead. Teenagers, who have not been able to use up enough energy during the day (they should be worked harder), turn at night to idiot vandalism. Later, if boredom hardens into frustration, some of them, too many of them, take to crime, all kinds, from petty shop-lifting to ferocious robbery with violence.

Life in fact was much rougher, harder, more superficially insecure, when I was young, but there seemed to be more honesty about, less constant cheating and pilfering and certainly far less vicious criminality. Other elements apart from boredom of course have been at work here. There is Iago's 'Put money in thy purse'; there is the false notion that the world owes you something while you owe it nothing; the other idea that so long as you are not found out, then all will be well – no final damnation threatening you any longer, and no understanding yet that there can be plenty of Hells on a do-it-yourself basis. Behind it all, whether people are sunk into almost mindless apathy or scream out of their frustration for violence, there is a feeling that everything is different now, that life has been 'found out' to be without meaning, without purpose, equally negative for all mankind or for your own nation. Naturally I am not saying all the English are down on this level. We still have some Englishness left, keeping our minds open to the past and retaining some faith in our future, rejecting the logic-chopping rational for the widely if hazily reasonable, refusing to be cut off from instinct and intuition.

Yes, Englishness is still with us. But it needs reinforcement, extra nourishment, especially now when our public life seems ready to starve

'Pupil Power' in London, 1972

it. There are English people of all ages, though far more under thirty
than over sixty, who seem to regard politics as a game but not one of
their games – polo, let us say. To them the House of Commons is a
remote squabbling-shop. Recognized political parties are repertory
companies staging ghostly campaigns, and all that is real between them
is the arrangement by which one set of chaps take their turn at ministerial
jobs while the other set pretend to be astounded and shocked and bring
in talk of ruin. The whole thing, in the eyes of these people, is an expensive
and tedious farce. In my view they are mistaken, indeed quite dangerously wrong, and I can only hope that no young demagogue of genius
and his friends are listening to them. Otherwise they could soon learn,
in the worst way, that heavy hands can fall on the shoulders that have
been shrugging away politics. You can ignore politics, taking what has
been gained for granted, only to discover your cousins have vanished
and you are being knocked up at three in the morning. Dictatorships
have thrived on majorities that are apathetic and then frightened, and
on minorities that are fanatically divided, brutally quarrelsome and
stupid.

At this time of writing, both the cynical or frivolous majority, which
imagines itself to be outside politics, and the stubbornly divided minority,
only agreeing in being myopic and entirely self-interested, exist in
England. But I believe there must also still exist, if only on a hidden
level, what remains of a characteristically English sense of community,

{247}

decent fellow-feeling, fairness. ('It isn't *fair*', children still cry.) In spite
of the Admass atmosphere, inflation, the all-round grab, all this must yet
exist even now, for there are deep roots here. But those roots must be
needing nourishment. Englishness cannot be fed with the east wind of a
narrow rationality, the latest figures of profit and loss, a constant appeal
to self-interest. Politicians are always making such appeals, whereas
statesmen, when they can be found, prefer to take themselves and their
hearers out of the stock exchanges, shareholders' meetings, counting-
houses. They offer men the chance of behaving better and not as usual.
They create an atmosphere in which the familiar greed and envy and
resentment begin to seem small and contemptible. They restore to
people their idea of themselves as a family. It has been done in England
over and over again. But not lately. There has been little or no appeal
from deep feeling to deep feeling, from imagination to imagination.
Recent years have 'robbed us of immortal things'. But we do not have to
go on like that, to enter a Common Market of national character. It is
now many years since I first declared in public my belief that the English,
despite so many appearances to the contrary, are at heart and at root
an imaginative people immediately responsive to any suggestion of
drama in their lives. Deprived of it, they drift towards boredom, sulks
and foolish short-sighted quarrels. And this is true, whether they are
wearing bowler hats or ungovernable mops of hair. To face the future
properly they need both a direction and a great lift of the heart. A rather
poorer and harder way of life will not defeat them so long as it is not
harder and poorer in spirit, so long as it still refuses to reject Englishness
– for so many centuries the secret of the islanders' oddity and irrationality,
their many weaknesses, their creative strength.

The working man's relaxation,
1973: strip-tease at a club in
the North of England

ILLUSTRATION ACKNOWLEDGMENTS

❈

(reverse of frontispiece) The English Cabbage Rose (*Rosa centifolia*) referred to by Chaucer and Shakespeare. Watercolour drawing by Alfred Parsons from *The Genus Rosa*, by Ellen Willmott, 1914 (Reproduced by courtesy of the London Library)

(frontispiece) Landscape study, water-colour drawing by John Constable. Victoria and Albert Museum, London (Photo S. Eost and P. Macdonald)

Page 10 'Unknown Gentleman with Two Children', 1799, by Henry Edridge. Victoria and Albert Museum, London (Photo S. Eost and P. Macdonald)

Page 13 'The Bench', Third State, 1758, by William Hogarth. British Museum, London (Photo J. R. Freeman)

Page 14 The British Officer in India, about 1870. Radio Times Hulton Picture Library, London

Page 17 'Making Game of Anything'. Radio Times Hulton Picture Library, London

Page 19 'A Country Girl', by Paul Sandby. Royal Collection (Reproduced by gracious permission of Her Majesty the Queen)

Page 24 'The Melancholy end of Corinthian Kate! – one of those lamentable examples of dissipated Life in London', by Robert Cruikshank, from *Life In and Out of London*. Radio Times Hulton Picture Library, London

Page 25 Title page and frontispiece of a best-seller of the eighteenth century, *The Complaint or, Night-Thoughts on Life, Death and Immortality*, by Edward Young, originally published 1742–5. Collection Mr John Hadfield (Photo Derrick Witty)

Page 27 Sir Benjamin Truman, by Thomas Gainsborough (Reproduced by courtesy of Truman Ltd)

Page 28 'The Ancestor' (Lord Ribblesdale), by Bert Thomas. Supplement to *The World*. Mander and Mitchenson Theatre Collection, London (Photo Derrick Witty)

Page 31 'Dr John Dee and Edward Kelly making a Dead Person appear in an English cemetery', from *Histoire Curieuse et Pittoresque des Sorciers*, by Mathieu Giraldo, 1846. Radio Times Hulton Picture Library, London

Page 33 Ladies playing cricket in 1890. Marylebone Cricket Club, London

Page 35 Mary Fitton, about 1595, from the Circle of George Gower. Collection Mr F. H. M. Fitzroy Newdegate

Page 37 Lady Jane Grey, about 1545, attributed to Master John. National Portrait Gallery, London

Page 38 'Conversation Group with Two Ladies and a Dog', by Daniel Gardner. Paul Mellon Centre for Studies in British Art (London) Limited

Page 39 (left) Lucy Hutchinson. Radio Times Hulton Picture Library, London

Page 39 (right) Dorothy Osborne. Radio Times Hulton Picture Library, London

Page 41 The Linley Sisters (Mrs Sheridan and Mrs Tickell), 1772, by Thomas Gainsborough (Reproduced by permission of the Governors of Dulwich College Picture Gallery, London)

Pages 42 and 43 A conversation piece depicting Edward Rookes Leedes, of Royds Hall, Yorkshire, and his family, by Arthur Devis. Collection of Major Sir Reginald and Lady Macdonald-Buchanan, Cottesbrooke Hall (Photo Mr John Hadfield)

Page 44 Staffordshire pottery chimney-piece group. Fitzwilliam Museum, Cambridge (Reproduced by permission of the Syndics of the Fitzwilliam Museum, Cambridge) (Photo Mr John Hadfield)

Page 46 Mary Wollstonecraft. Radio Times Hulton Picture Library, London

Page 47 Fanny D'Arblay Burney, by Edward Francis Burney. National Portrait Gallery, London

Page 50 Georgiana, Duchess of Devonshire and her Daughter, by Sir Joshua Reynolds. Devonshire Collection, Chatsworth (Reproduced by kind permission of the Trustees of the Chatsworth Settlement)

Page 53 George Anne Bellamy, engraved by Francesco Bartolozzi after Cotes. Mander and Mitchenson Theatre Collection, London

Page 55 Sarah Siddons as 'Lady Macbeth'. Mander and Mitchenson Theatre Collection, London

Page 57 Mary Robinson ('Perdita'), by George Romney. Wallace Collection, London (By kind permission of the Trustees of the Wallace Collection)

Page 58 Caroline Norton and her Sister the Duchess of Devonshire, attributed to Sir Francis Grant. National Portrait Gallery, London

Page 60 (left) Lady Oxford, by John Hoppner. Radio Times Hulton Picture Library, London

Page 60 (right) Emily, Lady Cowper, by J. Cochran after Sir Thomas Lawrence. British Museum, London (Photo J. R. Freeman)

INDEX

❊

Page numbers in *italic* type indicate illustrations. Entries for fictional characters and places include the names of the authors who created them.